Business Process Analysis
—including Architecture, Engineering, Management, and Maturity
2012 edition

Requirements Analytics Publishing Programme
2012-2014

This list shows the topics of planned books. The final titles will be decided immediately prior to publication

- Analyzing Requirements, Systems, and Processes Summary
- Analyzing Requirements, Systems, and Processes Advanced
- Business Process Analysis
- Competence - analysis, dictionaries, management, and modelling
- Emotional Abuse in the Classroom
- Enterprise and Information Architectures
- ICE Regulations
- Information Systems
- Meta Meta Modelling
- Modelling with PSL-lite and PSL/PSA
- Normalization Introduction
- Normalization Advanced
- Object Property Relationship Modelling
- PSL-lite User Guide
- PSL/PSA User Guide
- Research Methods Essentials

Further information can be found on the Requirements Analytics website: requirementsanalytics.com

Business Process Analysis

including Architecture, Engineering, Management, and Maturity

2012 edition

Geoffrey Darnton

Requirements Analytics

Copyright © 1995 – 2012 Geoffrey Darnton

First edition 1997
Second edition 2012

Published by:
Requirements Analytics,
Suite 59
2 Lansdowne Crescent
Bournemouth, BH1 1SA
UK

http://businessprocessanalysis.info/

ISBN: 978-1-909231-00-9

Contents

Simple process models: introduction to object property relationship (OPR)modeling

Business visions

Simple text analysis

Chapter 7

Analyzing diagrams

Chapter 8

Analyzing information

Chapter 9

Analyzing costs

Chapter 10

Analyzing organization

Business process architecture, engineering, epistemology, management, maturity, ontology, etc.

Journey's pause—epilogue

Acronyms

Appendix A
Process Description Forms

References and sources

Preface to 2012 Edition

"My boss has just told me that I am now a business process engineer— what am I supposed to do now?"

I have heard something like this many times in the past few years. I am not talking about the senior manager who has the inspiration that the best thing to do is redesign the business processes. I am not talking about the chief executive officer (CEO) who believes that the next major transformation of the bottom line will come from BPR. All such people will find something useful in the book.

I am talking about the person who actually has to figure out *how* to make those better, world-class, competition-beating, customer-satisfying, business processes that maximize the added value from refining core competencies that are driven by the most modern networked virtual knowledge-driven company!

It all started one day when I was given a project to train a group of people, spread around the world, in one of the world's largest companies, in the techniques necessary for business process engineering.

I was aware of the growing numbers of projects labeled BPR or such like, and already had several years of experience in relevant fields. However, this was an interesting assignment. There are various terms such as business process redesign, business process reengineering, business process improvement, in other words, business process work I have therefore decided to group them all together under the acronym BPW—for Business Process Work.

As the new process engineers were supposed to improve business processes, I started with a classical analytical perspective and assumed that the best thing to do at the beginning was to glean from the emerging BPW literature at least an operational definition of a business process—easy, right? After all, I should at least know what it is that is supposed to be improved, redesigned, or innovated. Once I understood the nature of a business process, I could then define the skills needed to improve one.

How naïve I was in those days! Either I missed something obvious or there really is a problem finding an operational definition of business process from the BPW literature.

Basically, it proved to be impossible—I could not find the kind of operational definition I was looking for, within the emerging literature, which would satisfy my need to establish some kind of professional foundation. I found lots of exciting stories about how this or that enterprise had achieved quantum level improvements by redesigning their business processes. I found glowing articles explaining how fee revenue in big consulting houses was experiencing double-digit growth from the push to improve business processes. I found many exhortations for enterprises to do BPW or die.

So, should I go back again for another look, or turn down the assignment? I was assured that those new process engineers were going to do "it" in any case, with or without my help.

Back to the drawing board! This was going to be harder work than I had expected. The groups that I had to train first came from software backgrounds. Therefore I decided to explore how their existing skills could be stretched and enhanced to deal with business processes. I built definitions of business processes and identified several existing disciplines that could contribute to understanding and improvement.

I was on very comfortable ground here. I suspected that all the analysis techniques used for developing software, whether structured or object orient approaches, all had the same ontological origin. I also knew that that ontological origin pre-dated the computer era and was applicable to a far wider range of systems than only computer-based systems. Software engineers were only using a particular form of an object-property-relationship view of the world. This was a good opportunity to check this out and explore if it could be extended easily to the wider organizational world.

I took an early decision about my approach. I decided that the first thing I would try to do was *describe* business processes. I already had considerable experience doing that with holistic definitions of processes which avoided the traps of structured and object-oriented approaches. I felt that would yield the source material for subsequent analysis. Initially, analysis follows description, then it may be an iterative process. The practitioner is usually looking to make recommendations of improved business processes and give some justifications for the proposals.

I have decided to retain the name of this book *Business Process Analysis*. As will be seen, there are now many alternatives: business process—architecture, engineering, epistemology, implementation, improvement, management, maturity, modelling, ontology, redesign, reengineering. Many of these have spawned since the book's first edition, and each has its own 'subculture', and in many cases, ideology. Therefore several of these are now included in the book subtitle. Therefore, the term BPW encompasses even more terms now than when the 1st edition was produced.

This book generally avoids specific methods and focuses on those analytical skills likely to be needed by the business process analyst, whatever the context for the work to be done. Professional analysis work is separate from taking the many business decisions that are needed.

I attempt here to sketch out foundations for the professional business process analyst.

Some approaches I have adopted are:

- I do not believe it is realistic to describe an enterprise by a small number of key business processes: it is more likely that hundreds or thousands are needed—of course, for some high-level presentations a small number may be enough;
- it is only partially correct that information technology is the

key enabler of radical business process change: information technology is along a much longer line of technological innovation, and radical business process change has accompanied all major technological innovation, not just information technology—and keep in mind massive technological convergence;

- despite the many exhortations to redefine the enterprise along the lines of key business processes, that is not being reflected in the boardroom, where functional and departmental heads rather than process managers are the usual members—substantial corporations with boards structured according to key business processes remain elusive;

- despite the popularity of graphical methods of analysis and presentation, they are not scalable to be able to manage the complexity of detailed enterprise-wide business process description, analysis, or redesign;

- there is a strong bias in implemented management information systems towards information attenuation rather than information amplification;

- I have encountered mainly "monolithic" approaches to business process analysis (with bias on information systems, cost, operations, or organization) but I believe the analyst needs a broad multidisciplinary literacy plus specialist skills in one or more relevant disciplines.

The first edition of the book attempted to identify many key founding books and papers that present ideas relevant to BPW. These have been retained. Some new references have been added. However, apart from the addition of new *terms* associated with business process, the underlying ideas have remained remarkably constant. The final chapter identifies ways in which the field could evolve, but they are more to do with improved cognitive models rather than some new breakthrough analytical technique.

My journey is not complete. The field is evolving, as it has done since the first edition. The techniques and approaches set out in this book have stood the test of time over the past 15 years and have been extremely useful on many projects in different parts of the world. The book has passed its critical tests, and I hope analysts will continue to find the book helpful—even if only a subset of the techniques described, are used. Good luck (or good skill!) with your next BPW project.

Where do I start with acknowledgments? So many people have helped, knowingly or unknowingly, in the development of my ideas and approaches. Of course, I take full responsibility for what has emerged in this book., but it stands on the shoulders of many who have gone before.

I break up the text and technical illustrations with more humorous cartoons. I am grateful to B.G. Gujjarappa who is much appreciated in South India for his cartoons and illustrations. He was able to demonstrate an excellent just-in-time business process to provide cartoons in the face of the quite unreasonably short period of time I gave him for his help! I am sure many readers will also appreciate his work. Strictly, they are not 'cartoons'; they are illustrations based on real experience while conducting a variety of consulting engagements.

The first edition of this book followed naturally from the earlier work on business and information architectures which was so well supported by Sergio Giacoletto, Jean-Claude Nikles, Alfonso DiIanni and other close colleagues. Much of that work remains as valid today as it did then.

One key theme of the book explaining the approach that has been developed for the analysis of thousands of processes is derived from the research work at the University of Michigan under the direction of Daniel Teichroew in the ISDOS project. He encouraged the approach taken in this book and gave many very valuable suggestions. Very sadly, he died in 2003 but his work lives on here.

Some of the examples used for the costs chapter were developed during a research project involving DEC, Lancaster University, National Westminster Bank, and Syncho Ltd. The contributions of John Hughes, Ian Sommerville, Mark Rouncefield, John Cullen, Steve Blythin, Raul Espejo, Tony Gill, Toni Gill, Dave Randall, John Williams, Gavan Burden, and Stafford Beer (indirectly) are very much appreciated. During a major project to investigate a generic model of banking, which was the first substantial test of the OPR approach to modelling a substantial organization, R. Sumanthra, N. Murali, Susan East, and Sara Oldham provided essential technical support.

Many students on undergraduate and master's courses, and organizations in a number of countries have used the book and its ideas. There has been a lot of helpful feedback, along with confirmation that this book is essential reading for the business process analyst.

Helpful feedback has been provided for some of the recent updates by Peter Merchant and Lynn Darnton (with whom a book about Normalization is in preparation).

A new publishing model has been adopted for this book because of the extremely long lead times between manuscript completion and final publication. This is to reduce time to market by at least a year. The main consequence is that there may be some typographic errors not yet discovered. Errata will be published on the main website associate with this book (businessprocessanalysis.info). Feedback, or discovered errors can be notifed via that website.

The next edition will be a lot sooner than another 15 years! The goal at this stage, is to incorporate more research into the next edition.

Geoffrey Darnton
Bournemouth, UK
July 2012

Chapter 1

The journey's beginning—introduction

The world of enterprise[1], or anginn, is a very turbulent one. It does not matter whether the enterprise is a multinational corporation, some other company set up to make a profit, a charitable society, a not-for-profit enterprise, or a government agency—radical organizational change is the order of the day.

Consulting firms, large and small, are doing a brisk business in helping enterprises to change. The popular and professional management press is full of stories about spectacular successes (and spectacular failures) from the latest trend to reengineer. Publishers scramble to secure the next book that can fuel the present reengineering fashion. There are many seminars and workshops about how to reengineer the enterprise.

Different authors and practitioners have coined slightly different terms, such as business process reengineering, business process improvement, business process innovation, and, business process management to describe what is going on.

Radical change and renewal are all around us; some enterprises are discovering their core competencies and outsourcing everything else. Just about every large corporation is shedding permanent staff even if the people return through the back door as contractors or temporary staff.

Many writers argue that we are witnessing an information technology based revolution just as profound as the industrial revolution. This book is set against such an exciting background. However, despite the huge amount of work going on under the BPW banner, overall the area remains problematic.

There are the senior managers looking out for the "silver bullet" that will take their enterprise into a world class. They need to squeeze every ounce of cost out of the enterprise and obtain maximum value from the goods and services provided. Then there are the hungry competitors scouring for every opportunity to take a greater piece of the market pie. There is sometimes a touch of political correctness because, every director or manager who is anybody is sponsoring an important BPW effort. These are the people who

---

1 Organization, business, or enterprise? This is a language difficulty that is not resolved easily in Modern English. We can talk about organizations and businesses. The problem with the word "company" is that it implies a for-profit enterprise whereas "organization" may include not-for-profit enterprises. The problem with the word "organization" is that a word is also needed to describe how a "company-organization-enterprise" is organized. Therefore the word "enterprise" is used for groups of people (incorporated, not incorporated, public body, charity, and so forth) with both profit and not-for-profit motives, and the word "organization" is reserved for talking about how an enterprise is organized. The term "enterprise" is intended also to cover virtual enterprises. A candidate Old English word is anginn.

sign the cheques for the BPW work, and the bigger the enterprise the more zeros on the cheque. They worry about receiving value for money—is the BPW project going to yield the kinds of impressive results demanded by many of the stakeholders? It is not just a matter of deciding strategy, as this can only be implemented by radically new business processes.

The functional or divisional structure of the company leads to stove-piped decision making rather than smooth business processes that span the supply chain from raw materials to customers. Therefore one task is to seek out those smooth, integrating business processes.

Consultants all have to make a living somehow. They are the other big group of players in this BPW world. At the top are the "gurus" who earn huge fees exhorting radical organizational change and threaten those enterprises that do not play the game with consignment into competitive oblivion—woe betide the enterprise or senior manager who does not embrace the BPW mantra!

The next level of consultants is more concerned with the sale and delivery of BPW services. They are the workhorses of the large consulting firms. They should not think too much or be very innovative in what they do because the firm has its method defined as a product; revenue and cost budgets depend on predictability and standardization as far as possible.

The "ordinary" employee just has to look on in fear that the next BPW project will chop the job, or depersonalize the work to such an extent that customer relations become mere words and concepts, and the new processes will prevent those long-term individual relationships with customers and other trading partners which collectively weave the fabric of work and customer satisfaction. Human beings are needed to make ill-defined processes actually work, and for a long time, the absence of mechanisms to enforce processes contributed to a breeding ground for enthusiasm and innovation. This work ecology is under threat from greater standardization of processes and a modern ability to enforce many more aspects of process than was previously possible, particularly when it is poorly defined processes that are enforced. There can be serious tension between mandated processes and enabling people to work 'professionally'.

Given this huge BPW industry, one could be forgiven for assuming that most of the participants have a clear idea of what it is about. I certainly started from that point, as described in the Preface.

Thus there are many dimensions and perspectives to BPW work: the whole industry itself; the managers who recognize the need for, and who sponsor the projects; the consultants advising on the tasks to be done; the analysts and other practitioners who are doing the detailed work, and don't forget the people at the 'coal face' who need to make processes work.

This book sets out to help the sponsors, consultants, and process engineers, each in their own way, not by addressing each constituency in turn, but by looking at the role of the professional business process analyst who provides key support. What this book has to offer is the result of coming to terms with the techniques, skills, and methods that are required by business process analysts who support BPW work.

Everything discussed has been used somewhere. There are many people who already have very good skills in some or all of the areas discussed, but producing excellent business process descriptions remains elusive for many. Recommendations for business process change are frequently vague and intuitive rather than well-supported recommendations based on a sound analysis. Indeed, even Davenport (1993) states, "... our belief in the importance of process innovation in management processes is necessarily based more on faith and intuition than on hard evidence".

The difference today is, perhaps, that the most senior business process analysts need a far wider range of skills and techniques than has been required of professionals in earlier generations.

BPW work results in new or modified human-created systems. As they are systems, the business process analyst needs to address the relevant human, social, and organizational issues along with the more technical process rationalization matters.

Does BPW work? Over the past few years it seems the jury is still out on this matter. Clearly the redesign of business processes is associated with many successful enterprises. Presumably it is also associated with many enterprise failures. The popular management press has many stories about BPR project disasters, and there are many case studies and anecdotes of spectacular success. Therefore there may be nothing inherent in BPW itself that leads to success or failure. The factors leading to success or failure may lie elsewhere. However, the redesign of business processes is going on all the time, and hence the need for relevant analysis will endure.

This book's journey is to seek out those techniques that support BPW work. The scene and context for this search are set out in the remainder of this chapter and in chapter 2.

In the remainder of this chapter, the question "what is a business process?" is explored. Given the difficulty in finding a good analysts' definition from the most popular BPW literature it is necessary to say how to go about finding business processes.

Several key BPW themes are explored in chapter 2, which is, in this respect, a miscellany of background issues.

The substantive analytical techniques start in chapter 4. The scene is set for one technique—object property relationship (OPR) modeling—that is particularly useful with a variety of analysis problems. The material developed in chapter 3 is supplemented in several others as the book proceeds.

In chapter 3 some of the analytical issues are side-stepped to take a long look at claims about BPW being new and driven by information technology. However, it is reasonable to argue that BPW has been undertaken in some form or other for several thousands of years, often linked to technical change generally rather than information technology specifically. Is anything new about the analytical foundations for looking at business processes? A wide range of techniques, most of which originated well before the currency of BPW, can be very helpful. What is perhaps new with BPW is the wide range of techniques needed, and a small amount of relevant innovation.

From where in an enterprise does the inspiration for BPW come? Usually BPW is related to something such as strategy formulation or a high-level radical review of processes. These are the business dreams, and a range of approaches is covered in chapter 5. The object property relationship model is extended by adding new objects and relationships which help to analyze items including critical factors, strengths, weaknesses, opportunities, and threats, which are typical for an enterprise vision.

Chapters 6 and 7 introduce approaches for the analysis of the most frequent sources for the business process analyst: words and diagrams. Words can be analyzed to produce a simpler OPR model of the underlying facts. How to handle more difficult aspects of text analysis such as synonyms, homonyms, ambiguity, equivocation, and anthropomorphism, is explored. The resulting OPR models are related back to business processes by explaining that processes are needed to handle the operations on the objects, as well as to implement all the relationships. The idea is developed of expressing diagrams in terms of meta models, which can then be represented easily by OPR models.

Information systems analysis techniques provided the initial substantive point of departure for the journey, and useful contributions to business process analysis are set out in chapter 8 using analogies from the ideas of cohesion, coupling, object-oriented development, and structured design. Information analysis at a strategic level can impact processes by a need to understand the information structure of the market situation facing an enterprise, and therefore the business process analyst needs some grounding in information theory. Social psychology is shown to be relevant because of an assumption that in performing their processes, people actually want to be informed, whereas in some cases people do not want to be informed correctly.

Some fundamental motives for changing business processes are rooted in classical microeconomic concerns such as cost, efficiency, effectiveness, production functions, and economies of scale. A range of approaches to understanding costs, is explained in chapter 9 primarily by exploring the differences between traditional and activity-based methods of cost allocation. An output can often be achieved in several ways. The alternative combinations of factor inputs can be represented by production functions. Choices involve factor substitutability. Achieving economies of scale is one motive that can drive BPW projects, which is related directly to costs, and sometimes technology. Potential economies of scale, or benefits from the exploitation of technology are often important aspects of BPW projects.

Many fine books have been written about enterprise organizational design. This area is more difficult for a conventional analyst because the subject matter is much less amenable to analytical techniques. Therefore the focus of this book is on describing organizational structures using more OPR model extensions. The question of relationships between organization and information technology is explored because there are many claims about this in the literature, and a framework is proposed to test assertions about their interdependence. The OPR approach to describing an organization helps the business analyst with tasks such as allocating process responsibilities and checking that a network is sufficient for the required business processes.

Many authors claim that information technology is the enabling technology for BPW. Their interrelationship is studied in chapter 11 using an approach similar to exploring connections between organization and technology, and some examples of IT-enabled processes are presented. Another theme developed here is that not only is IT an enabler for some business processes, but also many tasks of analysis require the use of IT.

BPW is usually about improving process performance. Approaches to performance measurement are examined in chapter 12, and a distinction is made between efficiency and effectiveness. The key technique explained here is data envelopment analysis, which is put into a broader process improvement perspective using themes from managerial cybernetics.

The real world is usually very expensive to play with. Therefore BPW projects frequently encounter the problem of establishing a basis for believing that proposed processes will be effective. A common approach to solving this dilemma is to use simulation, therefore the most common kinds of simulation and the differences between them are discussed in chapter 13. In the BPW world, event-based discrete simulations are the most common, but systems models may be more relevant in the longer term.

The work of the analyst needs to be represented in some way, usually in a report. In chapter 14, the idea of OPR modeling is taken to some depth by showing how it is possible to create checks for correctness, completeness, and consistency for such models. The presentation of analysis results then needs to be matched to audience and purposes by taking a subset of the underlying OPR models. A case study is presented of this approach applied in depth to information systems.

Chapter 15 explores the emergence of new terms (some of which are in the subtitle) since the first edition of the book.

Finally, chapter 16 contains more detailed descriptions of the work of the business process analyst, outlining skills and competencies. The question of techniques is addressed by providing a summary, and my view of an analyst's workbench is presented.

Perspectives

Different practitioners approach BPW projects from very different perspectives using a wide variety of techniques. Major perspectives are:

- information technology: this is portrayed by many writers as the enabling technology for BPW;
- information systems: information is seen as the major asset for enterprises and appropriate information systems are the key to radical enterprise transformation; additionally, many people see information systems analysis techniques as the main contributors to describing business processes;
- accounting: cost reduction is perhaps the greatest motivation for much BPW work and accountants are able to bring substantial analytical skills to bear on such a perspective;
- microeconomic: this is more extensive than an accounting perspective and includes the efficient and effective use of factors of production;
- operations: the rationalization of operational procedures can yield significant efficiency gains;
- organization: new organizational forms and the rightsizing of organizational structures make more agile firms that can harvest innovation more effectively;
- quality and total quality management (TQM): BPW projects are seen as a natural extension or component of quality programs;
- virtual enterprises: enterprises can be reduced to their core competencies with outsourcing of other activities; virtual enterprises emerge which are the core enterprises plus outsourced partners, supply chains, trading partners, and knowledge networks;
- social: emphasis is placed on human goals and organization, seeing an enterprise as a network of cooperating stakeholders.

What is a business process?

What is it that the business process analyst is supposed to analyze and can it be identified easily? Can an operational definition of business process be extracted from the key literature? The term business process clearly has two components: business, and process. What is a process? When looking at something, how to know that it is a process? What is the significance of calling something a business process—are there other kinds of process that are processes but not business processes?

Perhaps the most common other kind of process encountered during discussions with managers, is a set of steps needed to achieve a goal. For example, a quality process may be a way of carrying out a procedure that has been set down for the purpose of achieving quality certification. There are other connotations to process, such as a manufacturing process, a chemical process, and processing a document or transaction. At an international level, there are many times when a term such as "peace process" is used.

Before moving on to what other writers call business processes, how do dictionaries help with the concept of process?

Webster's Dictionary (Gove, 2002) identifies the word process as noun, transitive verb, adjective, and intransitive verb. The noun includes examples such as "a progressive forward movement from one point to another on the way to completion", "a natural progressively continuing operation or development marked by a series of gradual changes that succeed one another in a relatively fixed way and lead toward a particular result or end (the process of growth)", and "a particular method or system of doing something, producing something, or accomplishing a specific result". In its transitive verb form, there is the narrow connotation of legal process, and a broader concept including, "to prepare for market, manufacture, or other commercial use by subjecting to some process (efficiently processed the invoices)". As an adjective, one idea is, "prepared, handled, treated, or produced by a special process (process sugar process ink)". As an intransitive verb, it indicates moving towards something: "to move along in or as if in a procession (processed slowly through the town)".

B1

What is a Business process? — noun or verb?

The Oxford English Dictionary (OED, 2009) has an extensive discussion of the word "process" (almost three pages of small type!). There is a strong theme of the course of time, or a course of events: "The fact of going on or being carried on, as an action, or series of actions or events... ", "in the course of events, in course of time ... ". Then there is a sense of method, or continuity: "... a continuous action, or series of actions or events; a course or method of action ...", "The continuing interaction of human groups and institutions ...", "A continuous and regular action or succession of actions, taking place or carried on in a definite manner ... " (this may be natural or artificial); "a particular method of operation in any manufacture ... ". There are also the legal uses of the word, and the idea of a procession. The word is identified as substantive, hence it is used in different ways, such as noun, transitive, and intransitive verb forms.

Process is treated as a noun in this study because it is particularly useful to associate process with many other "things", and these associations are represented by relationships—verbs are the usual way in which relationships are represented. The problem of anthropomorphism[2] will be countered by adding requirements to identify the people who are involved in processes. Therefore it should be assumed that in many cases, people are part of any system or process, rather than being outside, or an interface to the process. This distinction is important.

The BPW literature uses the term process in ways similar to those implied by the dictionary definitions, although there is a narrowing of the concept, and perhaps a hardening of the results of process.

What does the literature say about business processes, and BPW? There is a variety of views, illustrated by quotations from several writers. This can be explored without any pretence of a systematic enquiry, as it is only some form of convergence that is sought.

The whole modern BPW thrust is assumed by many writers to have commenced around 1990 as a result of two key articles: Davenport and Short's The New Industrial Engineering: Information Technology and Business Process Redesign, (Davenport and Short, 1990) and Hammer's Reengineering Work: Don't Automate, Obliterate (Hammer, 1990). Both of those papers are important, and essential reading for everyone seriously involved in BPW. It became clear that there was a real possibility of the emergence of a new management fashion which would engage the attention of many people and much investment. Both papers drew on several emerging themes, including earlier use of terms such as "business reengineering" (for example, an article of that title published in Insights, Fall 1989).

Davenport and Short (1990) are brief in their definition: "We define business processes as a set of logically related tasks performed to achieve a defined business outcome". They say that their definition is similar to one by Pall (1987), who says, "The logical organization of people, materials, energy, equipment, and procedures into work activities designed to produce

---

2 The potential danger in thinking of process as a noun is that the process becomes the subject or object of some other verb (e.g. the order fulfillment process enters the orders ...). Anthropomorphism is discussed in more detail in chapter 6.

a specified end result (work product)". By implication they include human issues by asserting that their definition complements one by Schein (1988) who "focusses on human processes in organizations".

Following on from the 1990 papers, there were two key books published in 1993.

Davenport (1993) answers the question, "what is a process?" explicitly: "... a process is simply a structured, measured set of activities designed to produce a specified output for a particular customer or market. It implies a strong emphasis on how work is done within an organization, in contrast to a product focus's emphasis on what. A process is thus a specific ordering of work activities across time and place, with a beginning, an end, and clearly identified inputs and outputs: a structure for action". He suggests that "Our experience leads us to set the appropriate number for major processes at between 10 and 20".

According to Davenport, "... process definition is more art than science, boundaries are arbitrary".

Hammer and Champy (1993) define a business process, "as a collection of activities that takes one or more kinds of input and creates an output that is of value to the customer". They give the example of order fulfillment, "which takes an order as its input and results in the delivery of the ordered goods".

Although 1990 is a reliable date for the commencement of the current BPW fashion, there were earlier writers addressing similar themes, and also predicated on emergent computer-based technology as a key driver for process change. They did not quite use the term BPR, but they were pretty close.

As far back as 1947, a Systems and Procedures Association of America was founded specifically to encourage the examination and improvement of business procedures.

An example of an author who, for a period in excess of a decade, was involved in consulting and writing about procedure improvements is the McKinsey consultant who wrote about Streamlining Business Procedures as early as 1950 with a follow-up in 1960 (Neuschel 1950, 1960). This was very much concerned with the improvement of business processes, albeit called procedures by him. Neuschel was inspired initially by Elton Mayo's work in 1947. The two editions of his book (1950 and 1960) spanned the time when computing emerged as a virtually unstoppable driver of process (or procedure) change. The 1950 book has nothing to say about computers; the 1960 book refers explicitly to procedure changes being needed because of the application of computers. Of course, that early discourse should put the present-day practitioner on guard to consider business processes 'in the large', and not only those processes where computer-based technology has a major impact. BPW is much more extensive than only re-designing computer-based processes.

As far as any computer-based technology imperative is concerned, an early writer is Canning (1956: 226-7) who suggests: "...there have been a number of written and verbal statements by people working in the field of Operations Research to the effect that a company must change its methods and procedures before installing an electronic system...While the author does not agree that the sizeable procedural changes implied by some Operations

Research people are strictly necessary, there is no argument if it is pointed out that such changes may be very desirable".

Following on from those key 1990 papers, several writers strove to expand thinking about BPW. It is not asserted here that those post-1990 writers were primarily inspired by the 1990 papers; they had other sources of thinking about business processes and procedures to inspire them also.

Harrington (1991) is another writer who addresses directly the question, "what is a process?" his retort starts with an observation that there is no product or service without a process, and no process without a product or service. He builds up his definition with a series of terms. A process is "any activity or group of activities that takes an input, adds value to it, and provides an output to an internal or external customer" (using the organization's resources). He separates production process from business process: a production process is "any process that comes into physical contact with the hardware or software that will be delivered to an external customer, up to the point the product is packaged " and "A business process consists of a group of logically related tasks that use the resources of the organization to provide defined results in support of the organization's objectives".

Harrington proceeds to observe that almost everything done is a process, and that in companies there are "... literally hundreds of business processes...". He contrasts processes as flowing horizontally, with vertical organizations. Processes can be expressed in terms of a process hierarchy, by means of a de-composition. He refers to macroviews and microviews. Macroprocesses are made up of subprocesses which are made up of activities, that are in turn made up of tasks that make up "the very smallest microview of the process". Some processes are critical business processes. Processes should have owners, boundaries, and customers, and they should add value. They also have several characteristics: flow, effectiveness, efficiency, cycle time, and cost.

Johansson et al. (1993) also answer the direct question, "what are processes?": "A process is a set of linked activities that take an input and transform it to create an output. Ideally, the transformation that occurs in the process should add value to the input and create an output that is more useful and effective to the recipient either upstream or downstream". They also define a core business process as "a set of linked activities that both crosses functional boundaries and, when carried out in concert, addresses the needs and expectations of the marketplace and drives the organization's capabilities", and "a core business process combines both physical activity—the heart of core technology—with information flow, and addresses the needs and desires of the marketplace". They assert that in any company there will be a number of core business processes, usually limited to about six (five to eight).

Melan (1993) defines a process "as a bounded group of interrelated work activities providing output of greater value than the inputs by means of one or more transformations". He classifies transformations as: physical, locational, transactional, and informational Although his basic diagram shows a classical block diagram of inputs, transformation, and outputs, this is qualified by the recognition of feedback where the transformation process is regulated by output. Other terms are used by Melan, such as subprocess, activity, and task. Task is elemental work. Processes are part of a higher level object, a system. He refers to several different kinds of process such as manufacturing, transformation, service, continuous, cyclical, intermittent, chemical, and batch.

Born (1994) defines a process thus: "A process consists of a sequence of steps which transform information from an initial state (input) to a final state (output). A key characteristic of a process is that it can be broken down into less complicated processes ... ". He goes on to mention that the language in his book, quality process language (QPL), "does not deal directly with material objects ... but with information about such objects". He distinguishes between core and support processes where core processes provide added value to goods or services produced for customers. Core processes are also those on a direct path between source and destination (for example, order and customer).

Hammer and Stanton (1995) offer plenty of prescription about re-engineering errors, suggesting that "The verb 'to reengineer' takes as its object a business process and nothing else". They offer some rules of thumb to identify whether the object being dealt with is a business process:

- specific inputs and outputs;
- crossing organizational boundaries;
- focus on goals and ends;
- the process, inputs, and outputs should be comprehensible;
- relate to customers and their needs.

Ould (1995) paints a more implicit picture of what a process is. He identifies three types of process: core, support, and management. Core processes "concentrate on satisfying external customers", support processes "concentrate on satisfying internal customers", and management processes "concern themselves with managing the core processes or the support processes, or they concern themselves with planning at the business level". He resists the temptation to present a definition of process "We won't attempt a one-line definition of process straight off ... " and "... I have still not attempted a definition of the term process. This is intentional of course ...", but he offers a set of key features of processes: purposeful activity, it is done collaboratively by a group, often cross functional boundaries, invariably driven by customers.

It is surprising that there is not general agreement about the definition of business processes. This makes it more difficult for the analyst to know what to look for. When I first began to look for the meaning of business process, I anticipated finding more detailed, operational definitions, that is, a minimum set of information that would be needed by those who have to do the more detailed work, or implement new business processes. Clearly, the definitions obtained so far will require supplementary material before there is enough for the practitioner to handle in a rigorous, systematic way.

This is not saying that what has been found is particularly deficient. The material published so far has obviously proved immensely popular. Therefore there must be either minimum fitness for purpose or a total absence of clearly articulated alternatives. Most BPW literature is directed at senior managers, who require a very high degree of attenuation of process detail, therefore simple, high-level abstractions are probably appropriate.

After an initial search, and subsequent disappointment, it can be observed that the majority of approaches seem to fit into a monoculture, ignoring other existing alternatives (such as managerial cybernetics). The whole rich real world of enterprise seemed to be condensed into a few simple concepts, with substantial loss of detail. At times, there seems an almost religious fervor in some writers to eliminate existing processes and replace them with entirely new processes, preferably without much prior analysis—which might actually make you stop and think again!

Top-down approaches are particularly good at establishing an overall view that encompasses many key aspects of enterprise. Their most serious disadvantage seems to be their failure to represent the hard-learned detail of the real world of work "at the coal face". Bottom-up approaches are very good at capturing the day-to-day detailed experiences that need to be dealt with by the enterprise. Their most serious disadvantage is usually the absence of an overall perspective. Therefore there is a need for high-level, simple, abstract approaches, but it is disappointing to read comments to the effect that the detail does not matter—in many cases the detail matters a great deal, and one of the greatest skills of people at an operational level is making badly designed or incomplete processes actually work properly (they can also succeed sometimes in making well-designed processes work badly).

Much of the literature about business processes represents the abstract high-level visions of enterprise rather than the real world of work. The business process analyst needs to bridge these two perspectives.

Several important themes were detected in the literature and used in the search for business process definitions:

- improvement or innovation: are business processes changed by gradual improvement, or radical change?;
- levels: several writers allude to processes, sub-processes, activities, tasks, and such like;
- core or essential processes: an enterprise can be described with a small number of core processes;
- (re)engineering: are existing processes 'engineered' in some way?;
- management responsibility for business processes: the radical redesign of business processes has implications for continued management;
- input—process—output: this is the most frequent depiction of processes;
- purpose: if a high-level process is a system, then what is its purpose?;
- how many processes: different writers refer to different numbers of processes;
- microeconomic concerns: improving cost, efficiency, and effectiveness are prime motivators for BPW;
- binding time: process definitions imply abstract sequences of processes which may not be good representations of what happens in practise.

These themes are explored explicitly in chapter 2, with the exception of microeconomic concerns.

How to find business processes

Having extracted some key themes from the discussions about business processes, the literature has still not come up with a good operational definition. Therefore how does the analyst identify business processes?

The initial identification of candidate processes is usually arbitrary. Somebody says something like "order fulfillment is a core business process"

This is a common starting point. There is nothing wrong with such a starting point, but problems can arise when an initial and arbitrary identification of candidate processes is followed by analysis, but the initial processes are not revisited to check them for compliance against some completeness or consistency criteria. The main problem is that all very high-level processes need to be decomposed into smaller components. These smaller components may well be coherent processes that do something precise with clearly identified inputs and outputs. However, the high-level processes are then really abstractions, because the way in which the lower level components are chained together depends on circumstance.

Some useful starting points to identify processes are:

1. inputs and outputs: goods and services are generated and delivered by processes, therefore outputs indicate the existence of processes—the inputs of one process are generally the outputs of another therefore process chains can be constructed by working backwards;
2. revenue: income indicates that something was delivered, and the business process analyst needs to consider what generates revenue;
3. cost: expenditure indicates inputs to processes (and sometime it indicates outputs, see the discussion below about waste), therefore cost is a useful starting point to identify the existence of processes;
4. value: this is essentially the difference between cost and revenue (the higher the difference, the higher the added value)—the existence of profit indicates the existence of process.

It is tempting to suggest that the most important processes are those relating to the highest levels of output, revenue, cost, or value.

The identification of core business processes is not so clean. The concept indicates fundamental importance. Some writers emphasize core processes as chains of lower level processes which provide complete links between enterprise inputs and outputs, and some emphasize core processes as those that support handling enterprise critical success factors. Yet others relate core processes to core competencies yielding an identification of those activities that the enterprise should perform itself (the core competencies) and those that could be considered for outsourcing.

A simple input—process—output model defines an enterprise in terms of the transformations needed to convert the various inputs to the various outputs. The outputs indicate both objectives and processes. Somebody may be producing the wrong outputs (in terms of what is supposed to be produced), but behaviorally the actual outputs can be used as evidence of processes.

Start from the outputs of the enterprise, both products and services, to identify business processes. Not all outputs indicate core processes, and generally it is helpful to make some judgment about the relative importance of processes.

There is the obvious output of products that are exchanged for revenue. However, the process analyst also needs to look at all other outputs (that is, things produced by processes).

How, for example, should waste be treated? In many cases its value to the enterprise is negative because it costs money to deal with, and this negative sum is not likely to be represented in the accounts as a sale at a loss. It is more likely to be represented in terms of a waste service that is bought in, and hence represented as an input with costs attributed to overheads or costs of production. It is also unlikely that the production of waste is seen as an objective of the enterprise. However, despite these serious classification problems, waste must be considered from a technical point of view as a behavioral objective and an output that indicates the existence of processes.

The outputs of an enterprise should be considered both by revenue and physically. Examining outputs by revenue indicates the relative importance of outputs in terms of revenue for the enterprise.

Another source of symptoms of a core business process is cost. As part of an analysis of enterprise outputs by value, the analyst needs to examine costs in order of importance. However, it is necessary to be wary of existing cost classification and allocation schemes because they may not give the most suitable background for BPW work. After all, money is another output of the enterprise.

Concluding remarks

It seems that the key BPW literature extant today is aimed at senior management. From the literature it is possible to extract a few crucial points about what defines a process, but this literature is not intended to direct practitioners in the detail needed for business process analysis. From the point of view of the analyst, the characteristics of business process which have been extracted are necessary but not sufficient to support a serious BPW project.

There are some substantial themes that need to be addressed in analyzing business processes, which can be seen in the literature. These are described in the next chapter.

A broad range of perspectives has been identified. They are held by different practitioners in the BPW arena. There is some variety in the ideas of what a business process is, but so far, there is also a lot of uniformity.

There are several key ways in which the practitioner can set about identifying business processes, even if a clear definition has not yet been offered. Therefore there is a long way to go.

In the next chapter several key background themes are set out, which emerge from the BPW world. These provide an important background for the more substantive analytical techniques that follow.

Background themes

What is the overall aim of BPW—is it to achieve steady long-term improvement, or is it to achieve rapid and radical change? How many processes must the analyst take into consideration? These questions follow on from the view taken by an analyst of levels of processes. People talk about processes, sub-processes, tasks, activities, and so forth—are these levels identifiably different? Whether one takes only the high level processes as business processes or one takes all levels, there is a strong theme in the literature that the high-level processes are core in some way. The idea of common processes to accompany core processes is discussed in this chapter.

At the heart of most process definitions is the idea of input—process—output. This is described and set against a paradox of core competency. Directly related to this is the idea of process flow, which is used by many writers to depict processes. Here a very different view is taken of both the number of processes and the time at which lower level processes are chained together in response to a business event. This chaining together is called binding.

There is a brief excursion to consider the term reengineering and muse about the use of the word—does it convey anything in business process terms?

Central to the idea of BPW is the observation that many key processes cut across normal business functional departments, and it is the focus on business process which mitigates much of the dysfunctional aspects of analysis when organizations are viewed mainly in functional terms, or computer-based applications are functionally focused.

Finally, it is noted that the massive BPW effort made on the part of many enterprises, is not often followed by a corresponding change at the board level. Therefore it is not clear how new business processes will be managed cross-functionally.

Each of these themes is expanded in subsequent chapters, but in very different ways. The analyst needs to take note of these themes. They are of importance to senior managers and consultants, and the analytical techniques developed throughout the book are designed to help the analyst to take a more neutral stand with respect to them.

Improvement or innovation?

There is some discussion in the literature about whether business processes should be modified by gradual, step-by-step improvements to a whole range of processes, or by innovation of substantially different and new processes.

The debate between the two seems to be based on problems of change management. Some writers believe that it is better to take an existing process and improve different parts over time, so that the whole process becomes of higher and higher quality (and hopefully there will be improvement not only process quality, but also in the quality of the delivered product or service). Other writers believe that entrenched habits, politics, and organizational structure will make change much more difficult to achieve, therefore it is better to set up a new structure and innovate entirely new processes that are not encumbered by history.

Both positions could be tenable, but the concept of a general prescription that one approach is generally "better" than the other is inappropriate; deciding between gradual improvement or a "big-bang" innovation is unnecessary. One position or another should only be based on the facts of the situation facing the consultant who is doing the BPW. However, it should be noted that since the emergence of the BPW world after 1990, and the years that have elapsed since the first edition of this book, examples of organizations that have adopted the 'big-bang' approach remain elusive. This is not surprising; why would an organization just throw away processes that work and have been developed over a period of time incorporating real-world experience?

Many customers are wary of first releases of products and services, as there are still bugs that will not be detected and fixed until after some period of use, thus supporting an argument for incremental improvement.

Motor vehicles are a good example of products that have seen incremental improvement over a period in excess of a century. The motivation for improvements has come from many different sources, of which examples are shown in Table 2.1. Motivation comes from complex factors including technology, customer wants, and various environmental pressures.

Conversely, the installed base of a product may inhibit radical change.

For example, one of the most common combinations of personal computer (PC) operating system and chip design results in an appallingly inefficient use of the resources available in a modern PC, despite the fact that chip and software engineers know how such waste could be prevented—yet the installed base inhibits the required changes.

Motivator	Example(s)
Technical failure	redesigning components that fail most frequently or cause serious problems
New and emerging technology	plastics; electronics; ergonomics; fuels and lubricants
Standards	driving on the same side of the road; having the pedals in the same order; knowing the meaning of the various lights; construction and use regulations
Industrial and political pressure	persuade the politicians and civil servants that it is a good idea to take the necessary land and force the taxpayers generally to subsidize the required infrastructure
Environmental concerns	remove the lead from petrol; reduce exhaust emissions; reduce the consumption of carbon fuels
Competitiveness	reducing labor content; cost reduction; marketing

Table 2.1 Motor vehicles evolution—motivators for change

Levels and De-composition

One point of agreement among several writers is that high-level business processes can be de-composed into lower level processes as illustrated in Figure 2.1.

Several writers use the terms process, activity, sub-process, and task. From an analytical point of view, if these terms depict different things, then the differences between them need clarification. The only point detected from the definitions looked at is the assertion that core processes are related directly to customers. If a service approach is taken to all processes such that all recipients of goods and services (including internal) are viewed as customers, then even that distinction becomes untenable.

This kind of hierarchy may go even further. Some people consider that a process is internal to a company or organization, but what about an idea such as a supply chain? This may involve several legal entities in a sequence of supplies and transformations. Is the whole sequence a process, or just those parts inside one of the organizations? At the other end of the scale, is handling a telephone call to request a service a business process or not? Some say, "well, it is a process, but not a business process".

This book journey is to seek out a range of appropriate techniques and skills for undertaking BPW. Therefore, in the search for operational definitions, sometimes it is necessary to be boringly pedantic. For example, what is the difference between a process and a sub-process? What is the difference between activity and task? Many people will have experienced a similar discussion.

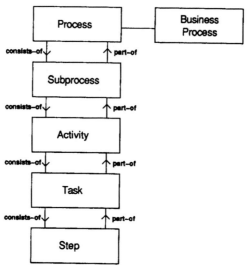

Figure 2.1 Process hierarchy.

Similarly to the question about innovation or improvement, the question of level in terms of this kind of hierarchy is also not particularly important. This point is covered in more detail later, but for the moment let's summarize the decision to work with a definition of process which is recursive. That is, the same definition is applicable at many different levels of detail. Therefore do not worry very much about the difference between a process and a sub-process, or the difference between an activity and a task.

Even the high-level processes sometimes need to be placed in wider, extra-enterprise, and environmental contexts, for example in supply chains.

The definitions identified in the literature do not persuade me to change my view that all that is needed is the concept of process, which can be viewed recursively to handle all the levels mentioned by writers.

Having said that, it should be noted that BPMN (Business Process Model and Notation) does draw a formal distinction between activity and process (Silver, 2011). The distinction is that an activity has a 'performer'. However, as noted in the discussions about OPR later in the book, the word 'processor' is associated with all kinds of processes whether the processor (or performer) is person or machine. Therefore, that BPMN distinction is not helpful, and really masks what should be expressed as completeness and consistency constraints.

There are two more points of importance to the analyst: (i) processes may cut across several business departments, therefore the analyst must understand the relationships between process and function, and (ii) if a process is a collection of activities, de-composition is implied and there is structure in terms of sequence: one activity can precede or follow another, or certain activities could be performed in parallel, with synchronization as necessary. These points are discussed later.

How many processes?

Several writers suggest that the number of processes for an enterprise is small. Harrington (1991) suggests the possibility of hundreds.

In a sense, the existence of only a small number of processes is tauto-logical in that if only the highest level objects in a hierarchical structure are called processes, then only a few are expected. If everything at a lower level is called for example an activity or a task, then a question of equal importance is: how many activities and tasks are expected in an enterprise? In general this question is not addressed by the literature directed at management.

The approach to process taken in this book is recursive, therefore activities and tasks are also defined as processes. Hence, the fundamental question needs to be asked: how many processes are needed for an enterprise—10-30 or 10,000-30,000?

In one example of a financial institution being audited it was estimated that there should be in the order of 20,000—25,000 processes. This number was estimated by taking the number of high-level processes, and calculating how many levels of decomposition were needed to reach elemental processes that could not be broken down meaningfully any further. Some of the high-level activities had already been broken down to that level, but others had not. Therefore there were examples to go by, and extrapolations were made from the already complete examples.

As a cross-check, there were just over 2000 procedures, each consisting of a sequence of elemental processes that were triggered in response to some event. A procedure essentially identifies what is to be done when various events occur. On average, each procedure required a chain of ten elemental processes. Therefore this provided an independent estimate of 20,000—25,000 elemental processes (or processes + activities + tasks + steps).

The implications of deciding that 25,000 processes are needed to model a large enterprise are serious for the analyst (and managers). The writers who make casual suggestions that existing processes should be abandoned, and completely new processes created, are not highlighting the reality that to reinvent a large enterprise would require the implementation of 25,000 processes. Clearly this does not happen and, despite what the BPW consultants might say, in all cases of "reengineering", substantial numbers of existing processes are retained, which cannot be ignored.

In practice, the analyst has a delicate job in deciding how far to take analysis. Despite the astonishing tirade against analysis by Hammer and Stanton (1995) ("There are two problems with conducting analysis in the reengineering context. The first is that it is a profound waste of time ... the second is that it can inhibit change"), it is necessary for the analyst to pay careful attention to detail and provide enough information about both the old and the new so that the final target system is understood and documented.

Of course, there is a difficult decision about how much analysis is appropriate. This has been addressed by Langley (1995) who identifies a set of contextual factors that affects the use of formal analysis. She asserts that "Thus managers need to navigate between two deadly extremes: on the one hand, ill-conceived and arbitrary decisions made without systematic study and reflection (`extinction by instinct') and on the other, a retreat into abstraction and conservatism that relies obsessively on numbers, analyses, and reports (`paralysis by analysis')". Table 2.2 summarizes her factors and indicates which extremes of these factors are more likely to contribute to extinction or paralysis. She goes on to identify several situations that contribute to paralysis or extinction, and she proposes ways to approach them.

Factor	Risk of extinction by instinct	Risk of paralysis by analysis
Participation	limited	widespread
Power	concentrated	diffuse
Opinions and motivations	convergent	divergent
Leadership style	autocratic	consensual or passive
Cognitive style	intuitive	analytical

Table 2.2 Factors affecting analysis (after Langley, 1995)

Core or essential processes

Another point of discussion is that BPW is concerned with *core business processes*. There is more than a hint that organizations embark on all kinds of activities, some of which are "core" and hence others which are more peripheral.

At least two important properties of core processes can be seen in the literature: the first is that they are fundamental and essential to the enterprise; the second is that the enterprise possesses some "core competencies" which means that the enterprise is relatively good at doing the activities, compared with other enterprises that do similar activities.

This kind of thinking drives many of the decisions taken by businesses today. There is a presumption that an enterprise adds most value by applying its core competencies, and other activities that are not core competencies are good candidates for outsourcing. Of course, outsourcing as an activity is not new but use of the particular term outsourcing is relatively recent.

Core business processes are essential not only to the survival of the enterprise, but also they cut across traditional departmental boundaries. For example, fulfilling customer orders is at the core of most enterprises that work in the trading or manufacturing sectors of the economy (frequently referred to as order fulfillment). It cuts across functional boundaries because meeting a customer order may involve activities related to selling, marketing, administration, law, purchasing, manufacturing, logistics, and accounting. Each of these may exist as a separate business function. Therefore in some sense an analysis of business processes requires an understanding of business functions and how they relate to each other.

Does anything special need to be taken into account for this? This is another point discussed in detail later, but essentially the issue was resolved by the earlier decision not to worry about levels of process as long as there is a definition of a process which is recursive. For example, if order fulfillment is broken down into pieces, one component is order entry. How does order entry relate to business functions? As a result of looking at a range of enterprises, it can be seen that some enterprises carry out order entry within a sales function, others have a separate administration function, and others give the responsibility to finance. Therefore, at one level, a process is orthogonal to the business function in that there may be several degrees of freedom available over the allocation of processes to functions. However, the key emerging theme is that these processes need to be organized in some way.

Is this why an 'object-oriented metaphor' is being applied with increasing frequency to BPW work? An order can be considered as an "object" in the object-oriented sense: it has data (the contents of the order itself), functions are applied to the data (validating, entering, reading, assigning, ...), and data and functions are implemented by methods (paper files, computer files, automated assignment, manual assignment, ...). In a deeper sense it does not matter which business function has responsibility for order entry as long as those who need the process to be performed can send an order message to the right place to have it checked and entered.

Figure 2.2 presents one possible de-composition of the whole order fulfillment process (that takes place within the enterprise). The de-composition of processes is discussed later, but for the moment a simple hierarchical de-composition is offered. It should be noted that hierarchical de-compositions may be common, but when designing business processes they may not be appropriate.

The diagrammatic way of presenting processes as shown in Figure 2.2 can be a simple indented list (such as is shown in Silver, 2011 p11).

When talking about business processes, it is useful to draw a distinction between core processes and common processes. For example, order fulfillment can be considered as a core process because it is of such fundamental importance to the enterprise. From the first column in Figure 2.2, there is a process "enquire". This is an example of a common process. To understand why it is 'common', identify it as "call handling". Call handling is necessary in an enterprise in many different circumstances such as: answering a request for information, dealing with a request to service a faulty machine, processing an order, or providing a support service. In all of these circumstances a common call-handling process would involve answering the call, acknowledging the call, logging the call, assigning calls to people who service the calls, managing calls, escalating difficult calls, and closing calls. Because call handling takes place in many parts of the enterprise, it can be classified as a common business process.

It is an essential part of the work in BPW to try and identify both core and common business processes.

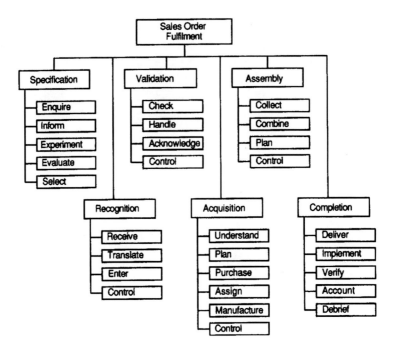

Fig 2.2 Order Fulfilment

Business Processes Cut Across Business Functions

An absolutely key point about BPW is that core business processes cut across traditional business functional departments in the sense that multiple departments are affected, or need to be involved in, the definition and operation of those business processes. In this sense, business processes can be considered to be orthogonal to business departments or functions. This point is illustrated in Figure 2.3[1].

In Figure 2.3 the horizontal businesses are core processes and (should) interact with all the departments shown vertically in the diagram.

One of the dreams of BPW was that the 're-engineered' organization would be managed in terms of business processes rather than departments. As is noted in the book in various places, that is something that does not seem to have happened. Although much BPW work has been done, it seems more organizations are very reluctant to go down the route of managing the business by having directors or VPs of processes rather than departments or functions.

---

1 Fig 2.3 appeared first in Darnton & Giacoletto (1992).

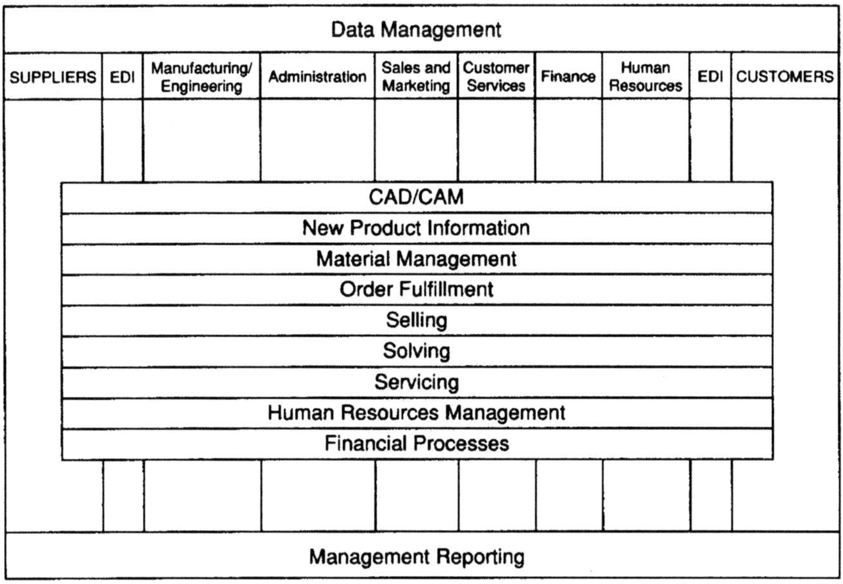

Data Management									
SUPPLIERS	EDI	Manufacturing/ Engineering	Administration	Sales and Marketing	Customer Services	Finance	Human Resources	EDI	CUSTOMERS

CAD/CAM

New Product Information

Material Management

Order Fulfillment

Selling

Solving

Servicing

Human Resources Management

Financial Processes

Management Reporting

Figure 2.3 Business processes and enterprise departments.

(Re)Engineering?

There is a lively debate in the software world about what is a software engineer, and why the work is called "engineering". This debate has been intensified in many US states where the term engineer is reserved for people who are certified or licensed in some way.

As far as business processes are concerned, the use of the terms engineering and reengineering are rather intriguing. The books by Davenport (1993), Donovan (1993), and Hammer and Champy (1993) all have the word "reengineering" in the title or subtitle. Davenport and Donovan do not have the term "engineering" in their indexes. Hammer and Champy have a fleeting reference in their index to "engineering, concurrent" in the context of a method used by Kodak. Donovan's index does not refer to reengineering. Davenport has two entries for re-engineering: one to discuss the differences between reengineering and innovation, including "Reengineering is only part of what is necessary in the radical change of processes; it refers specifically to the design of the new process", and the second, "innovation (or reengineering, as it was called there) ...". Hammer and Champy have a section for a formal definition of reengineering which includes: "Reengineering", properly, is "the fundamental rethinking and radical re-design of business processes to achieve dramatic improvements in critical, contemporary measures of performance, such as cost, quality, service, and speed". Hammer (Hammer and Stanton, 1995) even offers an Official Definition of reengineering as, "The fundamental rethinking and radical redesign of business processes to bring about dramatic improvements in performance". Would practitioners from traditional branches of engineering recognize such a general definition of reengineering?—probably not.

These references do not help the practitioner to understand why it is all being called "reengineering". Also, if the prefix "re" has any real meaning, were the processes 'engineered' in the first place?

The problems of these terms can be avoided by stating that although many uses of the term "engineering" are difficult or impossible to understand, it does not matter because the primary concern of the book is with techniques for the analysis of business processes. The books that were used to look for index entries are all fine books in their own way and are important reading. They do give a sense of the context for talking about engineering, but the impatient person who hopes to use an index as a fast track to operational definitions is in for a surprise. Is someone 'doing' BPW work who is not an engineer, supposed to know the essence of engineering? It is likely that a great number of business process reengineering practitioners have not had an engineering background.

Input—process—output

One point about which most writers agree is the simple idea that a process has one or more inputs and one or more outputs. The process performs some kind of transformation on the inputs in order to produce the outputs.

When the whole enterprise is viewed in such a way, there is no distinction between a BPW high-level view of the enterprise, and a classical economics view, which uses factors of production to produce goods and services. This is illustrated in Figure 2.4.

The analyst certainly needs to be concerned with the inputs and outputs of every process, along with details of the way in which the inputs are transformed to produce those outputs. However, the analyst also needs to be aware that although the concept is that an order fulfillment process receives as inputs customer orders and all the resources needed to process those orders, "order fulfillment" has no real existence beyond an abstraction; the analyst must find out what really happens to those inputs.

From a modeling point of view, the analyst will need to understand what triggers each process. For example, rather than seeing a customer order as an input to order fulfillment, it may be more appropriate to model the arrival of an order as a trigger for the process to start. The analyst should identify all possible triggers for every process.

It is not conceded, from an analytical point of view, that input—process—output is the most appropriate. There are alternatives. For example, many (most?) enterprises have intricate ways of cooperating together; when two companies agree to cooperate in a supplier—supplied relationship, what are the true boundaries of that enterprise? A vehicle manufacturer with intimate supplier relationships yields an enterprise larger than just the vehicle assembler or marketer—a virtual enterprise.

In this sense, enterprises may just be legal objects and span of control concepts rather than physical realities.

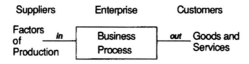

Figure 2.4 Enterprise as a business process.

The paradox of core competency

There are many exhortations to enterprises to concentrate on their core competencies. The existence of core competencies raises a serious challenge to the simplistic depictions of business processes. If a process can be represented primarily as the transformation of inputs into outputs, why is it often so difficult for one enterprise to emulate the efficiency of another?

Core competency often involves experience and organizational learning. In other words, as problems are solved, the enterprise is able to capture, share internally, and protect from external disclosure, knowledge of the most efficient and effective ways to perform processes. The efficiency of the enterprise over time is one measure of the enterprise's learning curve.

In reality, collective experience and learning are highly complex phenomena. They require careful attention not only to the technical aspects of processes, but also to the human, social, and organizational dimensions. In this deep sense, a business process is much more than a transformation of factor inputs. There is a serious risk that by using a reductionist approach of expressing business processes in terms of simple process flow diagrams showing flows of materials, flows of information, and sequences of activities, the whole essence of collective experience and learning is lost. It is impossible to find process flow diagrams and descriptions showing how to build up and exploit deep knowledge and competency.

Decomposition techniques of analysis by themselves are hopelessly deficient when it comes to identifying core competency. An organization is much more than a mere 'sum of the parts'. The sense in which an organization is more than the sum of the parts is referred to as the emergent properties of the organization as a system. Systems thinking is needed here, not reductionist or de-compositional analysis.

There is a very real risk that consultant prescriptions for radical reform of processes lose experience and learning, and disrupt essential, informal, and complex feedback loops that have evolved to capture and share essential experience. From an analytical point of view, when handling the subject of core competencies, rather than seeing business processes in simple, deterministic ways, systemic approaches are more appropriate to model the richness of the phenomena involved.

Binding time

Over simplistic high-level process flowcharts may be helpful in some situations, but generally are insufficient. The use of simple and highly aggregated charts as a symbol, or metaphor, for a hypothetical ideal form of the process presents no such concerns, since such charts are very useful to senior managers and those who need system overviews.

However, there should be concerns when people start to believe that these very simple, highly aggregated charts represent how the enterprise actually works. The real world of work is usually far apart from such simple charts.

25,000 processes may be needed to describe a large enterprise. In addition, predetermined process flowcharts, and procedures, represent ideal cases of how those processes "should" be chained together. In other words, the binding between processes is decided at the time of drawing the charts or defining the procedures.

However, the pool of 25,000 processes represents the possible ways in which inputs can be dealt with. In reality, they are not chained together until an actual event takes place, when the people managing the process and the context at the time are known. In other words, rather than the processes being bound together at design time, they are in practice bound together at "run" time.

There are some "process chains" that cannot be broken, either because there are absolute reasons (a telephone could not be connected to a distant place until a number had been dialed?) or because there are very strict rules in place. Apart from that, the real world of work is very much about people working together and deciding, as events happen and time goes by, how to handle the events, what to do, and in what order to do it.

Purpose

Many writers state that the purpose of business processes is to satisfy customer wants or needs. Several of the quotations above reference customers, even to the point of including customers in the processes.

It is undoubtedly a good idea to be concerned with the needs of those who are supplied with goods and services. It is even a matter of survival for many enterprises to supply products that people are willing to buy.

Sometimes there is more than a touch of political correctness in placing primary emphasis on customers. To say that my main goal is to satisfy customers can sound trite. This is not meant disparagingly, but attributing the purpose of business processes primarily to the satisfaction of customer needs is technically naïve.

Firstly, from an analytical point of view, enterprises do not have purposes; only people do. Galbraith (1967) articulated several motives (such as compulsion, pecuniary compensation, identification, and adaptation) in people who take part in corporate life. It is naïve to assume that those who control enterprises place customer satisfaction before their own welfare or survival (to do so would imply minimizing profits, not maximizing them). It is also naïve to assume that customer behavior is independent of corporate behavior—a large amount of marketing effort is expended to influence customer behavior.

In addition to the pioneering commentary by Galbraith, there has been much subsequent discussion in the management literature about the need to consider all stakeholders, or the "victims" of systems (see for example, Checkland 1981). Having said that, much extant literature places emphasis on customer satisfaction, even though the true picture is likely to be far more complex.

The business process analyst should understand the interactions between the enterprise, and the customers, stakeholders, and victims of processes, including ways to understand customer wants and the extent to which they are being satisfied by the enterprise, or by others.

The frequent comments in the literature about the mission and objectives of enterprises, and the purposes of processes, hint that perhaps the real scope of investigation for the analyst should be system rather than process.

Management responsibility for business processes

Business processes may be improved or innovated varying in how radical are the changes. Business processes can be considered as cross-functional chains of lower level processes which implement the core business processes.

Corporate responsibility is normally located functionally, although some enterprises give profit and loss responsibility to specific business units which may commission their own functional support or obtain it from corporate functional groups. If a for-profit enterprise is not making enough profit, is that usually the responsibility of the chief finance officer? Not usually, because profit and loss responsibility will lie with the business units. If there is poor performance by a particular employee, is that the responsibility of the human resources manager? Not usually, because it is the responsibility of the business unit where the employee is located.

What is still very rare following BPW exercises is a general trend towards the replacement of functional directors by process directors. When there is a problem in the order fulfillment process, is the order fulfillment director responsible? Usually not, as the responsibility will generally lie with functional managers. Perhaps fundamental reorganization of an enterprise's business processes does not require fundamental reorganization of responsibilities at board level, or maybe the political realities of enterprises mean that the boardroom is the last likely place for radical reengineering. Therefore there is a potential problem in overall responsibility for new or seriously modified business processes if the BPW exercise is not followed by an appropriate allocation of responsibilities.

Of course, identifying and organizing along the lines of core business processes does not eliminate the need for functional excellence. Therefore good functions will (should?) persist even following radical business process reform across functional boundaries.

Champy (1995) points out that it is not only the processes that need to be reengineered, but the high level management as well.

Concluding remarks

These background themes are developed in the next few chapters as specific techniques are explored. They are important because the analyst will frequently need to present the results of analysis in terms of some of these perspectives.

For example, it will often be necessary to extract from source material information about the highest level or core processes. The simple input and output models of process will need to be expanded to give much more detail. The analysts and their management will need to decide how much analysis is "enough".

The background has been set for this book's journey. The next chapter begins an exploration of substantive analytical techniques.

Lessons from history—the evolution of process analysis techniques

History repeats itself—those who do not learn from history, end up repeating it

Earlier, views of what various writers portray as business processes were set out. There is some incredulity expressed at those writers who dismiss the need for any analysis while proposing that the way to do BPW is only by radical design of new processes. If the order of magnitude of processes in a large enterprise can be 25,000+, then some kind of analysis is necessary along with accompanying technology to manage the volume of information involved, notwithstanding the suggestions of some writers not to bother with analysis—they are just plain wrong!

What is needed is an approach to the description of processes in a way that is completely scalable from a few processes to many thousands of processes.

In the search for business process analysis techniques, the key findings are simple. At the senior levels of management, most techniques seemed to be based on tapping into experience and intuition. There is nothing wrong with that, but following on from workshops to capture senior management ideas, something more analytical needs to be done. At lower levels of work, many published techniques seemed to be based on simple flowcharts of various kinds (for example, process or data), cost accounting, and very occasionally, operational analysis (but these last two occur rarely in the mainstream BPW literature).

Is there any more than that to the analysis of business processes? BPW is a new term, but does it introduce new methods of analysis? The investigation of this is an important part of the book's journey.

Despite some claims of contemporary radical redesign of the way in which enterprises work, there is nothing particularly new about this. It seems that since time immemorial, people have been taking advantage of new technology and ways of thinking to produce radically new ways of going about their work.

The world population is increasing rapidly, and the scale of enterprises is increasing to higher levels of size, complexity, and novelty in the things they are trying to do. Technology is deeply implicated in BPW, but are the claims justified that it is primarily information technology? For the analyst, it is necessary to know whether existing analytical techniques are sufficient, or is there something in the new size, complexity, and novelty that renders old techniques obsolete and introduces new techniques?

So far, there are no radically new techniques that are specific to BPW.

Indeed, several books often go back in time to the flowcharts and related techniques developed much earlier in the twentieth century. Accounting and operational research techniques have advanced (for example, activity based costing and data envelopment analysis), but more in response to drivers other than the BPW fashion.

History demonstrates the long-term intimate relationship between technology and business process. Examples such as Stonehenge, early calendar development, and ancient information technology illustrate this point. It is instructive to take a short journey back in history, before continuing with the examination of techniques useful for BPW work.

Technology, information, and business processes

Anthropology and paleontology include in their domains the study of the use of artifacts by human beings to help in the achievement of human goals. Humans live in their environments in groups and use communication. The organization of work by many individuals requires communication and information for coordination. Enterprise can be exercised either by individuals, or by groups that are organized in some way. Enterprise is about doing work, or trying to achieve objectives. In these senses, technology, information, and enterprise exist in all human cultures and have done so as far back as humans have been identified.

In chapter 2 it is shown that for many writers, business processes are concerned with delivering goods or services to customers. Presumably, this means work done by people for themselves is not the result of a business process, although it may involve other kinds of process. Therefore business process in this sense implies providing goods or services in some transaction for reward, either by barter or for cash (putting on one side, the complexities arising from slavery).

It is not clear whether humans were involved in this kind of business process more than, say, 10,000 years ago, but there is certainly substantial evidence of human organization and trade for the past few thousand years. Therefore enterprise and business processes have been around for thousands of years. Is the modern era unique in the radical redesign of business processes, or has it happened in the past? Did earlier business processes evolve very slowly until modern radical redesign, or were there earlier examples of radical redesign? Indeed, is the only new thing in the BPW world, the actual term 'business process'?

For the purposes of exploration, let us take the example of information technology, not only in the narrow sense of modern computing and communications technology, but also including all technology involved in performing operations on information. This is discussed in more detail by Darnton and Giacoletto (1992).

Early human enterprises have been concerned with matters such as food production, trading, warfare, ceremony and ritual, investigation of phenomena, and learning. In all of these, collaborative working has been necessary, along with division of labor, specialization, communication, and control.

Much ancient effort was put into knowledge of seasons, position of the sun and moon, time measurement and astronomy more generally, along with artifacts that can be a store of information or be used for estimating purposes. This knowledge has been, and still is, crucial for the organization of business processes.

Controversy about the purposes of the stone circle at places like Stonehenge continues, summarized by authors such as Burgess (1980). He points out that even if Stonehenge was used for various kinds of predictions based on astronomical observation, the degree of technology used was not necessary to achieve that purpose alone, and given the enormous coordination of collaborative effort needed to create such monuments there was probably more reason that merely the prediction of seasons. Astronomical observation was developed much further after Stonehenge, for example, in India. Basham (1967) presents an intriguing view of possible ways in which the development of astronomy involved various influences backwards and forwards between east and west.

Early developments of information technology beyond astronomical observation aids are in writing and the methods of storing writing. James and Thorpe (1994) discuss alphabets and codes, and identify a report of printing in India before 700 AD, and which was developed further in China. They also give an example of the application of movable type from Crete dated around 1700 BC. Printing and paper proved to be forms of information technology that have had a profound effect on business processes and many kinds of enterprise have been built up with the aid of books and documents. Indeed, earlier in the book, a focus on procedure change as a way of improving non-computer-based processes was identified.

It is a fundamental error in BPW work to focus only or primarily on computer-based activities.

The communication of messages is another form of information technology that has had a profound influence on business processes. James and Thorpe (1994) describe semaphore systems used by the Greeks in the second and first centuries BC. In the ninth century AD there was a substantial heliograph system used to communicate with Byzantium (Constantinople, Istanbul). In America, indigenous tribes used smoke as a form of communications technology. This was noted by Columbus, but there is no evidence on which to assess the age of the system.

The last few centuries have seen very extensive use of paper and printing information technology to revolutionize many enterprises.

Many early examples of communications information technology were related to warfare. However, some were also related to trading and associated accounting. Yates (1989) describes the use of early electrical forms of communication to help with the control and coordination of business that included facilities spanning large distances.

Needless to say, the second half of the twentieth century saw the massive emergence of information technology in the form of computers and electronic communications.

These comments should help to place information technology in a wide and historical perspective. Table 3.1 presents a summary of several key steps in the evolution of information technology and its impact on business processes.

So far, the discussion has focused on information technology, with the intention of establishing a broad base for the meaning of information technology.

Information technology is one way of viewing more general technology. The reality is that since time immemorial, there has been an intimate connection between technology and business processes. There are other views of technology, such as transportation, materials, manufacturing, electrical, and chemical. The introduction of new technology beyond an experimental stage has often resulted in massive and radical redesign of business processes. For example, the application of many different kinds of technology to agriculture has resulted in orders of magnitude greater output for substantially lower levels of labor input, delivered more reliably to orders of magnitude greater numbers of people. There is, of course, the industrial revolution itself which triggered the massive and radical redesign of business processes. Materials and manufacturing technology have delivered unimaginable changes in style and standard of living to billions of people by means of radically redesigned business processes in the course of the past few centuries.

The focus of system analysis

If there is a connection between the deployment of technology and business processes, evident for more than two thousand years, have any analytical techniques accompanied such changes? Are such changes helpful today?

Basic numeracy and geometrical skills are required, which can be taken for granted. Their origin is shrouded in the mysteries of antiquity, starting with glimmers of evidence from places as far apart as Ancient India (Basham, 1967) and Ancient Britain (Thom, 1967; Burgess, 1980), followed by the later and better documented examples from Ancient Greece.

A particular application of numerical skills of relevance to business process is accounting. James and Thorpe (1994) identify early forms that are possibly as old as 8500 BC.

Another application of numerical skills is to understand processes in terms of aggregated data and data distributions (statistics). Yates (1989) gives several early examples of the application of statistical techniques to early management problems, starting in some cases in the eighteenth century. These are associated with the rise of "scientific management", and include tabulation and graphical presentation.

Other analytical skills have been developed for different kinds of technology, but specific analytical techniques for business processes are not detectable until the late nineteenth century onwards.

Systems analysis has not always been called that, but it is a useful term to

Time period	Example problem	Information technology innovations	Commentary—implications for business processes
4000+ years ago	Knowing seasons?	Relative positioning of standing stones; microliths	An inspired guess at a reason for very ancient stone monuments; clearly some analysis performed; possible impact on processes such as agricultural production
2000+ years ago	Navigation of ships used for trade	Astronomical observation	Enabler of trade with a wider variety of places
2000 years ago	Building; military campaigns	Some automation of communication: Roman army mechanisms and bureaucracy; Egyptian geometry	Some sophisticated applications of technology to information operations; many analysts in formal jobs; changes to military processes; changes to building processes
1500+ years ago	Calculations, accounting, and abstract mathematics	Decimal number system combined with writing and recording	More efficient calculations and accounting
1300 years ago	Communication of religious ideas	Paper and printing	Improved consistency, efficiency, and productivity
500 years ago	Dissemination of information	Improved printing and paper	Much more information widely available to more people, more efficiently
200 years ago	Cloth manufacturing costs	Punched cards	Introduced for looms—usually there was only one analyst per factory; change to design and manufacturing processes

100+ years ago	Coordinate dispersed and complex firms	Typewriters, duplicators, telegraph	Emergence of systematic management used information technology to derive new kinds of business process
70 years ago	Optimize workflow such as office procedures, manufacturing, mining	Mechanical and electromechanical information and data processing devices	Arose because of machines: initiated by the availability of new mechanical devices, some of which dealt with data. This phase reached its height with data processing being done by punched cards—the data processes are things such as data entry, sorting, merging; the business processes are the coordination of complex manufacturing, logistics, etc.
40 years ago	Highly complex calculations; volume of business transactions; automated machine control	Electronic computer	The processes were redefined to those that fit the capability of the computer—the focus of that era of system analysis was to take data processing and automate it through computerized processes
Now	Business process reengineering; integrating the parts of large, complex, enterprises; changing patterns of work and leisure	Communication technology.	Systems analysis of today is BPR-communications technology is one driver of global competitiveness, which in turn requires the previous generations of system analysis results to have to be reorganized; it is not global competitiveness per se, it is the communication technology driving competitiveness
Future	Changing patterns of employment contracts; urban congestion; desired lifestyles	Massive convergence of technologies applied to information and knowledge	This will probably be a paradigm shift: since the creation of cities and the industrial evolution people used to move to where the work is located; more and more information and knowledge work will move to where the people are located

Table 3.1 Evolution of information technology and business process: examples

represent the fact that business processes are effectively human-made systems.

Apart from the early numeracy, geometrical, and presentation techniques, there was an early move to represent the production of goods as a series of flows. Scientific management was based on the idea of decomposing production processes into smaller parts, and then improving the efficiency of the parts, which in many cases has certainly yielded impressive productivity gains.

Apart from the evolution of approaches to process flows, there has been the emergence of practices such as systems analysis, organization and methods (O&M), and work study.

Workflow and process flow

There is a new enthusiasm for the idea of workflow as a way to improve manufacturing, business, and other processes. Although there is a new emphasis, the fundamental concepts of workflow have been evolving for a considerable period of time. The term Work Flow can be traced back to near the beginning of the twentieth century at least.

The essence of workflow starts from the recognition that enterprises produce some combination of outputs (goods or services). In the usual case, an enterprise is adding value to a set of inputs while producing the outputs. The added value may arise because the enterprise performs some transformation on the inputs to produce the outputs, or it may just be that the added value arises to the customer because the enterprise is able to supply at a rate which is likely to be exceeded if the customer tried to find alternative supplies directly (that was the reason early explorers found the American continent).

In some cases the enterprise never sees the products, and it supplies only a trading or brokering service.

Workflow has been applied traditionally to both materials and documents. The idea is that materials go through different stages of transformation, and hence the basic input materials flow through various stages of part-finished work-in-progress until final products are completed. Documents flow through different departments for different purposes, with the results of added information being coordinated and synchronized.

Workflow can be described with the aid of text descriptions and various kinds of "flow" charts—this applies to materials and documents. In recent years, technology has assisted in representing flows by means of more dynamic representations and animations (this is discussed further in chapter 11).

The analysis and modeling of workflow are really a subset of systems analysis techniques. The evolution of a wide range of these techniques has been described by Couger (1973). It is instructive to note his observations about the evolution of charting work and process flows. He identifies that pre-1920 the process flowchart was used primarily to show the flow of materials. Taylor (Taylor, 1911) and the Gilbreths (Gilbreth, F.B. and L.E., 1924) were the most widely cited people developing and using such process flowcharts. The Gilbreths developed the idea of a Therblig to represent "quantities" of micromotion. These were attempts to de-compose workflow into hierarchies of processes, in some cases to very low levels of detail.

Between 1920 and 1950 the volume of information flow related to workflow increased considerably, therefore there were developments of charts to show the flow of forms. Many business processes were controlled by means of forms that were used to initiate and synchronize tasks. Writers such as Neuschel (1950) discuss precisely this. For example, a sales person may use a form such as a traveling requisition to record visits and orders. An order would be entered, resulting in the generation of a series of further forms such as acknowledgment, bills of materials, requisitions, invoices, delivery notes, and so forth. The early forms of flowcharts were simple applications of the earlier process flow charts.

Early information processing technology included a large number of tabulating devices, so work flowcharts evolved to include depictions of activities performed by tabulating machines, and board wiring diagrams were added. As technology evolved further and was applied increasingly to the processing of information, charts evolved to include information about various information processing devices such as input and output, storage, and computation.

Couger's next phase is the period 1951-1960 which he characterizes as the period when " ... techniques especially suited for analysis of computer-based systems began to emerge". He gives the example of information process charts which were a combination of forms flowcharts and block diagrams. A text from this period is Canning (1956) who gives examples of flowcharts and explains a set of flowchart symbols.

For the period 1961-1970, Couger describes various ways to analyze greater complexity in computer-supported workflow by means of forms, and language-based system descriptions. Two examples of forms-based approaches from this period are NCR's ADS (Accurately Defined Systems, see Lynch, 1969) and Honeywell's BISAD (Business Information Systems Analysis and Design, see Honeywell, 1968). This was the period when the language-based descriptions began to emerge from the ISDOS research program at the University of Michigan (see Teichroew, 1974).

The descriptions of Couger and Knapp (1974) (along with Couger's associates) can be brought up to date. The early forms of flowchart have seen some recent evolution, but current forms of flowchart are usually the same or simple derivatives of these earlier forms. The 1970s onwards saw the addition of information flow diagrams (DeMarco, 1978; Gane and Sarson, 1979; Yourdon, 1989) and structure charts (Yourdon and Constantine, 1979). From recent publications about business processes, there has not been much evolution of the earlier techniques (see Harrington, 1991, and Born, 1994, for examples of established process and information flowchart techniques applied to business processes). A quick glance at a recent review of flowcharting tools by Rockman (1995) shows tools and symbols that are mainly derived from much earlier charting techniques. A somewhat different charting technique is described by Ould (1995), which uses a specific notation to chart some of the dynamic aspects of processes, along with identifying the kinds of people performing particular system roles.

There has been commentary in the professional literature for some time, about how work "flows" across traditional departmental or functional boundaries (corresponding to the comments noted in chapter 2 about business processes crossing functional boundaries). This has led to a long-lasting dilemma of organizational design, which recognizes that workflow lies at the core of enterprises in that the final deliverables can be seen as the very purpose for the existence of the enterprise, but it is often necessary to apply very different kinds of technical or functional expertise at different stages during the workflow.

Most enterprise boards of management comprise heads of functional departments rather than managers of key business processes, and this is often true even following radical business process reengineering that is supposed to give primary importance to customer-oriented business processes.

In contrast to the workflow analysis techniques described above a very different concept of workflow arises in conjunction with ideas about organizational design, and these are explored in more detail in chapter 10.

Current concerns with workflow have arisen in part from documentation handling. Despite the modern concern for document flow, this is not a new problem, and it has been mentioned earlier and explicitly as such. The need to manage documents other than the more standardized forms in forms flow systems has been described by Simon (1957) while discussing service organizations in general and insurance companies in particular. Other early descriptions of workflow include Chapple and Sayles (1961), Argyris (1966), and Holstein and Berry (1970).

The current concept of workflow is being merged increasingly with BPW and transaction processing ideas. There is also a merging with some key ideas from groupware and computer-supported cooperative work (CSCW).

There is a wider recognition that as computer-supported systems become more complex, and there is increasing novelty in the systems that are computer supported, more systemic interaction takes place between people and computers. This has more than a hint of the need in some instances for workflow to take into account needs of control and coordination of some tasks that are not performed by computer, within an overall flow of work.

Therefore, in a simple sense, workflow can be considered as the provision of optimum computer support of enterprise objectives, policies, and procedures—this provides a direct link between workflow and BPW. In a more complex setting, workflow can be seen as the provision of optimum computer support for cooperative work, by assisting human beings to do their work in a context of complex networks of tasks, groups, computers, and organizational units.

Workflow technology appears to have evolved in a different parallel line from "mainstream" software products such as operating systems, database management systems, transaction monitors, and communications systems.

The main impetus seems to have been the need to manage documents and the flow of documents. This is clear from many discussions about workflow technology and products.

The growth of PCs in parallel with mainframe processing, in part because mainframes were not delivering many of the functions wanted by end-users, is mirrored in the development of workflow tools (however, having said that, it must be recognized that the evolution of PCs is probably a spin-off from the military need for the miniaturization of control circuits in missiles). Mainframes and mainstream software were developed in part to manage the core business transactions of many enterprises, which often represent where most of the enterprise money is tied up. However, to perform all the associated tasks around the core transactions a great deal of information is needed, usually represented in the form of documents. The mainframe handles the highly structured records, but the surrounding documents are left to look after themselves. Indeed, one 'Achilles Heel' of activity based costing, is the absence of operational data to underpin the creation of cost-generating activities; there is plenty of financial information, but operational information can be very sparse. At a very simple level, how many companies know the value of all transactions executed but may well not have collected information about how many transactions were performed.

For many enterprises, the costs of managing information are an order of magnitude greater than expenditure on IT—and the order of magnitude may be a factor in the range 5-20 (Darnton and Giacoletto, 1992; Vincent, 1990). Much of this information is in documents of some kind, which has not so far been well supported by computer applications. It is this recognition that so much workflow involves so much information which is not yet handled by today's information technology which leads to "documentation in the large" posing such a challenge for workflow technology. As if it were not a great enough problem that the management of information costs several times more than the management of IT, at the computer level itself " 98% of business computer users employ word processing software on their PCs ... at least 80 percent of corporate electronic information is in the form of documents, as opposed to structured database records...", according to Reinhardt (1994) while discussing various reports about the role of documents.

Workflow and transaction processing

Workflow is not the same as transaction processing; or workflow and transaction processing are the same concepts. These two opposite views were encountered during the search for ideas behind BPW.

One basis for distinguishing transaction processing from workflow seems to lie partly in the nature of the data involved, and partly in the kind of processing operation applied to the data. Those who distinguish between the two have remarked that transaction processing systems handle highly structured data with a clearly defined set of operations in well-defined sequences, whereas workflow deals with many different kinds of document and perhaps ill-defined, or more ad hoc operations to be performed. If that is really the extent of the difference, then at a meta-modeling level, there may not be much at all to distinguish transaction processing from workflow.

The concept of workflow involves an abstract high-level process that is broken down into a series of smaller processes performed on materials or information. There is usually a finite set of possible ways in which the smaller processes can be linked together while the overall inputs are used to generate the required goods or services. The materials or information being worked can be viewed as going through a series of state transitions. There are no general rules about which state transitions are permanent, and which can be reversed on a change of mind, or unexpected event.

The concept of a transaction involves an abstract high-level process that can be broken down into a series of smaller processes or tasks. There is usually a finite set of possible ways in which the tasks can be chained together to complete the required transaction. There are no general rules about which tasks are permanent, and which can be reversed. At this level of discussion, there is very little indeed to distinguish transactions from workflow.

There are some more subtle aspects to transactions which have arisen as a result of the need for precision before transaction processing systems could be written as computer applications.

Gray and Reuter (1993) describe the technical problems and decisions needed for the implementation of chained transactions. In a transaction processing and database management environment; care needs to be taken before a transaction is considered complete and "committed". There are certain circumstances when not all changes required for a transaction have yet taken place. For example, a computer may fail in the middle of processing a transaction, or someone may be able to change their mind until the last moment. If there is a machine failure or change of mind then any changes that have taken place so far may need to be restored, or returned to their original state. In a complex transaction, the designer will attempt to break a transaction down into smaller pieces, each of which can be committed in sequence, so that in the event of system failure, recovery is much easier and is only needed from the last "save-point" when the changes so far had been saved in some known and non-volatile state. If there is a sequence of save-points, then the design of the transaction processing system needs to take account of any rules about how far a transaction can be rolled back before it is completed.

In the non-computer business process world, these concepts of save-points and committed transactions have a parallel in the legal world where lawyers have well-rehearsed rules about when an agreement actually comes into existence. Anthropologists have a useful construct of human ritual.

Conceptually, there is virtually no difference with a workflow system that deals with either materials or information. In materials workflow, there are points where the use of materials is committed and cannot be reversed, and in some cases design can yield components that could be re-used if a part-finished product is abandoned.

In this way, Gray and Reuter give a technical explanation of a workflow structure as a set of chained transactions, with particular characteristics of save-points and database context. The rules relating to partially complete workflow situations have close parallels in the rules that need to be understood for the variants of chained transactions models. A discussion about the relationship between workflow and transaction processing, with a touch of middleware, can be found in Schreiber (1995), who proposes workflow as a means of linking together various transactions through what he calls a transaction workflow manager (which is the middleware).

The kind of reconciliation between workflow and transaction processing by means of something like Schreiber's transaction workflow manager is not needed for Nippon Telephone and Telegraph's (NTT) Multivendor Integration Architecture (MIA) component called Structured Transaction Definition Language (STDL) for distributed transaction processing. As a model, STDL is able to represent the concepts of workflow discussed above. NTT's MIA STDL effort represents probably the only international effort to define an open transaction processing standard.

If the key difference between workflow and a transactional system is reduced to the kind of data manipulated, then, fundamentally, the metamodels are the same. If the difference lies in transactional systems being purely computer based and workflow consisting of both computer-based and manual tasks, then again the meta models are the same.

Classical process analysis techniques

There is a very rich pool of techniques available to the business process analyst based on more classical practices of:

- systems analysis;
- organization and methods (O&M);
- work study;
- operational research.

Sources for these provide the majority of the basic skills needed by analysts. The skills are needed both for the description of processes and for the analysis of processes to propose various process rationalizations or improvements. These practices have seen substantial evolution during the twentieth century by applying earlier mathematical, statistical, and management approaches to the redesign of business processes at many different levels.

There are many excellent texts available. The business process analyst's library should include core books from all of these practices (in addition to basic statistics and mathematics).

The goal of the analyst is to produce process models such as classified in Table 3.2.

Type of model	Explanation	Examples
Descriptive	Mainly as implied by the word—a description of a process usually using some combination of text and diagrams summarizing a larger volume of source material	Explanatory text; charts; diagrams
Iconic	Some form of physical representation of what is being described	Scale model; photograph; video; animation
Symbolic	Creation of some abstract representation of a system or part of a system	Highly abstract graphical depiction; equation; statistical distribution and characteristics; simulation

Table 3.2 Types of process model

A summary of the approaches found by the author to be particularly useful is presented in Table 3.3. This table presents classical techniques because they are the techniques described in many textbooks. Additional techniques are described elsewhere in the book, including a formal analysis of text and diagrams (chapters 6 and 7), information (chapter 8), organizational and social factors (chapter 10), performance measures (chapter 12), and costs (chapter 9). The techniques are brought together in the next chapter using a metamodelling approach.

The most widely used techniques for BPW projects are those derived from the systems analysis field applied to the development of computer-based systems (supplemented by flowcharts of various kinds). It is useful to outline a history of those:

- 1967 - initial ISDOS proposal (Stieger and Teichroew, 1967)
- 1969 - Bachman (1969)
- 1971 - Teichroew and Sayani (1971), and, PSL v2.0
- 1976 - Chen (1976)
- 1977 - Teichroew et al. - most widely cited paper about PSL/PSA (1977)
- 1979 - Yourdon (1979)
- 1979 - Gane and Sarson (1979)

Category	Example techniques	Issues
Fact finding	Questionnaires; interviews; examination of existing process descriptions; observation	Rules and conventions; reliability; validity
Interviewing	Formal; informal; factual; attitudinal; open; confidential	Cognition; motivation; accuracy; adequacy of responses
Charting	Process flow; physical layout; organization; function allocation; work distribution; scheduling	Diagram semantics; adequacy of diagram vs text; completeness
Analysis of objectives	Output analysis; strategy formulation	Traceability; transformations known; assumptions known
Statistics and probability	Classical; empirical; subjective	Theoretical outcomes known; sample of historical data; knowledge of real distribution
Forecasting	Judgmental; extension of past history; causal	Experienced panel available; time series data available; evidence of relationships
Matrices	Input—output analysis; object life-history; process-function	Meaningful axes; classification system for each axis

Table 3.3 Process analysis: classical techniques

Many readers have probably not heard much about ISDOS and PSL. That is discussed in the next chapter.

An emergent 'fashion' in the modelling world is the Unified Modelling Language (UML), and there are attempts to apply this to BPW (see, for example, Holt, 2009). However, as noted in the next chapter, it is essential that a business process analyst adopts tools that are able to manage process definitions for thousands of processes, and not just relatively trivial classroom sized examples. Thus UML must be rejected as a serious contender for providing a BPW analysis toolkit. Some of the diagram types for UML may be helpful at a conceptual level for some audiences.

It would have been immensely helpful if standards organizations such as the International Standards Organization (ISO) had put its mind in a well-disciplined systematic way to come up with helpful standards for activities such as BPW and systems engineering.

Unfortunately, it now seems that ISO is subject to a barrage of various interest groups trying to have their own idiosyncratic approaches defined as an ISO standard. It is the humble opinion of the author of this book, that ISO is now in serious danger of bringing its standards activities into disrepute by allowing so many new inconsistent and competing standards take on the aura of an international standard. As far as ISO standards that may have a bearing on BPW are concerned, the problems of reconciling recent standards that have been permitted to be promulgated by ISO is illustrated well by Holt (2009: pp105ff). Taking the sum total of ISO standards that have emerged in recent years, it is now safe to say that there are no standards, simply because of the serious inconsistencies and deficiencies in those that have been promulgated. It can only be wished that those heavily involved in such standards activities were able to enjoy any expense accounts made available as a perk of the standards definition work! Sadly, it is prudent these days to pay little attention to ISO standards that affect the BPW world, and indeed may even provide a warning to be very cautious of any approaches that are now standards, because they may well be the result of considerable pressure by interest groups, rather than being something that has been thought through carefully and independently of particular interest groups.

Extreme caution should now be exercised before any ISO standard is adopted as a standard by a particular organization.

Systems, complexity, and de-composition

As far as analysis is concerned, mainstream BPW conveys the distinct impression that the key techniques to be employed are the analysis of process flow, and the decomposition of higher level processes into lower level "things", such as activities and tasks.

Such a view can leave us deeply troubled. Large enterprises are highly complex systems. If a system is "more than the sum of the parts", then after de-composition of a system into parts, what happened to the bits of the system that represent the essence of the "more than the sum of the parts?"

Hall (1989) defines a system thus: "A system is a set of objects (elements or parts), with relations between them and between their attributes (properties, or qualities). It is embedded in an environment containing other inter-related objects". He goes on to define objects (or elements), attributes (properties, or qualities of objects), and relations (which tie the objects of the system together).

Hall's object property relationship approach adds an interesting perspective to Teichroew's object property relationship approach (Teichroew et at., 1980). Hall's area of concern has been with systems generally, whereas Teichroew's has been principally with information systems. However, in both cases, the analyst obtains assistance from the observation that it is the relations that represent how a system is more than the sum of the parts. Teichroew's OPR provides a meta language for the definition of system languages implemented in a tool developed under the ISDOS program, called System Encyclopedia Manager (SEM). Hall gives an interesting list of relation occurrences of relevance to systems: "Some kinds of relations include: spatial, temporal, causal, random, equivalence, logical, semantic, and emotional ... ". Klir (1991) defines a system as a set of things and relations on those things.

What are the basic skills needed by the analyst who wants to approach business processes from a systems perspective? In a brief survey, Bertalanffy (1968) enumerates them as: cybernetics, information theory, game theory, decision theory, topology, factor analysis, and general system theory in the narrower sense. Bertalanffy's "narrow sense" covers the question of interaction by defining system: "as a complex of interacting components, concepts characteristic of organized whole such as interaction, sum, mechanization, centralization, competition, finality, etc., and to apply them to concrete phenomena".

An identification of the significance of relations is not quite sufficient for the analyst's examination of business processes. Enterprises consist of various operational units which may be more or less self-sufficient. The aggregation and disaggregation of enterprises (which may be simply to build up or reduce conglomerates, or it may be to outsource various functionality) is facilitated by identifying components that are viable in their own right. Similarly, some systems writers see the world as hierarchies or networks of different levels of system. For example, the heart is part of a person who is part of a social system who is part of the local life system which is part of the global ecology which is part of the solar system ... .

There are different levels and degrees of viability. Hence Beer's (1985) idea of a viable system is another idea that some analysts have found particularly useful (for example, Hoverstadt, 2008). Also, given the approach here of treating the concept of system as recursive at many levels, the idea of recursion in viable systems as expressed by Beer and other authors such as Espejo and Harnden (1989), and, Hoverstadt (2008) is particularly useful. This approach was coined by Beer as managerial cybernetics.

Concluding remarks

BPW can be seen in a long historical context by linking changes in business process design to the evolution of technology.

Business processes have been undergoing radical change since there have been enterprises, and that is for at least the last few thousand years. Each new generation or category of technology has been followed by new business processes. There is a broad spectrum of analysis techniques that has developed within well-known practices. These should be part of the business process analyst's toolkit. However, most of the more traditional techniques seem to be appropriate to the examination of specific and localized processes rather than overall business processes.

Some BPW literature talks about processes and workflow, and there are some hints that workflow and transactions are not the same thing. So are there any fundamental differences between business process, workflow, and transaction? At a meta-modeling level, it is very difficult to identify any such differences. The OPR approach introduced next is particularly helpful to the analyst for depicting high-level processes, workflow, or transactions. The other more traditional techniques are complementary in that they can be used as appropriate, to produce more detailed descriptions of the components of the overall processes.

If there is any fundamental difference between the older techniques and the problem of business process analysis it is to do with scope. In the 1950s and 1960s, it was fashionable to conduct a feasibility study and a cost-benefit analysis. It was recommended that one of the alternatives that should be considered was to redesign the present system without necessarily adding automation. Then it became fashionable to argue that the analyst should concentrate on the proposed system and ignore the present system because that would amount to putting on blinders. Now it is fashionable to recommend BPW. BPW is in some sense just the re-emergence of the feasibility study, but on a spiral, rather than a circle, because the scope is not just one application (which is the usual scope of the more traditional systems analysis techniques) but is now enterprise-wide or even used for a virtual enterprise.

For the description of business processes, OPR modeling provides a very useful framework for the overall enterprise, business processes, workflow, and transactions, with traditional techniques filling in the detail.

In earlier days, the systems analyst or requirements engineer developed a model by abstracting from a number of examples to a meta model and in many cases used a computer to create instances of the model, increasingly with the help of the business user who wanted the results of the analysis.

Now the business user has immediately available a large amount of data, can perform many "what if ... ?" investigations, and when performing a series of operations several times, wants to (and frequently can) create a macro to have that series performed automatically. The business, or end, user is assuming more of the role of the analyst by developing models for individual cases. There are more PC tools available to help with this kind of investigation, thus genuinely empowering senior enterprise managers.

This means that the business process analyst must now shift to specifying requirements for systems which produce models as outputs. The process engineer must state requirements for meta-metamodel systems. In terms of the levels presented in the next chapter, this means the meta language level rather than the model language level. The process analyst previously used a model language, but must now use a meta language. The business process managers are now likely to have access to some kind of model language, manual or automated.

Despite claims that today's situation is new because of the emergence of information technology, the fundamental skills needed by the business process analyst are derived mainly from techniques developed before the widespread deployment of computer-based information technology. What is new for the process analyst is the need to have meta language skills in addition to in-depth skills from one or more of the practices, and literacy in all of them. It seems that most of the current approaches to analyzing business processes were established before the ubiquity of the computer.

Simple process models: introduction to object property relationship (OPR) modeling

The previous chapter clarifies that the link between technology and business process is 'as old as the hills', or at least as old as humans have been doing business! Of specific relevance to BPW work, the chapter explains that most of the techniques advocated by writers in the BPW field use a range of techniques from the systems analysis world (system in the sense of computer-based system, or prior to the computer era, some system analysis techniques used in areas such as operations research).

In this chapter, the likely origin of the computer-based systems analysis techniques is identified. Other techniques are analyzed, and one overall approach is set out, which is able to bring all of these systems analysis techniques together in a systematic way, so that any organization is able to define how it would like to perform its own BPW work.

In identifying an overall scheme of analysis to integrate process description and analysis techniques, it is important to do so in a context of some important principles:

- the descriptions should be standardized according to some predefined notation;
- the notation has to be understandable by nontechnical people, even if they could not apply the techniques themselves;
- the notation should be scalable to help the analyst who needs to manage the descriptions and interrelationships between hundreds or thousands of processes;
- 'analysis' means it should be possible to define a range of completeness and consistency criteria for process descriptions, apply those criteria to a large number of process descriptions, and have a report on the overall state of completeness and consistency—analysis also means identifying possible candidate improvements;
- it should be possible to define a process description document schema and generate process documentation[1] from a database of process descriptions;
- it should be possible to have an approach that can yield different levels of system detail for different audiences (the information needed

---

1 using the term 'documentation' in the widest sense—it may not be only paper.

by senior managers who want an overview of business processes is generally much simpler than that needed by the process analyst who is looking at detailed improvement methods).

The world of developing computer-based applications has been subjected to waves of fashions over more than half a century, in seeking the 'silver bullet' for system definition and development. These 'waves of fashion' are psychological epidemics in that so often they are based more on an ideological commitment to a particular approach, than to well-researched ideas or rational choice of appropriate techniques to solve particular kinds of problem.

It is beyond the scope of this book, and unnecessary for its purposes, to explore further into the waves of fashion that have swept the world of computer-based application development (and hence many approaches to process analysis). However, in the search for a credible origin for many description and analysis techniques, it is worth noting the major fashions in the computer analysis and design worlds, of relational databases and object-oriented techniques. As will be seen, this helps to triangulate a likely origin.

Problem Statements and Requirements

The previous chapter presented some key points from the analysis techniques paper by Couger (1973). Having documented and classified a variety of analysis techniques into 3 generations, he identified a fourth generation as the ISDOS project at the University of Michigan (discussed in more depth shortly). He cites Teichroew, the ISDOS director as saying about the Problem Statement Language (PSL) that it is "a generalization of Information Algebra, TAG and ADS".

In the 1950s and 1960s there were several published papers and articles about the term 'problem statements'. At one level, a natural language understanding of that term can be at a simple very general level such as 'the problem is to automate the system for shipping goods and invoicing customers, as far as is feasible'. That is undoubtedly a useful starting point, but it is not what key writers about problem statements had in mind; they envisaged a problem statement as a collection of inter-related, formally constructed, information, in some detail, setting out what the problem is. There should be enough information in the problem statement(s) for a system designer to start making progress with the design of a computer-assisted solution, or even look only at the computer-assistance and leave more general system issues to others.

Perhaps the earliest substantive paper referencing 'problem statement' is Young and Kent (1958) following the very strong hint at such a term in Canning (1956). They distinguish an abstract statement of a problem from a verbal statement.

"An abstract statement of the problem can be made by preparing two lists: one of the information sets and the other of the documents... Thus the output documents are completely specified in terms of the transformations which are applied to the inputs. At the same time, the relationships among the information sets enable logical substitutions to be made in the input to achieve the same outputs." (p472).

They go on to provide an example verbal statement of a problem. It is unnecessary to quote that here, but suffice it to say that it is a set of precise, well constructed, natural language statements about the problem for which computer systems are required.

Young and Kent proceed to set out a formal notation to define symbolic representations of all items in the verbal description. Equations are presented to show relationships between inputs and outputs.

Thus, the approach proposed by Young and Kent involves problem statements which are detailed and precise articulations of the requirements of the proposed system. This is a far cry from a simplistic high-level statement of a problem to be solved.

Around 1961, there was work on an Information Algebra (IA) (Bosak et al., 1962). IA was not developed or used much. However, of particular interest in a discussion of correspondence between methods of system analysis and Carnap (discussed below) is the IA concept of a property space.

A property space is a set of all possible points that are a combination of possible values on a set of properties expressed as an n-dimensional space for n properties. McGee (see below) gives a simple example of a 3-dimensional property space: employee number, employee age, and employee sex. If there are 10,000 possible employee numbers, 45 possible ages of employees, and 2 possible sexes, the 3-dimensional space has 900,000 possible points in its property space. Is this a reflection of what is described by Carnap (1937) as an example of a coordinate-language that sets out coordinates whether or not objects exist at each coordinate?

Another influential paper from the same period is that of McGee (1963), continuing the theme of data processing problem formulation ("The principal function of data processing is to create output files from input files" - p42). He spends much of his paper discussing the emergence of a 'Data Processing Theory' and the Information Algebra that emerged from some CODASYL work. It is worth noting that McGee identifies some key high-level objects: entity, property, and measure (with associated datum, unit record, and file).

This earlier work about problem formulation and problem statements was followed in 1967 by the start of what is probably still the world's most extensive applied research project into requirements modelling and analysis. At Case Western Reserve University, there was a proposal for "A Research Project to Develop Methodology for the Automatic Design and Construction of Information Processing Systems" by Teichroew and Stieger (1967). This was the birth of the ISDOS (Information System Design and Optimization System) project. A key element in that proposal was for a Problem Statement Language and a Problem Statement Analyzer, which became the very widely known PSL/PSA. The ISDOS Project was born at Case Western Reserve University, but moved very quickly in 1968 to the University of Michigan (UoM), where almost all of its work was done.

The choice of the term 'Problem Statement Language' should be no surprise when looking at the background. Teichroew (and hence ISDOS) had been influenced strongly in his early years by Young and Kent (1958), and Canning (1956). He had worked with Young and Kent at the National Cash Register Company; he had worked with Canning at the University of California. McGee's work (1963) figured in the original ISDOS proposal. Teichroew already had students working in classes in 1966 on problems based around Young and Kent's work, prior to the 1967 ISDOS proposal. A summary of "Problem Statement Languages in MIS" was produced by Teichroew (1971).

The development of problem statement languages was also recognized in Sammet's seminal work on the history of programming languages (Sammet, 1969).

Some of the PhD work that underpins ISDOS has a smoking gun pointing at Carnap as the source of several key concepts as well as articulating a set of constructor principles that apply to a series of analysis 'layers': the part of the real world to be analyzed, the model of that part of the real world, a meta model or language that sets out what should be contained in a model, and a meta-metalanguage used to create meta languages or models.

Exactly that kind of language is used for a current fashion, UML, used in the computer-based system development world. UML is asserted to have been derived from a higher level metametalanguage. Holt's book (2009) about business process modelling is based on the application of UML.

The very close links between deMarco, Yourdon, Gane and Sarson are well known. In terms of data flow diagrams, the differences are primarily notation. Yourdon provides another 'smoking gun' in terms of links to Carnap. Yourdon and Constantine (1979) are dependent on Martin and Estrin (1967) in their discussion of graphs. Martin and Estrin refer explicitly to Carnap. Therefore, Yourdon and Constantine are acknowledging, albeit indirectly, an influence by Carnap on their approach to graphs.

For relational databases and the underlying relational theory, there is also no doubt that probably the most prolific writer on the subject, Date (2007), recognizes explicitly the contrbution of Carnap to relational theory. Date uses Carnap as an exception to "Most logic texts pay little or no attention to the notion of types...", using Carnap (1958).

In 1928, Carnap had laid down, albeit in German, many of the fundamental building blocks used today for various purposes related to systems analysis.

Carnap's starting point is to the effect that there are certain fundamental concepts that underpin all science, commencing with his choice, 'object':

> "The present investigations aim to establish a "constructional system", that is, an epistemic-logical system of objects or concepts. the word "object" is here always used in its widest sense, namely, for anything about which a statement can be made. Thus, among

objects we count not only things, but also properties and classes, relations in extension and intension, states and events, what is actual as well as what is not...the present study is an attempt to apply the theory of relations to the task of analyzing reality" (Carnap, 1967:5-7).

If there is any doubt about Carnap's use of the terms mentioned above because his 1928 book did not appear in English until 1967, that doubt can be dispelled because he also discusses the terms object, property, class, extension, intension, and relation (that may be one-one, one-many, many-one) in other works prior to 1967, in English (Carnap 1936, 1958). Carnap discusses relational theory (Carnap, 1936) and various kinds of relations (Carnap, 1958). Systems and database analysts would recognize many core concepts in those discussions, and indeed would probably find Carnap's treatment much more rigorous than normally found in today's practice (and literature).

Thus, Carnap articulated object-property-relationship (OPR) modelling, and that was followed by entity-relationship-attribute (ERA) where objects are called entities (Bachman, 1969, does this explicitly). and properties are called attributes. Object oriented analysis can also be derived from Carnap who has thorough discussion of objects and classes, as can the underpinnings of relational database theory by his explicit discussion of relational theory and use of so many terms in use today for database analysis and design.

Carnap's meta-meta-modelling (he does not use that term per se) of the world commences with a very general concept of 'object' which is instantiated as a set of objects which can be used in combination to provide lower levels of model. Thus he talks about objects not only as things, but other objects as set out in the quotation above, including properties, things, relations, classes, and so forth.

The key point being made in this book is that many of the terms used by systems analysts, object-oriented designers, and relational database designers are used by Carnap, and prior to the modern computer world. There are some clear 'smoking guns' referencing Carnap explicitly in some of the literature. Hence, Carnap is proposed as the most likely origin for all these key concepts.

Table 4.1 sets out an illustrative list of concepts and where they can be found in Carnap. This list is not intended to be exhaustive or to present all occurrences in Carnap's works.

Implications of Identifying Carnap as the Origin of Analysis Techniques

Having identified Carnap as the most likely foundation for most extant systems analysis techniques, along with related concepts such as relational theory and object-oriented analysis, the implications are both profound and practical for the person doing BPW work.

All systems analysis techniques offer some kind of system modelling language, whether that language is linguistic or graphical. All system modelling languages can be abstracted to a metametamodelling language which is object-property-relationship modelling derived from Carnap. This applies to systems modelling languages whether they are used for pre- or post-computer process descriptions. They work whether the domain of analysis is only the computer-based applications, or the more general field of business process analysis which includes manual and automated elements.

Concept	Carnap Source
Class	(1937) p134ff; (1958) p 77, 109; (1967) p57, pp68ff
Domain	(1958) p34; (1967) p 29, 59ff
Extension	(1937) pp240ff; (1958) pp40ff (1967) p56. 59
Intention	(1937) pp245ff; (1958) pp40ff; (1967) pp72ff, 261
Many-to-One	(1937) p222; (1958) p75;
Object	(1937) 13; (1967) pp31ff, 43ff
One-to-Many	(1958) p75
One-to-One	(1937) p223; (1958) p75;
Property	(1937) 13; (1958) p40, 109; (1967) p51
Property Space (as coordinate language?)	(1937) 141;
[Ir]Reflexive	(1937) p261; (1958) p120; (1967) pp166ff
Relation	(1937) p13; (1958) p40; (1967) pp21ff
Relational Theory	(1937) pp 260ff; (1967) pp59ff
Thing*	(1958) pp157ff; (1967) p32
[In]Transitive	(1937) p261; (1958) p119; (1967) pp166ff
Tuple	(1958) p75

* Carnap does not use the term 'entity'; he talks about 'thing' and a thing-language. The earliest formal and explicit definition of Entity as a word for Thing the author can find is in the definition of Information Algebra (Bosak et al., 1962:191)

Table 4.1 - Key Terms in Carnap's Works

UML asserts it is derived from a metametalanguage (identified as Level M3).

Following Carnap's constructor principles means that there must be one higher level above that (UML's Level M3), a metametametalanguage (or meta[3] language) resulting in 5 layers of model, as shown in Figure 4.1.

Five levels of model have now been identified, as illustrated in Figure 4.1 and set out in Table 4.2:

- model instance: the order-entry process;

- model language: the possibility to define sources, inputs, processes, transformations, outputs, and destinations;

- meta language: the language to define the objects, relationships, properties, text, and statements;

- metametalanguage: the language that sets out all kinds of object and relationship that can be defined with the language;

- meta[3] language: the pinnacle of the modelling pyramid.

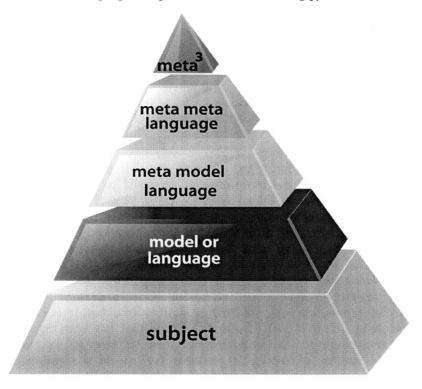

Figure 4.1 - Levels of Languages and Models

The significance of these different levels of model is discussed in later chapters. In Table 4.2 BPL refers to a Business Process Language developed to describe and analyze business processes. metaPSL is tool developed to implement some of the research done in the ISDOS project.. It is a tool used to define languages[2] of many kinds.

---

2 There is a wide variety of languages produced by this tool, covering many modeling problems such as the requirements for information systems, devices for compliance with standards for connection to public telephone systems, real-time devices such as electronic watches, system development methods, business systems, information architecture, and so forth.

Level	Example	Pyramid Segment
Metametametalanguage (meta³ language)	Object, thing	
Metametalanguage - metametamodel	metaPSL	
Metalanguage - meta model	BPL (Business Process Language)	
Language or model	Order fulfillment	
Real world or subject of model	Business activity for order entry	

Table 4.2 Instances, languages, and meta models

Key elements of an object property relationship language: a simple example

An OPR language is a formalized subset of natural language. It should have eliminated ambiguities and inconsistencies. It should be reasonably easy to understand by its readers. Taking an initial simple view of natural language, expression is a series of sentences, which have various components, such as nouns, verbs, adjectives, adverbs, and so forth. Therefore a sentence such as "*a process takes a set of inputs from various sources, performs some efficient transformation on those inputs to generate outputs, and those outputs go to various destinations*" contains several such components. The sentence is clearly abstract because it is not talking about a particular process, particular inputs, outputs, sources, or destinations, but it does imply a process model; it is part of a metalanguage that has been created by a metametalanguage. This model could then be used to describe an indefinite number of particular processes (i.e. model the real world).

To consider the sentence in more detail, the key components are set out in Table 4.3. Some parts of the sentence have not been included in this initial analysis. Notice that in Table 4.3, only the singular has been included. For this reason, the noun "set" can be omitted as it implies the plural of input.

There are several possible ways to model such a sentence. Use source, input, process, output, destination, and transformation, as shown in Figure 4.2. The convention being used is that a box indicates an object, and the name of the object appears in the box.

As far as relationships are concerned, some verbs were added to this model, in order to complete it unambiguously. This led to Sources creating Inputs, Processes receiving Inputs, Processes generating Outputs, Processes performing Transformations, and Destinations taking Outputs.

Component	Instances
Nouns	process, set, input, source, transformation, output, destination
Verbs	take, perform, generate, go-to
Adjectives	various, efficient

Table 4.3 Sentence components example

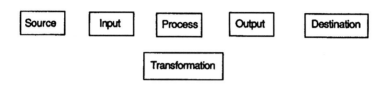

Figure 4.2 Simple process: initial objects.

All of the verbs in these relationships are in the active voice. Each relationship can be seen the other way round, and an appropriate name for such complementary relationships can be obtained by converting active verbs into passive verbs. This yields created-by, received-by, generated-by, performed-by, and taken-by. Figure 4.2 can now be supplemented by these relationships that are represented by lines between the boxes, as shown in Figure 4.3. Each line can have an arrow indicating direction, implying the subject and object of a sentence using either the active or passive form of the verb. This has introduced objects and relationships. It has also hinted at sentences.

A property, or attribute, is used to provide more information for a structured definition of an object. For example, an Input may have a name, description, and type. Properties of the categories of information needed to describe and identify an object. So if Person is an object, the properties or attributes of person would include given-name, family-name, date-of-birth, gender, address, and so forth.

The OPR model introduced by Teichroew et al. (1980), adds TEXT, KEYWORD, OPTIONAL WORD, and STATEMENT to the main building blocks of an OBJECT, PROPERTY, and RELATIONSHIP language (model).

Information about an object may involve a lot of descriptive text. For example, a Transformation may require a description of how the transformation is performed, and a statistical distribution may be associated with a Process to summarize its behavior.

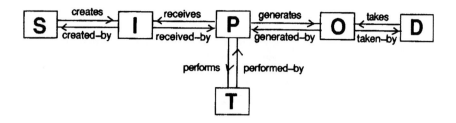

Figure 4.3 Simple process: initial objects and relationships

Ultimately, the idea of OPR language modeling is to produce a simplified natural language that can be used to describe situations and provide information in a way that can be checked for completeness and consistency. They can be understood by many stakeholders who should be involved in modelling business processes.

OPR modeling has the concept of a STATEMENT, which is how the parts of a model are brought together into a language that can be used for analysis and understanding. STATEMENTs join together the Objects, Properties, and Relationships. In the example so far, there are now several possible sentences that can be constructed:

- Source S1 creates Inputs I1, I2, ... In
- Inputs I1 ... In are created_by Source S1
- Process P1 receives Inputs I1 ... In
- Inputs I1 ... In are received_by Process P1
- Process P1 generates Outputs 01, 02, ... On
- Outputs 01 ... On are generated_by Process P1
- Process P1 performs Transformation T1
- Transformation T1 is performed by Process P1
- Destination D1 takes Outputs 01 ... On
- Outputs 01 ... On are taken_by Destination D1.

Where a graphical notation is to be used, the metametalanguage would be used to define graphical elements that are part of the modelling language. Thus, the diagram shown in Fig 4.3 is an example of a graphical language.

The approach to OPR set out by the ISDOS project provided a suite of tools to define a modeling language that could then be used for system description purposes. For instance, the above simple example of a model derived from the definition of a process led to a simple language to describe processes. How would such a language be used in practice?

The analyst needs something like a language reference manual (or a set of computer-based forms) that can be used to describe a set of processes. Taking a purely linguistic approach (as opposed to, say, a graphical approach), what is needed is an ability to define the various objects in a system, along with the associated relationships and properties. Therefore it is necessary to be able to say something like:

DEFINE PROCESS order-entry;
RECEIVES sales-order;
GENERATES order-record;
PERFORMS order-validation;
DESCRIPTION IS;
text-of-description;

DEFINE SOURCE customer;
CREATES sales-order;
DESCRIPTION IS;
    text-of-description;

DEFINE INPUT sales-order;
CREATED-BY customer;
RECEIVED-BY order-entry;
DESCRIPTION IS;
    text-of-description;

DEFINE TRANSFORMATION order-validation;
PERFORMED-BY order-entry;
DESCRIPTION IS;
    text-of-description;

DEFINE OUTPUT order-record;
GENERATED-BY order-entry;
TAKEN-BY customer;
DESCRIPTION;
    text-of-description;

DEFINE DESTINATION order-scheduler;
TAKES order-record;
DESCRIPTION;
    text-of-description;

Several observations can be made about this exercise. First, it has produced a number of definitions, because all the combinations have been presented. Because the objects at both ends of each relationship are completely unambiguous, software that accepts one definition should have no problem in creating all relevant corresponding definitions. For example, the DEFINE PROCESS order-entry statement contains enough information so that sales-order, order-record, and order-validation did not need to be defined explicitly. The underlying model defines what type of object each of these must be. Second, other analysts may have produced a perfectly valid alternative model. For example, the transformation may have been a property of Process rather than being a separate object. In all cases, the object instances had at least names as properties.

Obviously, this simple model can be used to describe as many combinations of source, input, output, process, destination, and transformation as desired.

Object property relationship modeling: more advanced rules

Having introduced the basic points about an OPR model, what are some of the substantive rules that help the analyst? Many of these rules are similar or identical to rules found in some data modeling techniques.

The analyst who needs to follow any of these points in more detail should consult literature about data modeling.

Objects
So far, nouns have been equated to objects. This is a very useful starting point, but there are difficulties to be overcome by the analyst.

For example, in conducting a study, an analyst may encounter reports and statements that refer to employees, managers, contractors, instructors, and so forth. Initially the analyst will treat each as a separate noun. The problem to be resolved is how far these objects are different. It is clear that one option available is to create an object PERSON, and have a property such as person-type or person-status.

Therefore one task of the analyst is to examine all candidate objects and make sensible decisions about simplifying the list of object types.

There is a more subtle problem in that what is seen initially as a noun may be modeled as a property or a relationship. For example, employees and managers may have been detected. Clearly they are both nouns and hence initial candidate objects. However, the list of objects may have been simplified by having one object type, person or employee. In most cases, managers are also employees. The difference between someone classified as an employee or manager is the relationship between employees. Therefore the noun manager is likely to be changed by an analyst into a relationship MANAGES or MANAGED-BY.

Properties

Properties provide the more detailed information about objects. The most common way to see this is to use the analogy of record and fields: records correspond to objects, and fields correspond to properties.

A frequent problem to be resolved by analysts is when to treat an item of information as an object, and when to treat it as a property. The data modeling conventions of normalization are helpful here. This means that any property that could have multiple values for a particular object instance should be modeled as a separate object. For example, if there is a rule that every employee can have one and only one address then address can be modeled as a property of employee. However, if it is permitted for employees to have more than one address, it may be advisable to model address as a separate object, and introduce a new relationship such as LIVES-AT.

In the business process analysis world, the same considerations should be taken into account. For example, if it is certain that in a model of business processes each process can only be triggered by one event, then it may be more efficient to model event as a property of process. However, if some processes can be triggered by more than one event, or if events can trigger more than one process, then it is better to model event as a separate object, and not as a property.

For every identified property, it is helpful to show which object(s) it applies to, and what kinds of values can be assumed for the property. Hence, there are some more technical points to be made about properties:

- some properties can only take on specific values: gender can only take one of three forms, male, female, and hermaphrodite; department can only be one of the defined departments;
- some properties must be expressed as a particular kind of information: names can only be alphabetical (and cannot include numbers or non-alphabetic characters except hyphens); length can only be a number;
- some properties can only have values within a particular range: age must be greater than zero.

In practice, when applied to the analysis of business processes, most objects have a very simple set of properties and a larger number of relationships, and this improves flexibility and modularity.

The main rules and practice for the analyst with reference to relationships also follows data modeling closely.

An important contribution from data modeling is to understand the cardinality of a relationship. Cardinality is usually expressed as one to one (1:1), one to many (1:M), or many to many (M:M). Therefore for every relationship, it is important to know how many of one object can be associated with how many of the other object(s) in the relationship. Taking the earlier example further, this would mean understanding whether a process can have only one, or many inputs. Can a process produce only one output, or several outputs? Does a process perform one transformation, or more than one? In my experience with modeling business processes, the higher the level of abstraction, the higher the likelihood that relationships are M:M. Towards the end of the book the extent to which this information in the models of business processes can be used to identify candidates for process improvement is discussed.

The example shown above contains only two-part relationships. While analyzing business processes, particularly at higher levels of abstraction, workshops tend to produce relatively high numbers of n-part relationships. It is part of the analyst's task to investigate these relationships to see how far they could be de-composed into less complex relationships.

Two examples are presented to illustrate the point. The first concerns a simple educational example, and the second is concerned with distributable systems.

A core business process for an educational establishment is to fulfill training requirements. Consider a very simple statement that "classes are taught by lecturers and one or more books are specified for use by each class" There are three nouns here: CLASS, LECTURER, BOOK. There are two verbs: TEACH, USE.

The potential analytical problem arises through constructing appropriate statements, for example, "Lecturer L1 uses Books B1 and B2 to teach Class C1. An appropriate three-part relationship for this is shown in Figure 4.4.

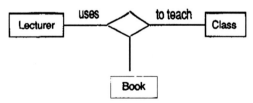

Figure 4.4 Three-part relationship: lecturer, book, class.

The analyst will try to break down such a model into a set of two-part relationships: book—class, lecturer—class, and book—lecturer being the three candidates. What should the analyst do? The dilemma is that the answer lies not in the inherent nature of the information, but in the actual business rules.

If the educational institution gives no freedom to lecturers who must use the prescribed books for each course, then it is meaningful to state that lecturer and book are independent; it is not necessary for a student to know anything other than the courses being followed to know which books to purchase. Similarly, each lecturer only needs to know which classes are to be taught. In such a case, the three-part relationship can be represented quite satisfactorily by using two two-part relationships: class—book, lecturer—class (the third possible relationship, lecturer—book, is not necessary as the objects are independent).

However, if the institution allows freedom to lecturers to decide which books to use for each course, then students cannot buy their books safely until they know not only the classes to be taken, but also the lecturers who are giving each class. Books and lecturers are no longer independent. Therefore the three-part relationship cannot be de-composed. This is where the problem begins for relational database management systems, because they are not really suitable for n-part relationships where n is greater than 2. Normalization[3] is the data modeling technique that is most useful for de-composing relationships.

The second example concerns an interesting problem that arose from a shortcoming in most information system development methods, that no help is given for the design of distributed systems.

The problem to be solved was to produce a set of OPR components that could be used to model distributable systems. A typical scenario is an enterprise that is dispersed with various kinds of facility in different geographical locations. Within such an enterprise, some processes, such as nominal ledger maintenance, would be centralized in one location. Other functions, such as selling, would be distributed by replication in different geographical regions. Yet other functions may be inherently different, such as manufacturing and training, and distributed to different facilities in different geographical locations. The enterprise, in designing its organization, wishes to produce a logical model in the first instance which is independent of implementation, so that the business needs can be understood. Then decisions can be taken about how and where to implement the organizational structure in real life, that is, perform design and implementation. In addition, the enterprise, understandably, wished to retain as much flexibility as possible so that various activities could be moved, centralized, or dispersed, according to current thinking about the best way to manage the work to be done.

3 For the reader who has experience of the data modeling technique called normalization, it will be found that n-part relationships occur frequently, particularly with business processes, despite the many texts about data modeling which assert that normalization beyond third normal form is usually unnecessary. For the reader who is not experienced in normalization the technique is recommended, but caution that it is necessary to understand normalization to fifth normal form, particularly when the technique is to be used to construct OPR models of business processes.

In conducting this analysis, the client agreed some rules:

- there were tasks to be performed, some of which could be dispersed, and others that should be centralized;
- there were many different kinds of facility envisaged (such as regional office, factory, garage, training center and headquarters);
- people performed tasks, and what was required may depend on the place where the work is being done;
- performing a task requires the use of various resources;
- there are various "properties" that may apply to the other system components (such as ownership, or consistency).

To support an analysis of the business needs, five logical objects could be used for analysis independently of implementation: logical role, logical location, logical task, logical resource, and logical property. Examples of these are set out in Table 4.4. This set of logical components could be combined into an appropriate OPR statement giving a five-part relationship (Figure 4.5):

Person R1 performs Task T1 at Location LI using Resource RI subject to Property P1

Model component	Explanation	Example
Logical role	similar to job description, but with the emphasis on the role being performed; there is likely to be a many to many relationship between person and role; the role is expressed in a general form	local office sales order entry; instructor; laser printer repair; cost center management
Logical location	the type of location, independently of the physical implementation (that is, where the type of facility is actually placed	manufacturing plant; regional headquarters; training center; sales office; warehouse
Logical task	the tasks done, independently of how or where they are done, or who does them	order entry; accounting; service design; managing a group of sales people
Logical resource	the kinds of resources used, rather than the specific resources that are actually employed	people with business process analysis skills; manufacturing equipment; computing capability; capital
Logical property	characteristics that apply to the overall process, independently of the other dimensions	performance characteristics; standards compliance; consistency

Table 4.4 Distributable system model components

It is interesting to note that the five-part relation shown in Figure 4.5 was developed to model distributed systems. Exactly the same kind of model, but with a different set of verbs in the associated statements, can be used to model security requirements.

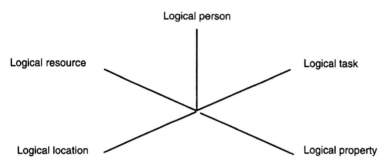

Figure 4.5 Distributable system five-part relationship.

One key problem for the analyst is to know whether this five-part relationship can be de-composed into less complex relationships. This could only be done by establishing complete independence between some of the parts. One example could be if each task is already defined in terms of the resources to be used. This would be taking an essentially object-oriented view. In other words, the method for performing the task is "invisible" to the rest of the system. This would make resource related to task, but nothing else, thus simplifying the five-part relation to one two-part and one four-part relation. In the information processing world this is easier to achieve, because it may be possible to impose strict conditions that certain data items can only be maintained by a particular module. Then if one knows the module, one knows which data items are involved. In the business process world this is not so easy because a task may be performed with different combinations of factor inputs; for example, in a high-wage country, road building may use substantial equipment, whereas in a low-wage country, road building may involve substantially more labor.

It is not only objects that can be simplified; relationships should be simplified by the analyst as well. Four tests are proposed for the simplification of relationships:

■ similar or identical object types are connected;
■ temporal dependence: two objects are connected by more than one relationship, but the relationships may change independently of each other at different times (for example, an employee may be a member of a department and a consultant to a department, and the participation of each object—person, department—in those relationships may change over time, that is both member and consultant for one period of time, and only consultant after

moving to another department);

- the structures of the relationships are identical (with respect to cardinality, insertion, and retention)[4];
- one relationship implicitly contains information that is explicit in another (for example, an explicit relationship showing that Person P manages Department D at Salary S with Job-title T also shows the implicit relationship Person P manages Department D).

There are some relationships that can occur in a model several times because of identical inherent relationships. For example, processes can be de-composed, and data items can be de-composed. In both cases it is meaningful to use the pair of relationships, CONSISTS-OF and PART-OF. Thus a high-level process may consist-of lower level processes, and some processes may be part-of higher level processes.

A simple business process meta model

Discussions with many people about business processes identified a lot of common ground about the basics. There are processes, inputs, outputs, transformations, events that trigger processes, effects of processes, and so forth ... and of course there may be frequencies and distributions associated with all of these.

There may well be thousands of processes at various levels, which are all linked together. When people talk about processes they may describe different aspects of different processes at different levels, all within the same discussion. However, for all the possible thousands of processes, there is a range of useful meta models to be used for their description.

BPW engagements usually involve helping people to describe and analyze business processes. In some cases, the analysts have very little prior experience of producing consistent, systematic descriptions. Although many people are very willing to offer some very good ideas about how processes could be improved, there was generally much less rigor behind describing and improving the processes.

Generally, the best way to proceed is by iterations, increasing the amount of detail with each successive iteration. It may be helpful to have an idea of Level I, Level II, and further levels of Process Descriptions. Each level adds more objects and relationships to the previous level. This way, Process Engineers are able to develop analytical skills very quickly. There are much more complex business process descriptions beyond Level II, but rather than having a set of higher categories, by the time analysts are working at that level of complexity, they no longer need specified levels and can work with an appropriate level of detail. The following sections build up the suggestion of basic business process definitions.

---

4 Cardinality is discussed earlier in this chapter. Retention and insertion are discussed in chapter 14.

Level I process descriptions

The idea of a Level I process description is to describe one process that is not part of a more complex process structure (other than the source and destination of inputs and outputs). A minimum set of objects and relationships has been identified and developed as a result of working with several groups of people in different enterprises in different parts of the world. There is general agreement that the objects and relationships in Level I are a bare minimum to understand what a process is about.

There was also general agreement that a process is the transformation of a set of inputs to produce one or more outputs. Something triggers a process. The running of a process may depend on one or more conditions, and when a process terminates, there will be a control effect elsewhere. This is the basis of Level I process descriptions.

There is a form (appendix A, Figure Al) for analysts to collect this basic information. The idea is to complete a form for every process. Examination of this form yields a set of objects:

- PROCESS
- PROCESSOR
- INPUT
- OUTPUT
- EVENT
- CONDITION

There are several relationships:

- TRIGGERS
- RECEIVES
- GENERATES
- PERFORMS
- USES ... TO DERIVE
- ON TERMINATION TRIGGERS
- ON BECOMING {TRUE/FALSE} TRIGGERS
- ON CHANGING TRIGGERS

There are perfectly reasonable alternative ways to model some of these components and their relationships. My goal was to provide one consistent starting point that analysts find useful. It has proved very difficult to derive even this basic amount of information from many different wordy process descriptions I have examined. This set provides a minimum completeness standard.

Level II process descriptions

Level I descriptions are concerned with one process in isolation. The next step was to place each process in a broader context. It is also important to collect quantitative information for many of the objects.

The additional points to bring a Level I description to Level II are:

- a process may be part of a higher level process;
- a process may be capable of de-composition into several lower level processes;
- processes occur in some sequence, therefore there is a sense in which one process can come after another process and before yet another;
- events, processes, inputs, and outputs occur with some frequency per period of time;
- it is useful to identify who is responsible for the definition of the various objects.

This means that a Level II form needs some modification to collect this additional information. In addition, there need to be some extra objects and relationships:

- UNIT (to represent the period of time for frequency information)
- PART-OF
- CONSISTS-OF
- COMES BEFORE
- COMES AFTER
- HAPPENS ... TIMES PER
- DEFINES

A suggested modified form is shown in Figure A2 (appendix A).

Further levels of process descriptions

There are many possible ways to extend the Level I and II process descriptions. Problem Statement Language/ Problem Statement Analyzer (PSL/PSA[5]), has 21 objects and 105 relationships.

Important additions to Level II descriptions include allocating attributes, defining system parameters that can be used to describe a range of system characteristics, and capturing assertions that are made about different objects.

Business Process Language

A linguistic approach to modeling is illustrated earlier in this chapter. Although many writers and practitioners work today

---

5 PSL/PSA is the most widely known and cited product of the ISDOS project, as described in Teichroew and Hershey (1977) and described in a research report as early as 1967. Comments are occasionally made about this technology being old, but it continue to be very useful. See, for example, Sayani (1990).

in the belief that "graphical is best", graphical techniques are simply not scalable beyond relatively simple cases. Understanding and comprehending large and numerous graphical illustrations just does not seem to work well with human beings.

For this reason, a Business Process Language (BPL) has been created for use in BPW analysis work. This approach is scalable to thousands of object and relationship instances-it has been done. Some of the graphical tools that are currently applied to BPW work are not scalable because they are unable to handle the complexity of some models (despite the claims of some tool vendors).

There is another very significant example of adopting linguistic rather than graphical or graphical user interface (GUI) approaches.

The task of preparing complex computer chip designs was becoming more and more difficult because of the problem involved in managing and checking diagram designs involving thousands of logic gates. The US Department of Defense funded a very high speed integrated circuit (VHSIC) program. As explained by Perry (1991), "Creating designs of hundreds of thousands of gates using gate level tools was an extremely challenging task, and therefore a new method of description was in order". One result of that program was the definition of a new standard (IEEE Std 1076) for a VHSIC Hardware Description Language (VHDL), which has now become an industry standard.

Carlson (1991) suggests that, "Being able to predict the outcome of any process is fundamental to the most efficient use of that process". Although he is talking in a context of hardware description languages, his sentiment can be echoed with respect to business processes, although the specification of business processes poses very different problems from specifying application specific integrated circuits (ASICs).

The use of VHDL requires the specification of a set of circuit requirements by means of the language. This needs to be followed by using that information to compute optimum circuit designs. Then final designs can be generated, down to the gate level.

Another example of linguistic definitions being used on a world-wide scale is the language for defining World Wide Web (WWW) pages—Hypertext Markup Language (HTML). HTML is itself a subset of SGML (Standard Generalized Markup Language), which is discussed further in chapter 6. SGML is a language used to describe documents, and a variant of SGML can be used for a process specification generation environment so that documentary output can be computed[6].

Linguistic approaches to analysis are discussed further in chapter 5, with a description of a Business Architecture Language (BAL).

Concluding remarks

This chapter introduces the building blocks of object property relationship modeling. OPR models have a lot in common with data models, but

---

6 For a discussion of this, see Alshuler (1995)

there are some significant differences in practice. Therefore the analyst, especially one already versed in data modeling, needs to be wary.

In OPR modeling, the analyst is producing a language that is sufficiently meaningful to be applicable to the area of work under investigation. Such a language should be a formal subset of natural language containing nouns and verbs that are near to the vocabulary used in the situation to be analyzed. The data analyst is producing a model that can be implemented in a database management system with all the constraints that implies.

The data analyst is likely to be concerned more with well-structured data and relationships that can be de-composed in many instances to two-part relationships. The business process analyst must deal with more variety in the types of information to be handled. Many n-part relationships will be encountered which cannot be de-composed safely without substantial investigation and proof (by means of understanding the real business rules that apply), and they need to be incorporated into the business process models.

Frequently, the business process analyst will not have access to software that implements OPR modeling directly[7]. Nevertheless, simple tables can be constructed to hold the acquired information, and the analyst will usually benefit from the design of forms that help to collect definitions of objects and the relationships in which they participate.

The ideas introduced in this chapter are developed as the book proceeds. More objects and relationships are suggested for additional process description topics.

Language modeling skills, and associated meta modeling skills, of the kind needed to produce or use languages such as OPR, HTML, and VHDL are core skills for the professional business process analyst.

The next chapter develops OPR modeling further incorporating a way to bring together the results of high-level strategy studies, which are often the starting point for BPW projects.

Practical Advice

This chapter covers lot of ground and introduces approaches that are not (yet) common. However, if you are likely to be responsible for BPW work in any real world organization, and not just a classroom situation, you need to be able to manage hundreds or thousands of process definitions in support of efforts to improve efficiency or effectiveness.

Real world situations involving large numbers of processes cannot be handled primarily with graphical techniques. It is not possible to perform sufficient completeness and consistency checking on diagrams. There would need to be a very precise mapping from diagrams to some other form that can render the process descriptions amenable to the analysis required for serious real world organizations.

---

7   Organization who wish to have their own language for analyzing business processes are welcome to contact the author who has considerable experience of doing this.

Chapter 5

Business visions

Where does the inspiration for BPW come from? It is usually triggered by some senior management vision that the enterprise, or some part of the enterprise[1], could be "better" than it is at present. The most common techniques encountered for articulating that vision are high-level management facilitated workshops and discussions, with various frameworks introduced to stimulate thought. Generally, these techniques are derived from approaches to strategy studies and large-scale complex business design.

Some approaches are based primarily on the facilitation of senior management meetings, followed by the consolidation and reporting of results. Other approaches are based on a wide range of available "frameworks" that are used frequently for business analysis and strategy.

Ultimately, business vision involves the creation of a "dream" about where it is believed the enterprise should be going. The business literature over the past few decades is very rich in ways to approach articulating the enterprise dream.

Techniques include:

1. techniques that are primarily facilitative in that they help to clarify a problem situation and perhaps define a way forward;
2. techniques that present a prescriptive or analytical framework as a focus for the vision work;
3. a formal analysis of the results of high-level workshops.

There is a great deal of material available to aid the practitioner in this aspect of BPW work. Many consulting organizations have proprietary techniques they apply in their engagements.

However, this book concerns tools to help the analyst, rather than tools to help the facilitator. It is the third category in the above list with which this book is primarily concerned. This chapter identifies and discusses briefly, other well-established techniques listed in 1 & 2. There are actually very few formal approaches to analysis following the creation of a vision. In this chapter is a description of some work to try and define a flexible approach that can be used to provide an analytical underpinning to the results of facilitated workshops. Many enterprises have some difficulty in proceeding from a strategy study to

---

1 In reality, it is rare to see a BPW project undertaken for the whole enterprise; it is much more common to see focus on one or more particular processes.

new business processes. Therefore in this chapter is an approach to this class of problem, which can provide a very solid foundation for implementation and subsequent BPW work.

The approach presented here involves defining and using a business architecture language[2]. Different enterprises usually approach strategy exercises in different ways, therefore there is an uniqueness in each. Many of the building blocks are common, but tied together differently. This approach is completely scalable from the modest to the very large.

This chapter illustrates the application of OPR modeling to the components of a business vision.

Background

Most of the techniques for creating an enterprise vision have been derived from general management literature, particularly with reference to strategy formulation, and information systems or information technology planning.

These techniques are an important part of the business process analyst's toolbox. In general, they are "softer" techniques than those elsewhere in the book, in that there is frequently a lack of deterministic or analytical rigor to underpin conclusions and recommendations. Another characteristic of many of the techniques is the absence of solid empirical evidence to justify their advocacy and use.

The 1980s saw considerable effort to find the characteristics of excellent companies, as evidenced in the management bestseller by Peters and Waterman (1982). They advocate a balance between quantitative and qualitative analysis, saying "What we are against is wrong-headed analysis, analysis that is too complex to be useful and too unwieldy to be flexible, analysis that strives to be precise (especially at the wrong time) about the inherently unknowable ... ". Of course, there is an irony that Peters and Waterman were looking for what makes enterprises 'excellent'; after some time, many of the enterprises asserted to be excellent, were in deep difficulty, and some difficulties were fatal to the organization. Therefore, it is only extreme optimism that could claim Peters and Waterman found any silver bullets for making enterprises 'excellent'. However, that book was successful in terms of royalties earned by the authors (and, of course, it is an important book for identifying many things to look for in an 'excellent' enterprise).

The "dream" is all about how to create successful enterprises. In one sense, much management literature in the past century has been about finding the elixir of success. That search continues today. BPW is about how to put in place the processes that support the successful enterprise.

Apart from techniques based on an analysis of data, the most common approach is probably to try and capture the collective wisdom of senior executives. This is where what can be termed facilitative techniques are used.

---

2 Business architecture is described in more detail in Darnton and Giacoletto (1992). It is concerned with the *information relevance* of overall enterprise vision and strategy. A new version is expected late 2012.

They are called that because the principal role of the consultant is to facilitate workshops and discussions to obtain the necessary source material.

Where there is not yet even agreement about the nature of the problem to be solved, there are techniques such as Soft Systems Methodology (SSM) by Checkland (1981) and Checkland and Scholes (1990).

General facilitation techniques exist, such as: wall-charting, process mapping, and the Delphi technique.

Wall-charting techniques are common, and there are numerous suppliers who provide different kinds of kit. Typically, a kit would contain cards of different colors and shapes, pens, various kinds of adhesion, and mounting sheets. Boards of various descriptions may also be available (e.g. pin- boards). In a wall-charting session, participants will put their ideas on cards, using different shapes and colors as a simple classification scheme. These cards will be placed on mounting sheets. The facilitator will be responsible for timing, encouraging participation and involvement, and moving from one stage to the next.

Process mapping is a specific variant of wall-charting. Participants will use cards for the lower level components of business processes. These will be arranged on a wall, in an appropriate sequence. Then information about the flow of resources and outputs can be added to the maps. If required, control information can also be added. This is a wall-charting equivalent of IDEF (mentioned in chapter 7).

Producing a vision of an enterprise usually means articulating several categories of information such as mission, objectives, strengths, weaknesses, opportunities, threats, critical factors, strategies, core competencies, roles, organizational units, and key processes.

An enterprise can be seen as a viable purposeful system. This means that enterprise purpose can be implied whether or not it is articulated. It is also possible that real enterprise purpose is not necessarily the same thing as the articulated purpose. For example, an enterprise may exist to perform a particular kind of business (say, card tabulating machines), but in the event of a substantial decline in that business, may diversify or move into something else (say, computers). Thus the real purpose may be survival, independently of the stated purpose.

A common way of expressing an enterprise's purpose is through statements of mission and objectives. A mission statement expresses the overall objective of the enterprise. For example, "we aim to be the most innovative company that is valued by its customers as the first choice for the provision of widgets".

Following on from a mission may be an overall vision of how the participants in the strategy formulation exercise see the enterprise. A vision is likely to have many facets representing the perspectives of different enterprise stakeholders.

The objectives, or goals, of an enterprise (either profit or objective oriented) are detailed statements of what it wants to achieve or how it wants to behave. Typical enterprise objectives include:

- relative size in an industry (being the largest, the second largest, and so forth);
- market share (achieving, say, a 10% share of a particular market);
- public perception (being perceived as the foremost provider of widget services);
- service level (providing the fastest response in the industry to special customer requests);
- service depth (providing support to a particular group of people).

Statements about objectives are often derived from a vision of a desired future state. Some writers distinguish objectives and goals[3], but what is often important for the enterprise is an agreed definition that can be used both for understanding and for directing strategizing activity.

A technique that has achieved widespread use in classifying the situation of an enterprise, combining both external and internal views, is to identify threats, opportunities, weaknesses, and strengths. The internal attributes of an enterprise are classified as strengths or weaknesses. The external attributes are threats or opportunities. Several texts refer to this approach as a SWOT (strengths, weaknesses, opportunities, threats) analysis, and many analysts stop at just producing a list for each of those characteristics.

The origin of SWOT is obscure. However, the origin of SWOT reversed (TOWS) is not; Weihrich (1982) expresses the concept as a TOWS (threats, opportunities, weaknesses, strengths) matrix. He presents an analytical process to examine the situation of an enterprise, and articulates a method in terms of a series of steps to follow. As far as the TOWS classification is concerned, a matrix is drawn up with one axis the internal classification (strengths and weaknesses) and the other axis the external classification (opportunities and threats). The body of the matrix is then populated with strategies that take advantage of the intersections. In this sense, TOWS requires much more analysis than a mere listing of SWOTs.

For an example based on a TOWS matrix developed for a small engineering company, see Figure 5.1. This was produced after a series of workshops and interviews with management, staff, and customers. The strengths, weaknesses, opportunities, and threats are listed in the margins. Then at the intersections (SO, WO, ST, WT) are strategies that were considered both realistic and appropriate. The strategies are intended to take advantage of the appropriate SWOT characteristics. The most difficult task is to find strategies that exploit the combined threats and weaknesses. Where there are common strategic elements in the body of the matrix, it may be possible to draw out an overall enterprise strategy. In this example, diversification was considered to be the most common strategy that would help toward several of the others.

Another approach used often is that of identifying critical success factors (CSFs), which are "those few critical areas where things must go right for

---

3 For example, Martin (1989) defines an objective as a "general statement about the direction a firm intends to take in a particular area without stating a specific target to be reached by particular points in time", and a goal as "a specific target that is intended to be reached by a given point in time. A goal is thus an operational transform of one or more objectives".

the business to flourish" (Rockart, 1979). Rockart is usually credited with originating the term, which appears with varying frequency in management literature. The obvious corollary to CSFs is critical failure factors (CFFs), which can be defined as, perhaps, "those few critical areas where, if things go wrong, the business will fail to survive". An enterprise can, of course, remain static as well as flourish or decline. Hence, between critical success and failure factors, there may exist critical existence factors (CEFs), which are "the few critical areas where things must go right for the business merely to exist" (Figure 5.2).

In addition to the classification techniques are frameworks, many of which have been proposed in the popular and professional literature. Frameworks are generally very popular. Perhaps this is because they provide a simple, easy-to-use, overview and classification of a range of issues. They often provide essential key points to think about in enterprise planning. For the professional analyst, they are often problematic because of an absence of empirical foundations, or even conflicting empirical evidence.

OVERALL BUSINESS STRATEGY To focus on diversifying the company into a wider range of mechanical products	Internal Strengths (S) • Engineering capabilities • Strong sales force • Efficient production • Good service an • Experienced designers	Internal Weaknesses (W) • Financial management poor • Short of cash • Inefficient use of stock/labour • Expensive Chairman • Catering for a single customer
Opportunities (0) • Growing market demand for new product • Identified customer • Development of International market • Production of an augmented product	SO 1. Develop and produce flexible new product 2. Expand Into foreign markets	WO 1. Develop flexible machines for different price levels 2. Increase stock turns 3. Increase the PR role of Chairman
External Threats (T) • Competition • EC rules • Economic condition (Recession)	ST 1. New product 2. Meet competition with advanced design and technology 3. Adapt to new rules 4. Diversify Into products that support recession-proof sectors of the economy	WT 1. Define and Implement appropriate metric 2. Restructure the capital base of the Company 3. Optimize the stock 4. Attract institutional share holders 5. Reduce threat of competition by developing flexible product line

Figure 5.1 Sample TOWS matrix.

The use of frameworks is often a valuable facilitative technique to achieve consensus. In a deeper sense, the result of applying a framework is often the construction of a complex icon or symbol. Those involved in the work understand the meaning of the symbol, but those who were not involved in the consensus formation are likely to find the symbol difficult to understand without considerable additional explanation.

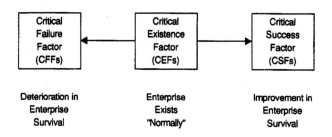

Figure 5.2 Critical success, existence, and failure factors.

The business process analyst needs to have a range of these frameworks in the toolbox. Here is a list of other frameworks used in a context of articulating a business vision. It is not a complete list, and there is no claim that the frameworks listed are the most frequently used (because data has not been found to justify such a claim), or even the most useful. Generally, the results of applying these frameworks are interesting and useful notwithstanding a lack of empirical foundations:

- Anthony's pyramid (or triangle)—strategic, tactical, operational levels of management (Anthony, 1965);
- McKinsey 7-S (Peters and Waterman, 1982, Pascale and Athos, 1981);
- environmental scanning and monitoring—political, economic, social, technological, environmental, legal (PESTEL) analysis;
- review of competitor activity (Porter, 1980);
- information intensity matrix (Porter and Millar, 1985);
- five forces model (Porter, 1985);
- value chain (Porter, 1985);
- IT strategic grid (Cash et al, 1983);
- systems audit grid (Earl, 1989);
- Nolan's stage model (Nolan, 1973, 1979);
- assessing your IS strategy (Galliers and Sutherland, 1991);
- information management (Synnott and Gruber, 1981);
- IT strategy framework (Earl, 1989);
- balanced scorecard (Kaplan and Norton, 1992);
- viable systems model (Beer, 1985; Espejo and Harnden, 1989; Hoverstadt, 2008).

Mintzberg's work, starting with the summary of different approaches to strategy formulation (Mintzberg and Quinn, 1991), is particularly interesting.

There has been an absence of clear empirical data to show that enterprises with an articulated strategy are more successful than those without, and Mintzberg (1994) provides a useful discussion around this point.

Business Architecture and Strategy Modeling

There are many ways in which the results of a strategizing exercise can be brought together. The interesting question is: how can all the many statements made about the enterprise in the course of relatively "soft" approaches be examined more rigorously? The various elements such as CSFs, processes, objectives, strategies, and so on, should be related together in some formal way in order to have a check on:

■ the internal consistency of the various statements which have been made;
■ the use of all the items of information which have arisen as a result of the various investigations and analysis.

Starting points could be the identification of:

■ statements about the state of the enterprise which is desired for different points in time; these statements will incorporate many different ideas and intuition about what is possible, what is desirable, and how the enterprise could look in relationship to the environment and other related enterprises; the identified objectives of the enterprise are important components related to this view;
■ statements about the state of the enterprise with respect to its present position; this will include an analysis of thinking about strengths, weaknesses, opportunities and threats; it will also identify perceived general trends which are likely to affect the enterprise's mission.

The consistency between critical factors and SWOTs can be analyzed. This could involve a matrix to show how the SWOTs are likely to have an impact on the various critical factors which have been identified. Another matrix could be developed to show the relationships between SWOTs and Objectives. This would help to identify the possible impact of SWOTs on achieving or inhibiting different objectives.

The different statements about the desired future state can be checked against objectives for consistency. Dissonance between the future and present states can be noted, because eventually it will be necessary to define a migration path for the enterprise to evolve from its present state to the desired state.

The business processes can be de-composed into smaller tasks. The resources needed to perform these tasks can be quantified, and responsibility for performing the tasks identified. This will enable a cross-check later between tasks, people and organizational units when organizational design is done.

Strategies could be defined either to take advantage of strengths and opportunities or to overcome weaknesses and threats. A cross check can be made to ensure that strategies have been identified to handle all the SWOTs.

OPR modeling has been used as a vehicle for this exploration. Each strategizing element is defined as an object, then relationships are constructed between the objects. It should be emphasized that there are several possible ways of putting this information together, and the model produced for each enterprise is likely to be different. What is presented here, is one example that has been used successfully in several enterprises.

Consider possible relationships between critical factors and SWOTs. These could be expressed as "a factor can be caused by a SWOT" (and of course factors have subtypes CFF, CEF, and CSF; SWOTs have subtypes strength, weakness, opportunity and threat). Strategies are designed to overcome weaknesses and threats or to take advantage of strengths and opportunities, so it could be said that strategies overcome factors. A SWOT is derived from some statement about the present state. If all of these statements are correlated together, they can be represented as shown in Figure 5.3.

This idea could be extended to take care of possible additional relationships where an objective is influenced by a factor, and an objective is implied by a statement about the desired future state. This extension is shown in Figure 5.4.

The application of a more rigorous approach can be demonstrated by means of a formal language modeling technique. Discussions are held to determine the scope of the business architecture or enterprise strategizing objects. Agreement should be reached about the range, names, and meanings of the different objects (for example, objectives, mission, strategy, SWOT, principle); then it is necessary to agree on the kinds of relationships between the various objects.

The agreements about the objects and relationships are used as the basis for a consultant or methods engineer to create a formal language. A subset of objects and relationships used for BAL (Business Architecture Language) is set out in Table 5.1. A formal language in this sense will consist of specific statements that can be used with the language to describe an enterprise. These statements, along with the objects and relationships, will then form a multidimensional model stored in a database. This set of steps is shown in Figure 5.5.

The Business Architecture Language is defined using a tool metaPSL®. BAL is used to model the specific business. Reports and other outputs are defined to report on the enterprise's Business Architecture.

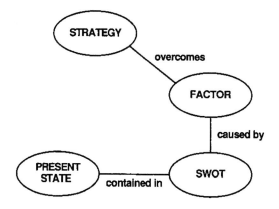

Figure 5.3 Strategies, factors, SWOTs and the present state.

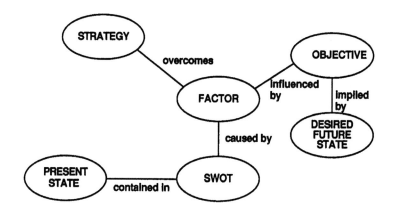

Figure 5.4 Factors, objectives and the desired future state.

Objects

Business-Process	Business-System	Data-Subject
Deliverable	Desired-Future-State	Event
Factor	Method	Metric
Mission	Objective	Organizational-Unit
Person	Present-State	Principle
Problem	Procedure	Resource
Solution	Strategic-Business-Unit	Strategy
SWOT	Task	Technique
Unit		

Relationships

Achieves-Relation	Attributes-Relation	Causes-Relation
Consists-of-Relation	Consumes-Relation	Depends-on-Relation
Establishes-to-Fulfill-Relation	Equivalent-to-Relation	Experiencing-Relation
Formulates-Relation	Happens-Relation	Identifies-Relation
Implements-Relation	Implies-Relation	Influences-Relation
Maintains-Relation	Measures-Relation	Memo-Relation
Overcomes-Relation	Owns-Relation	Performs-Relation
Requires-Relation	Solves-Relation	Supports-Relation
Triggers-Relation	Uses-to-Derive-Relation	

Table 5.1 BAL sample objects and relationships

BAL is used in the following ways (as shown in Figure 5.6):

- when the results of studying the business are available (or even only a few of them to begin with), the analyst uses BAL to create a source file which describes the enterprise;
- BAL checks these statements, and when all the statements are syntactically correct, a business specification database is created;
- completeness and consistency checks are performed on the business specification database, and reports produced;
- the consultants and analysts, in conjunction with relevant business people, decide whether more investigation is needed or whether the existing incompleteness and inconsistencies are acceptable;
- if necessary, more investigation is carried out and the specification database updated accordingly;
- when the business specification database is considered sufficiently complete and consistent for the purposes of the modeling, a series of reports on the business is generated;
- these reports are used (the reports at this stage are technical and not normally suitable for the business or management end-users) by the consultants and analysts to support writing the business architecture documents which will finally be delivered to represent the results of the business architecture work;
- in preparing final reports, nonspecific sources of diagrams and information will be used in addition to the technical reports from the specification database;
- the business specification database can be used to support any subsequent work from systems architecture right down to the specification of individual applications (this adds considerable traceability).

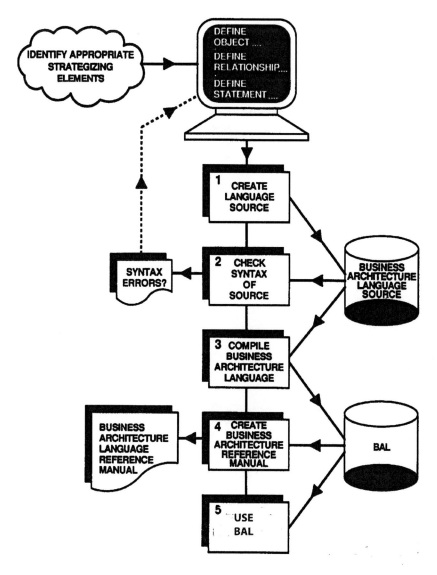

Figure 5.5 Creating a business architecture language.

Concluding remarks

A practical way of determining a business vision is to have senior managers, and any other appropriate stakeholders, work separately on defining vision and objectives, CSFs (along with CFFs and CEFs), and TOWS. In each case, identify strategies: what strategies are suggested to achieve objectives; what strategies are proposed to deal with CSFs etc; what strategies emerge from a TOWS exercise?

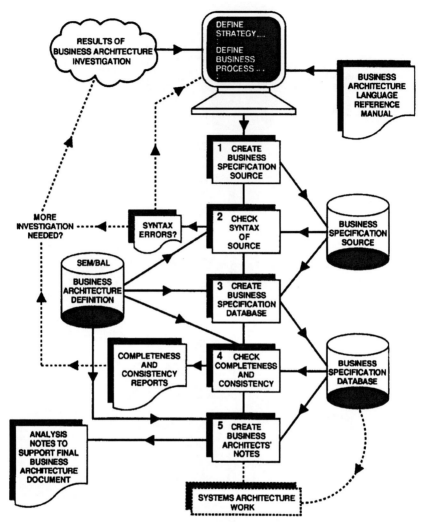

Figure 5.6 Using a business architecture language.

The business process analyst can then support an enterprise strategy study by at least five key contributions:

1. facilitate workshops and suchlike to obtain the key ingredients of an enterprise strategy;
2. analyze the results of strategy studies for completeness and consistency, and relevance for business processes;
3. clarify any issues of inconsistency or incompleteness with business people;
4. triangulate strategies articulated when deciding TOWS, CSFs, and Objectives;
5. prepare appropriate reports for stakeholders involved in preparing the vision.

In these cases, the analyst needs a grounding in the key techniques likely to be used or encountered.

The usual approach approach is to define a set of objects and relations and then create a language for the underlying meta model. A language reference manual will help the analyst greatly by providing a mapping from diverse source strategy material to a standard OPR model that can be checked for completeness and consistency independently of the number of objects and relations involved. Alternative to a language reference manual is a set of computer screens that can be used to input and manage all the business architecture information.

This approach is suitable for analyzing the results of a wide range of approaches to business vision. An OPR approach to analysis is sufficiently independent of any specific business vision technique to provide the analyst with a good foundation.

The Business Architecture work can then be enhanced by follow-on architectural work defining such things as systems and processes needed to realize the vision, objectives, and so forth.

Chapter 6

Simple text analysis

This chapter starts with two examples of relatively informal descriptions of processes or events. These are used to identify and explain how to use documents as sources of information about business processes, and how to consolidate that information.

There are many ways in which textual sources can be analyzed. Therefore the way the analysis has been exemplified is written in the first person, from the author's own perspective. This is not intended to be a statement about how it should be done. Others may approach the analysis with completely legitimate alternative approaches.

Example one

> Couple intending to travel to the USA in two days time, want £1300 worth of Traveller's Cheques in Dollars. Cashier: "£1300 ... just a moment ...". Goes to desk and picks up two 'crib sheets' on which both daily Rates of Exchange and Charge Schedules are printed. Cashier to ethnographer: "It's easier when they're ordered ... we try to discourage them from doing this ... (coming in on spec.) ... we have to work it all out like this ... I got the rates off the screen earlier ...". Cashier calculates on pen and paper, using multiples of £200. Cashier: "That's ... $2400 for £1300 ... and the charge will be uh £12.20". Cashier gives customer form to sign and gets up, goes to cupboard and collects Traveller's Cheque Register and Traveller's Cheque File. Writes Customer names; Currencies; a balance; and initials it in the Register, The Register's filled in separately for each packet of US Cheques (in $500 packets), and code printed on each packet is written in the Register. Asks customer to sign Customer Receipt Form and to sign the top left hand corner of each Cheque plus counterfoils. Asks customer's wife to do the same. Cashier puts society's copy of Receipts in Traveller's Cheque File. Borrows further 'crib sheet from next door cashier and enters 'Nominal Receipt-cash' screen. Cashier: "It's come out of our stock so I have to put the money through to T.C. sales, and 1% ... through to T.C. Commissions ...".[1]

---

1 This example comes from the draft of a CSCW paper entitled Customers and Cooperation, by Geoffrey Darnton, John Hughes, and Dave Randall. It is based on field notes taken during an ethnographic study in a financial institution in the UK.

Example two

> Our order entry system works like this. We don't do any cold-calling. All our leads come from advertisements. The telephonist receives an enquiry from a potential customer. This is noted on an Enquiry Sheet. That sheet is passed to a sales manager who manages a group of sales people and their assistants, and who assigns it to a particular salesperson depending on the products mentioned, and the manager's impression of who would be best to do the selling. The sales person then makes contact and arranges a visit. If the customer orders, then we try to get an official order from the customer on their own stationery, but in any case the sales person fills out our own internal order form. That is handed in to the office here and an order entry clerk enters the order into the computer. The computer checks the customer details. If this is a new customer, a record is created and we may need to get some more information to set a credit limit. If the customer is verified, the order is then validated to make sure that what has been ordered are goods and services we actually supply, and a delivery date is calculated. We try to get in orders and agree a delivery date of 28 days or sooner, so we need to notify the customer of the expected date. Following on from this order entry, the order will be processed[2].

Fundamentals

Perhaps the most frequent source of information for the business process analyst is words in some form or other; they may be printed, or they may be spoken during meetings. If it is not words, it is probably diagrams or pictures, which are discussed in chapter 7.

    The two examples that start this chapter, demonstrate the difficulty for the analyst of constructing a model of business processes from such text. This is not an unusual situation. In fact, it is probably the most likely

---

2 This example comes from a set of interview notes from an interview session with a senior manager in a large European manufacturing company.

starting point for business process analysis work. Even if it is not the starting point in a project, then text sources will probably form a substantial part of all sources.

The analyst will usually have to deal with considerable variety in the available sources. Many statements will be written down in some form, but not many enterprises have adequate formal descriptions of their processes. Of those that do, the most common form is a book of procedures, explaining how an employee should handle a particular situation, what policies are involved, and what matters need to be attended to. For example, a bank may well have in excess of 2000 procedures.

Therefore, the analyst will frequently need to examine memos, notes, various documents, and multitudinous pieces of paper. It is also likely that the analyst will attend meetings and interview people. The results will then appear either as notes, transcripts of meetings or discussions, or tape recordings of meetings.

Text analysis

The objective of the analyst is to create a machine-processable model of processes derived from statements about those processes.

Machine-processable models will eventually be required because for any significant enterprise it will be necessary to manage information about hundreds or thousands of processes, and the interrelationships between them. This is a task that cannot be done adequately by manual means.

Whenever process descriptions have been produced primarily by manual means (including text and diagram processors), *there are usually serious deficiencies and inconsistencies in the descriptions.*

High-level depictions of processes must be tolerant of incompleteness and inconsistency, but the nearer to implementation the process descriptions are, the more careful they need to be. For these reasons, any technique employed by the analyst must be scalable to be able to check the completeness and consistency of hundreds or thousands of process descriptions. That does not mean using only word processors and graphical editors—far more analytical capability is needed.

The technique explained in this chapter is the construction of a set of objects, properties, relationships, and statements from verbal sources (written or spoken) into a structured formal language that can be used to standardize the information about a set of business processes—in other words, producing an OPR model.

In implementing this kind of analysis, several key problems are usually encountered:

- objects, properties, and relationships can be represented using a remarkable variety of expressions, therefore the analyst needs to exercise much judgment;
- validity: the words used may not say what was intended to be said,

therefore on occasions the analyst must infer intention and ignore some specific words used;

- reliability: the words used may be idiosyncratic and understood by people working in some subculture (for example, the word "process") in a particular way, but their meaning is not necessarily shared by others; one dimension of corporate culture is the idiosyncratic way in which various words and terms may be used, therefore the analyst needs to pay attention to the general and specific meanings of words;
- synonyms: it is often taught in language lessons that it is a bad writing style to repeat the same word several times in the same sentence or paragraph, therefore it may be a requirement for good language grades to introduce synonyms deliberately; the analyst must seek out synonyms and try to produce one agreed term to resolve them;
- homonyms: we all use some words to mean different things in different contexts; when talking about business processes, there is often some relationship between the level of abstraction and number of homonyms (the higher the level of abstraction, the higher the probability of a word having more than one meaning); the analyst needs to introduce more words and terms to account for all the meanings of a word or term;
- ambiguity: words and their context can be ambiguous in their meaning, and this ambiguity may be patent or latent; the analyst needs to recognize ambiguity and resolve it where necessary;
- anthropomorphism: "the company's objectives are ..."—companies do not have objectives, but people do; in management literature it is very common for abstract entities to be attributed with human desires and goals; the analyst needs to identify anthropomorphisms and resolve them (usually by identifying the particular stakeholders or people concerned);
- redundancy: human language is very rich, particularly when spoken; spoken language often contains repetition, hesitation, incompleteness (and often sentences may not be completed), and the same things said in different ways; the degree of redundancy in the spoken word is often so high that it is possible to obtain the essence of what is being said from a subset of the conversation; the analyst needs to handle this incompleteness and redundancy.

Therefore any model will inevitably be the result of many arbitrary decisions. Such arbitrariness is unavoidable and is not a problem in itself. It is important for the analyst to present any proposed formal language to the client in order to establish an agreed way to produce formal process descriptions. In practice, this is not usually as difficult as it may sound.

The remainder of this chapter discusses these key problems in more depth, in addition to addressing the basic construction of OPR models from words.

A full analysis of all parts of speech in verbal sources is not usually necessary, so restrict the analysis to a limited number of parts of speech. The omissions may be of use in the resolution of ambiguity or taking a decision where there are genuine modeling alternatives available. The parts of particular interest, are nouns, verbs, adjectives, and adverbs.

The starting rules of thumb are: nouns indicate objects; verbs indicate relationships; adjectives and adverbs indicate properties. Each of these may be a single word, a phrase, or perhaps even a clause. Sentences are constructed from the objects, properties, and relationships into statements that are understandable to the originators of the source statements.

In practice, a set of highlighter pens can be very valuable in starting this kind of analysis It is also useful to have clean copies of the text to allow for changes in the classification of words and phrases.

Simple Example

Try this simple exercise before reading much further. Take a clean copy of the two examples at the beginning of this chapter. Take three different colored highlighter pens—one for nouns, one for verbs, and one for adjectives and adverbs. Take three pieces of scrap paper, one for nouns, one for verbs, and one for adjectives and adverbs.

Identify the parts of speech in the examples by using the highlighter pens. Transfer the results to the pieces of paper. On the paper, write down possible names for the objects, relationships, and properties.

The following subsections present versions that I have created for the examples. Yours may not be the same, but that does not necessarily matter; there are several "correct" ways to do this, and some arbitrary decisions are required. Please note that for reasons of space, I have not completed the exercise, but have gone about half-way for each.

You will have encountered some of the problems I identified in section 6.2 while deciding possible objects, relationships, and properties. These are discussed in more detail in the following sections.

Nouns and objects

Table 6.1 shows the first pass at identifying several objects from the first example. Nouns are put in the first column of the table, then possible object types are put in the second column. The third column is reserved to enter analysis notes (such as why a particular arbitrary object name was chosen, or how synonyms or homonyms were resolved).

This is now repeated for the second example, and results for the first part are shown in Table 6.2.

Noun(s)	Object(s)	Comments
couple	PERSON	implies marriage/partner relationship
USA	COUNTRY; PLACE	perhaps a structure needed for "place", e.g. hierarchy?
check	DOCUMENT; BILL OF EXCHANGE; PAYMENT	classification not straightforward—perhaps should be modeled as an attribute or subtype?
sheet	DOCUMENT; REPORT	may contain many objects and relationships, and sheet is a user view of a subset of more information

Table 6.1 Nouns and objects: example 1

Noun(s)	Object(s)	Comments
system	PROCESS	Implies several components interrelated
lead	CALL	similar to enquiry—but what makes the difference is higher probability of an order?
advertisement	OUTPUT; INTERFACE	Implies more complex set of processes, outputs, inputs
telephonist	PERSON	also implies other objects such as telephone
enquiry	CALL	Similar to lead-but what makes the difference is lower probability of an order?
sheet	DOCUMENT; REPORT	may contain many objects and relationships, and sheet is a user view of a subset of more information

Table 6.2 Nouns and objects: example 2

Verbs and relationships

The identification of relations is similar to objects. Verbs are entered in the first column, possible relation types in the second, and explanatory notes in the third. I show my first pass for the first example in Table 6.3.

Verb(s)	Relationship(s)	Comments (objects implied)
travel to	TRAVEL	A three-part relationship? (person P travels to place PL using method of transport T)
ordered	ORDERS	verb or noun (therefore, relationship or object)?
calculates	CALCULATE	person or mechanism P calculates metric or set of values M; a relationship or a process?)

Table 6.3 Verbs and relationships: example 1

This is now repeated for the second example, and I show the first part of my approach in Table 6.4.

Verb(s)	Relationship(s)	Comments (objects implied)
works	PROCESS	replace with full process description
come from	GENERATES	interface INT generates input INP
cold calling	VISIT	person visits (potential) customer?
receives	RECEIVE	process P receives input I?

Table 6.4 Verbs and relationships: example 2

Adjectives, adverbs, and properties

Adjectives and adverbs qualify nouns and verbs, respectively. Therefore in terms of OPR modeling, there are possible qualifications for objects or relationships. These are more complex to handle than nouns and verbs as the impact on the model may be subtle. Table 6.5 summarizes the adjectives and adverbs found in the first example. These are listed in the first column, and in the second column I give suggestions for impact on the developing OPR model.

The exercise is repeated for the first part of example 2, and the result is shown in Table 6.6.

High-level models may start life with only objects and relations (for example, the simple process shown in Figures 3.1 and 3.2). As shown in more detail in chapter 8, entity-relationship diagrams do not usually show attributes or properties. This is also the case for OPR diagrams: they usually show only objects and relations.

Adjective or adverb	Impact on model
traveller's (checque)	document subtype needed?
crib (sheet) of objects and relationships on each	complex structure of objects and relations on each sheet? User view subtypes needed?
separately	implies a collection of records (entries)?

Table 6.5 Adjectives, adverbs, and properties: example 1

Adjective or adverb	Impact on model
order entry (system)	description of system implying other objects
Mentioned (products)	topic of a communication?
crib (sheet) of objects and relationships on each	complex structure of objects and relations on each sheet? User view subtypes needed?

Table 6.6 Adjectives, adverbs, and properties: example 2

However, it is necessary for the analyst to identify the properties of each object. This corresponds to identifying the attributes of every object (or entity). In many cases, the properties of objects are not all obtainable from source text. Therefore in the initial modeling stages, the analyst will need to infer, to guess, or to interview, in order to create a list of the properties for each object. The analyst *should create* such a list for *every* object or state that an object has no properties (this is extremely doubtful, as every object should have at least a name). This is one of the most important ways for the analyst to resolve synonyms and homonyms. Obviously, inferred or guessed properties need to be checked with the client at some stage.

The examples in this chapter are short on properties, therefore in cases such as these, the analyst can infer or guess certain properties. Table 6.7 shows some specimen inferred properties for the first example, and Table 6.8 for the second example.

Object	Inferred properties
person	name; address; status (e.g. customer or not)
document	owner of set of document elements; name; description; type
register	name; date commenced; column names; amount; currency

Table 6.7 Inferred properties: example 1

Object	Inferred properties
person	name; address; status (employee or temporary)
document	owner of set of document elements; name; description; type
register	name; date commenced; column names; amount; currency

Table 6.8 Inferred properties: example 2

Processes

The question of process identification will be revisited later in the chapter, but for the moment it is helpful at the beginning of the analysis to make some arbitrary selection of appropriate process names to cover the material in the text sources.

For the first example, the following process names are suggested:

■ calculate exchange rates;
■ issue cheques;
■ transaction entry.

For the second example, the following process names are suggested:

■ order entry;
■ call handling;
■ manage team.

Following on from identifying candidate processes, each process should be described by starting with the Level I and Level II process descriptions explained in chapter 4.

At this stage there is no clear connection between objects, relations, and properties on the one hand, and processes on the other hand, as described in this chapter. The connection is explained later.

Synonym and homonym detection and resolution

As mentioned earlier, writers of prose are encouraged not to use the same word too many times in the same sentence or paragraph. This means that a writer will frequently introduce synonyms for ideas in order to improve readability.

The goal of the analyst is almost the opposite; by careful naming and avoidance of synonyms, the model can become a much more precise rendering, and remove doubt. The person reading a set of sentences constructed from an OPR model can obtain a very precise description of processes.

Similarly, a writer may use a term more loosely, so one word may have several valid meanings (that is, the word is a homonym). Synonyms are different words that mean essentially the same thing; a homonym is a word used to mean different things. The analyst can start synonym and homonym detection and resolution at the level of natural language. That will deal with many problems quickly and easily.

Following on from using natural language, the most useful technique to identify synonyms is the comparison of properties.

Every object should be defined also in terms of a set of relevant properties. Where there is more than one object (that is, different object names are used) and assertions are made that the objects really are different, the analyst can test the assertions by comparing properties. Let us illustrate this point by looking at one issue that is at the heart of business process analysis: what is a process?

In an earlier chapter (Figure 2.1), a hierarchy of "processes" is set out along with the question, from an analytical perspective, are process, sub-process, activity, task, and step, different objects or the same kind of object? Is there any difference between a business process and an activity?

The key to unravelling such a question is to understand the properties of the objects. The analyst should set out definitions for each of the objects. Each has a name and various other attributes. It participates in a range of possible relationships, such as TRIGGERED_BY or PERFORMS. Chapter 4 mentions Level I and Level II process descriptions. Are those descriptions valid for business process, sub-process, activity, task, and step? If they are, then the objects are synonyms.

There are two important tests for synonyms. Two terms are synonyms if:

1. the properties (or attributes) of the objects are essentially the same;
2. the objects participate in essentially the same relationship types.

If the first condition is true, but the second is false, then the analyst needs to create two objects with different names.

Homonyms are detected beyond the natural language level by identifying inconsistent properties. Then the analyst resolves the problem by creating enough objects with unique names so the set of properties can be allocated among the objects eliminating inconsistency.

A problem of *classification* may arise, which looks initially like a problem of synonyms. For example, an examination of an enterprise may yield a set of objects such as employee, manager, and contractor. An examination of the properties (name, address, gender, date-of-birth) suggests that they are in fact synonyms because the properties are mainly identical. A new object such as "person" with an identical set of properties would resolve this. However, it is not so much that person is a synonym; it is more that the different kinds of people have been classified into one group. This is also known in the object-oriented world by terms such as genericity. Person then becomes a class of object types. Similarly, in several clients, the properties of customer and supplier are identical. then perhaps create a new object type called something like TRADING PARTNER—whether that partner is a supplier or customer depends on other matters such as relation, or the direction of flow for goods, services, and cash. Of course, some trading partners can be both customer and supplier.

Ambiguity and equivocation

Incompleteness and inconsistency could almost be the most important problems to be solved by the analyst (apart, that is, from the problems of defining completeness and consistency criteria in the first place!).

People do not always say what they mean, and do not always mean what they say. Statements about processes may be incomplete, and a range of possible meanings may lead to potential inconsistency. Actual inconsistency can arise when different descriptions of the same process depict it in different ways.

The analyst has a difficult facilitation role to perform by interacting with a range of people to try and produce process descriptions that are complete and consistent. People need the assistance of a good analyst, because it is not reasonable to expect the beneficiaries of analysis to intuit what is required of them.

Ambiguity and equivocation occur frequently in text sources, even when the texts were produced by experts in the drafting of documents. If this were not the case, there would be far fewer legal disputes about the meaning of statutes or contracts! In looking for techniques to support the business process analyst, it can be seen that lawyers have long experience in recognizing and dealing with ambiguity and equivocation in documents.

Ambiguity can be classified as either patent or latent. According to Dworkin (1967), "a true patent ambiguity will exhibit on the face of the deed an uncertainty or inconsistency". In BPA language, an example would be "a purchase order is then sent to A or B". An ambiguity is not the same an an incompleteness, although it is a symptom of incompleteness. For example, "a purchase order is then sent" is clearly incomplete. In the prior example of being sent to A or B, the ambiguity can only be resolved by knowing how to decide between A and B, and it may also be the case that A or B are alternative names for the same supplier. There the legal analogy ends. In English law, rules have evolved for the admissibility of evidence to deal with patent ambiguities, and normally such stringent rules are not needed to deal with patent ambiguities in process specifications—unless, that is, they relate to processes to implement statutory or contractual requirements.

According to Dworkin, "in a latent ambiguity the sense *seems* perfectly clear on a perusal of the document. It is not until further facts are disclosed that the ambiguity appears". For example, while describing a process for project initiation, there is a statement such as "the project initiation document must be approved by the Corporate Project Review Board". That seems very straightforward until it is discovered that the Corporate Project Review Board was disbanded three years previously.

That leaves the question of equivocation which, according to Dworkin, " ... arises where the description employed seems to be applicable to more than one person or thing, it being clear that only one was intended". For the business process analyst, equivocation can arise from the linguistic convention of introducing synonyms, thus requiring the analyst to think carefully about whether it is really only one thing being described or several things.

A further discussion, also from the legal world, is provided by Bennion (2008), considering grammatical and trained constructions. He classifies grammatical ambiguity as general or relative. Bennion is looking at grammatical ambiguity in the UK legal statute world, buit his codes can be adapted to any situation where an organization has evolved its own use of language into idiosyncratic strained uses.

The approaches used in the legal world to problems of ambiguity and equivocation are useful. The rules of evidence around those principles are less helpful, but worthy of consideration as they can guide the analyst in the nature of material that may be needed to deal with ambiguity.

The other contribution from the legal world which is helpful, is to use a gentle cross-examination technique to facilitate the production of good process specifications.

Anthropomorphism

Anthropomorphism is the "ascription of a human attribute or personality to anything personal or impersonal". For example, "this organization values its employees". Anthropomorphic writing is a common feature of writing about business processes. Whilst anthropomorphism is a reasonable and succinct writing device for high-level summaries, it generates problems for the analyst, especially if modeling under the constraints of a technique such as OPR (and this is necessary if hundreds or thousands of objects and relationships need to be managed).

For example, "The Mortgage Centre performs the lending control functions for the branches in the Central European Region; has a Personal and Small Business Lending Section; and does any necessary Debt Recovery".

This kind of sentence is meaningful to many people; however, it is strictly anthropomorphic because in reality an organizational unit does not perform anything. People perform functions, or in some cases, a mechanism may, but not an organizational unit. Therefore the analyst must decide among (i) should the organizational units be modeled as interfaces (ii) should they be modeled as processors, and (iii) should people be introduced into the model as processors with the organizational unit being modeled as some high-level aggregated object such as a process?

The analyst needs to identify all cases of anthropomorphism. The most satisfactory way to deal with them is by adding logical roles to the model, acting as processors, and adding logical people who perform the roles. For example, in the mortgage center case, the analyst should identify who takes the lending decisions and who does the debt collection. These people can then be mapped in some appropriate way to the mortgage center. The Level I and Level II process descriptions require that processor(s) are identified for every process.

Constructing object property relationship models

When the analyst has extracted all the relevant objects, properties, and relationships from the text, and dealt with synonyms, homonyms, ambiguity, and anthropomorphism, work can continue by producing a more polished OPR model, represented by the kinds of statement given in chapter 4.

The usual preference is for an OPR model to be represented by means of an OPR language. However, an alternative diagrammatic approach is suitable when dealing with:

■ high-level process descriptions;
■ local models of parts of processes;
■ small and simple processes.

It is usually helpful to produce an entity relationship attribute (ERA) diagram for the simple OPR models. This will prove to be a very useful reference during subsequent analysis work.

A sample OPR model expressed as an ERA diagram is shown in Figure 6.1.

A complete OPR model expressed as an ERA diagram will not be particularly easy to read by those who are unfamiliar with the approach. Therefore it may also be necessary to produce simple, expressive, diagrams that are suitable for audiences who need only an overview.

Developing such OPR models is usually an interactive process. The objects and relations need to evolve as the analyst puts more precision into the model. It is important that the client understands and approves the model.

Model testing

The penultimate task for the analyst is to test the OPR model. My preferred way to do this is to create a language reference manual and check that the language is capable of accounting for all the source material that is considered relevant.

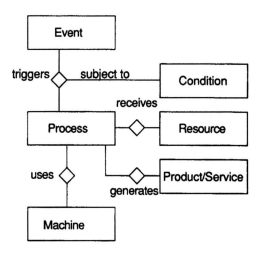

Figure 6.1 Example ERA diagram of OPR model.

Text analysis and business processes

So far, the analyst has produced an OPR model based on an agreed set of objects, relations, and properties. A list of process names will also have been chosen to encompass the sources used to produce the model.

What is the connection between the OPR model and business processes? Surely, the OPR model is only a static structural representation?

After constructing the OPR model, the analyst can define a set of business processes based on implementing the model. A summary of the way to do this is:

1. for every object in the model, define the operations that need to be performed on it;
2. each operation will need to be implemented by one or more processes;
3. every relation requires processes for implementation.

As a simple rule of thumb, every object will require at least four processes (create, use, modify, delete) and every relation will require at least two processes, and perhaps three (connect, disconnect, reconnect).

The largest known model built with the most famous OPR language, PSL, had 25,000 objects and 65,000 relations. Therefore that model would need at least 230,000 processes and probably a lot more than that. Try managing 230,000 processes with UML or any other diagram technique!

This yields a list of processes to handle the OPR model. Those who are familiar with the information systems idea of object-oriented analysis will notice that here, we are effectively constructing business objects as a combination of objects and constructing business objects as a combination of objects and the processes performed on those objects. Notice also that this result is achieved, not by a top-down functional de-composition of an arbitrary view of processes, but by a careful consideration of operations to be performed on objects.

In this way, a well-formed OPR model is a very powerful assistant in the identification of business processes, or the building blocks of business processes.

Document analysis

Often the analyst will be faced with documents that provide much of the source material. So far this chapter has discussed the analysis of the document contents. It is also useful for the analyst to analyze the documents themselves, in other words, to do *document analysis.*

A useful summary of approaches to this is provided by Alschuler (1995) who explains that "The purpose of document analysis is to build a model of document structure and content that can be translated unambiguously into an SGML document type definition ...". Although this sounds like a very mechanical exercise, she goes on to explain that "The objective is to capture what is known about the document and its uses ... identify and define the document life-cycle questions—Where does information come from? What do I do with it? Where does it go? ...".

This means that document analysis is concerned not only with the technical content and structure of the documents themselves, but with all the major aspects of document life-cycles, such as origination, use, modification, and retirement. In chapter 14 the need to match purpose and audience when defining standards is discussed, and this approach to document analysis is a very useful addition.

A simple method

The principal approach to the analysis of text sources identifies objects, properties, and relationships from the parts of speech found in the text. An initial set is refined to resolve problems such as synonyms, homonyms, and ambiguity. The refined set is used to build an OPR model, which can be expressed either in linguistic form by means of carefully designed statements, or in diagrammatic form by means of an ERA diagram.

The analyst identifies processes that are required for every object in the set. Every relationship needs to be implemented by means of processes also.

The resulting process descriptions are refined further by bringing them up to at least Level I or Level II.

This chapter is concluded by bringing together the steps outlined, into a simple method for analysts to use. This is summarized in Figure 6.2.

Text sources are usually about specific processes and other objects. The analyst will usually want to create a meta model of which any situation is an instance. Therefore, there are initial steps of examining and understanding the source material, but this is simplified and generalized to create a meta model, which can then be used to identify a minimum set of required business processes.

The discussion in this chapter has focussed on an analysis of text, and the next chapter shows how a similar approach can be taken for the analysis of diagrams, pictures, and charts.

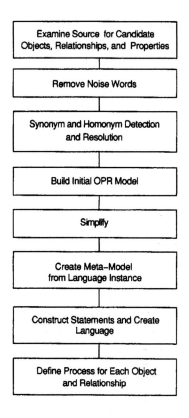

Figure 6.2 Method of identifying processes from text.

Analyzing diagrams

If words are not the most common information sources encountered by analysts, then probably diagrams are!

Diagrams used to depict business processes can take many different forms. They may be produced as a result of either senior strategizing exercises or prior process analysis work. The conventions in the diagrams may be either formal or informal.

"A picture says more than a thousand words"—a frequent rallying call exhorting people to present their work in some graphical or pictorial way. The rationale is that a picture conveys the equivalent of a large number of words, but more effectively. In many ways, pictures and illustrations are very useful ways to build good cognitive models of business processes. However, the riposte to the above saying, is "a picture may say more than a thousand words, but with some pictures you also need the thousand words!"

The business process analyst faces a serious dilemma over language versus diagrams. The debate over the number of business processes in an enterprise is discussed in chapter 2. The answer depends on the acceptability of an arbitrary level of abstraction. So, a high level of abstraction which accepts something such as order fulfillment as a business process will yield a total number of processes for an enterprise within tens, such as 10— 30. If this level of abstraction is sufficient, then it is likely that each of the 10-30 processes can be described by relatively simple process flowcharts. Indeed, for senior audiences who only need a high level of abstraction, that is what the analyst should deliver. Pictures will say more than a thousand words, and there is a good chance that they will be sufficient. The work of the business process consultant may well end there.

However, the work of the business process analyst may hardly have begun. A process such as order fulfillment needs considerable decomposition to design ways of implementing it. As this de-composition proceeds, the number of process descriptions will move much nearer to the 10,000-30,000 order of magnitude.

One piece of advice frequently encountered while drawing diagrams is to apply the magic number, 7+2, objects on each page. Fewer than five objects indicates insufficient grouping or leveling, and more than nine objects makes the picture too detailed for people to take in.

Obviously, descriptions of 10,000 processes cannot be managed effectively by means of diagrams. There must be some way to store and process that information, and produce diagrams for small subsets and aggregations of the information.

Typically, diagrams of business processes are much easier to analyze than text. This is because there are far fewer degrees of freedom available for the representation of processes. Most diagrams are constructed using some kind of formal notation to begin with. Therefore the principal problem for the business process analyst to solve is producing a meta model of the diagram notation. That meta model can then be applied to diagram instances.

Diagrams will generally originate in one of four different ways:

1. relatively simple diagrams drawn using some established notation;
2. diagrams drawn with no preconceived notation, using whatever symbols are agreed by those involved;
3. diagrams with high symbolic value and low semantic value;
4. complex diagrams drawn to represent part of the contents of some large store of information (e.g., a large data model).

Most process flow diagrams fall into the first category. The analyst should not have too much difficulty in establishing an underlying meta model for the notation involved (bearing in mind that there may be several possible and equally valid alternative meta models).

In the second case, there are generally more degrees of freedom involved because the final notation used may not be predictable before the diagrams have been produced. These diagrams are referred to usefully as "rich pictures", a term used by writers such as Checkland (1981) and Wilson (1984). One way round this problem is for analysts to have a predefined form of "rich picture" (for example, Digital Equipment Corporation developed a consulting technique known as TOP MAPPING[1] - see an example in Darnton and Giacoletto, 1992). Where there is a predefined notation for rich pictures, the meta model becomes relatively easy to define and apply.

The third case is where a formal analysis of the diagram yields very little information, and visual effects such as juxtaposition and linking have no clear meaning. In such a case, the diagram is really more of a symbol for some decision or approach, and formal analysis is not appropriate.

In the fourth case, the analyst should proceed by determining the meta model of the diagrams from the underlying tools used for the information base. Unfortunately, very few tool vendors have documented the underlying meta model.

Diagram analysis

As with an analysis of text, the objective in analyzing diagrams is to produce machine-processable process descriptions by means of a technique that is scalable to hundreds or thousands of descriptions.

My approach is usually to create a meta model of the diagram type. Each separate diagram can then be described by means of the meta model, and appropriate completeness and consistency checks can be carried out. The principal technique here is also OPR modeling. This makes it easier to merge the analysis of text with that of diagrams.

In doing this, the most common problems are:

- boundaries: diagrams often include enclosed objects—is there any significance to the boundary?;
- juxtaposition: what is the significance of placing one object next to or near to another?;
- lines: often there are devices used to connect objects in some way—what is the nature of the connection?;
- shapes and symbols: there may be a formal convention for the use of different shapes for specific purposes—where these are defined in advance, producing meta models is much easier;
- topology and morphology: the way in which all the objects in the diagram have been laid out as a collection (for example, is a chart to be read top to bottom, left to right, or some other way?);
- underlying assumptions: in addition to a diagram, and possibly an associated legend, there may be background material that is needed to understand a diagram (for example, boxes further from the top of a piece of paper are de-compositions of boxes nearer the top).

---

1 TOP MAPPING was a registered trademark of Digital Equipment Corporation. It has been difficult to verify its current status, but it is safest to assume the existence of some registered trade mark covering its use.

Producing meta models of diagram types is usually easier than for text because diagrams already have classes of objects indicated by the diagram components. There is usually little need for generality (unless the diagrams are free format, with much variability in the way in which components have been used).

Process diagrams

The most common diagrams I have encountered are:

- simple flowcharts showing a complete process broken down into a series of lower-level processes;
- process flowcharts based on standard American National Standards Institute (ANSI) notation;
- process flowcharts based on more traditional program flowchart notation;
- UML diagrams.

Examples of these diagrams are given on the following pages, along with an indication of how the analyst can construct and apply meta models for each. Please note that there is insufficient space to give complete listing or development of these diagram types, and what is provided is for illustration, not a representative or complete survey.

Simple flowcharts

Figure 7.1 shows a simple process flowchart of the type that Harrington (1991) calls a *block flow diagram.* He asserts that this type of diagram is "the simplest and most prevalent type of flowchart".

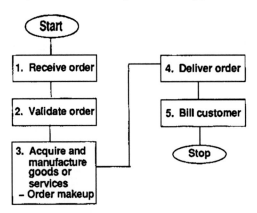

Figure 7.1 Simple flowchart: example.

These charts are very easy to read. A high-level process, effectively the whole chart, is broken down into smaller processes (called activities by Harrington). The lines on the chart indicate the sequence of these lower level processes.

Much detail is missing from these charts. They convey a high-level view, but frequently, the real world of work does not follow such neat, simple sequences. They may have heuristic value, but their analytical value is very restricted. The chart has only boxes and lines between the boxes. Each box indicates a process that is part of the overall process. The lines indicate sequence. A line entering a box from the left (or top) indicates that the process comes after the process at the other end of the line. A line leaving a box from the right or bottom indicates that the process comes before the process at the other end of the line.

Therefore in such a diagram, there is only one object, Process. There are four relations in two pairs (pair because of two directions to the relation): {part of; consists of}; {comes before; comes after}. An ERA version of this model is shown in Figure 7.2.

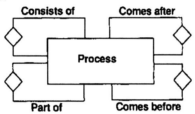

Figure 7.2 ERA model of a simple flowchart.

As a linguistic form of description, the PSL equivalent of the diagram is:

DEFINE PROCESS order-fulfillment;
    CONSISTS-OF receive-order, validate-order, order-makeup, deliver- order, bill-customer;

DEFINE PROCESS receive-order;
  PART-OF order-fulfillment;
  COMES BEFORE validate-order;

DEFINE PROCESS validate-order;
  PART-OF order-fulfillment;
  COMES BEFORE order-makeup;
  COMES AFTER receive-order;
  ....
  ....
  ....

DEFINE PROCESS bill-customer;
  PART-OF order-fulfillment;
  COMES AFTER deliver-order;

Process charts

The evolution of flowchart techniques is outlined in chapter 3. One of the most widely used techniques is the process chart. There is an ANSI Standard (ANSI, 1980) for process charts, and this is referenced or used by many authors. The Standard itself acknowledges that it is based on the work of F.B. and L.M. Gilbreth, with some modification. The Standard also anticipates and gives examples of similar charts, including use of the term *flow process chart*.

Figure 7.3 shows a sample process chart, using all the activity symbols from the ANSI Standard (which also discusses some additional combined or modified symbols not included in the example here). Figure 7.4 summarizes the main symbols used in compliant process charts.

The ANSI Standard defines a process chart as " ... a schematic or tabular representation of the sequence of all relevant actions or events—operations, transportations, inspections, delays, storages (and the like)—occurring during a process or procedure ...". It is interesting to note, following the discussion in the previous chapter about the introduction of synonyms into written descriptions, how the ANSI Standard refers to operations, etc., in this quoted list as actions or events, but then defines each as an activity— analyst beware!

The meanings of the terms in Figure 7.4 are:

- *Operation:* occurs when an object is intentionally changed in any of its physical or chemical characteristics, is assembled or disassembled from another object, or is arranged or prepared for another operation, inspection, transportation, or storage. An operation also occurs when information is given or received or when planning or calculating takes place.
- *Inspection:* occurs when an object is examined for identification or is verified for quality or quantity in any of its characteristics.
- *Transportation:* occurs when an object is moved from one place to another, except when such movements are part of the operation or the inspection, or are caused by the operator at the workstation during an operation or an inspection.
- *Storage:.* occurs when an object is kept and protected against unauthorized removal.
- *Delay:* occurs to an object when conditions do not permit or require immediate performance of the next planned step.

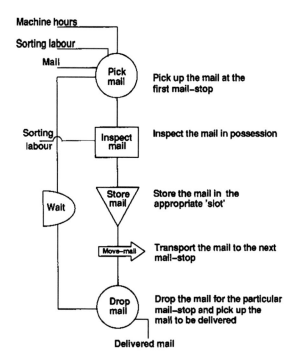

Figure 7.3 ANSI process chart: example.

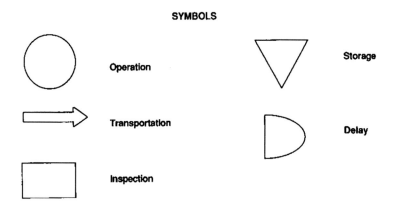

Figure 7.4 Process chart symbols.

The Standard distinguishes between horizontal lines that indicate material feeding into a process, and vertical lines indicating chronological sequence. Therefore horizontal lines require an object such as "Resource" and a relationship such as "Consumes". The vertical lines can be modeled by means of the "comes before" and "comes after" relations. For good measure, another object has been added, "Unit", with relationships {measures; measured by} to allow for adequate quantification of resources (but this is not part of the Standard). There is another synonym to deal with in the Standard, as vertical lines may also be used to indicate the flow of materials.

Therefore the Standard has an hierarchy, where the top level is a process, which can be broken down into actions or events or activities (where the terms action, event, and activity appear to be used synonymously). To add another synonym, the Standard later explains lines with arrowheads shown, but arrowheads do not appear in most of the illustrations in the Standard.

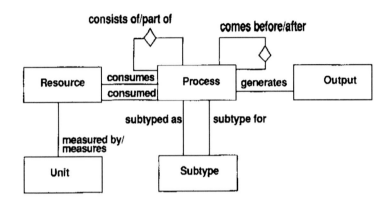

Figure 7 5 ERA Metamodel of process chart.

It is interesting to produce a meta model for this type of chart. An initial approach would be to choose object types for each kind of symbol, but the Standard itself has operation, transportation, inspection, delay, and storage subsumed under "activities". Therefore a relation "Subtype is" is added to handle the classification or subtyping (Figure 7.5).

The linguistic equivalent of the example process chart is:

DEFINE PROCESS mail-handling;
    CONSISTS-OF pick-mail, inspect-mail, store-mail, move-mail, drop-mail, wait;

DEFINE RESOURCE sorting-labor;
    CONSUMED-BY pick-mail;
    MEASURED-BY person-hours;

    ...

DEFINE PROCESS pick-mail;
    PART-OF mail-handling;
    COMES BEFORE inspect-mail;
    COMES AFTER wait;
    CONSUMES mail, sorting-labor, machine-hours;

...

DEFINE PROCESS drop-mail;
   COMES BEFORE wait;
   COMES AFTER move-mail;
   GENERATES delivered-mail;

IDEF diagrams

Many organizations make use of IDEF in their business process modeling.

IDEF originated from a US Air Force program for Integrated Computer Aided Manufacturing (ICAM) by taking a subset of SADT[2] called IDEFO. According to Marca and McGowan (1988), SADT "was developed specifically to help people describe and understand constructed systems that fall into the spectrum of 'medium' complexity". In this sense, IDEF means Icam DEFinition method. The aim is that both SADT and IDEFO can be used to model systems generally. There is a derivation, IDEF1, that can be used to produce an information model.

Therefore, from the point of view of the business process analyst, IDEFO is aimed at systems and can be used for all kinds of resources and processes employed within business processes.

IDEF diagrams consist of rectangular boxes and arrows, along with a title and identification information. An example is shown in Figure 7.6.

There is an SADT rule that each diagram has no fewer than three and no more than six boxes, except for the top-level diagram which is a single box for the overall system. The meaning of an arrow depends on which side of the box it is connected to. Inputs are at the left side of the box, and outputs at the right side. Arrows at the top of a box indicate controls, and those at the bottom indicate mechanisms. Hence these diagrams are not flowcharts and the arrows indicate interfaces between activities or subjects. The relationships are: control, input, control-feedback, input-feedback, and output mechanism. The restriction on the number of boxes means that decomposition is an inherent part of the method. Each box is an activity or subject which may be de-composable.

The complexity of IDEFO and SADT diagrams means that only a partial meta model is presented here. The basics of an IDEFO system are shown in Figure 7.7.

Following the earlier decision about processes, activities, and so forth, activities are called processes. Therefore the main building blocks are Process, Input, Condition, Output, and Mechanism (along with diagram and its description). The feedbacks allowed are cases where the output of one process can be control, input, or mechanism of other processes. In examining various diagrams, including the illustrations in Marca and McGowan (1988), from

---

2 SADT: Structured Analysis and Design Technique, produced by SofTech.

an analytical point of view, there is insufficient precision to model control and mechanisms. For example, many cases were encountered where control is expressed as a document or drawing. More accurate modeling of such things needs the addition of objects such as Event and Condition, and relations such as Triggers, On becoming true/false triggers, Interrupts, Terminates, and so forth. Therefore when the output of one process affects the control of another, this should be represented by the output changing various conditions or causing certain events, and it is the impact of the conditions or events that controls the following process.

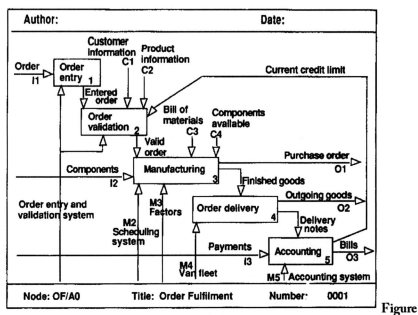

Figure 7.6 Example IDEF diagram.

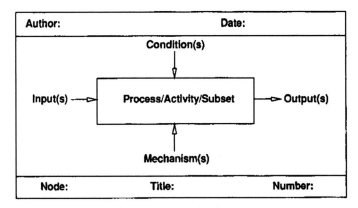

Figure 7 7 IDEFO system.

One approach to producing a meta model for an IDEF system diagram is shown in Figure 7.8. The meta model for a more complex IDEF diagram may be slightly more detailed.

The following is a partial listing of the modeling language equivalent of the IDEF example.

DEFINE PROCESS order-fulfillment;
CONSISTS-OF order-entry, order-validation, manufacturing, order- delivery, accounting;
...
...
...

DEFINE CONDITION customer-credit-limit;
ALLOWS order-validation **TO GENERATE** valid-order;
...
...
...

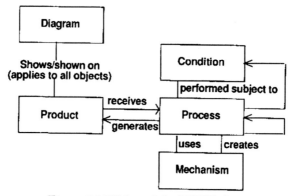

Figure 7.8 ERA model of IDEF chart.

DEFINE PROCESS order-validation;
PART-OF order-fulfillment;
COMES BEFORE manufacturing;
COMES AFTER order-entry;
ALLOWED-BY customer-information, product-information, customer-credit-limit;
RECEIVES entered-order;
GENERATES valid-order;
UTILIZES order-entry-and-validation-system;
...

DEFINE PROCESS accounting;
PART-OF order-fulfillment;
COMES AFTER order-delivery;
RECEIVES delivery-notes, payments;

GENERATES bills;
MAKES customer-credit-limit **TRUE;**
UTILIZES accounting-system;

UML Diagrams

According to a recent publication by the Object Management Group (OMG, 2009) there are 14 UML document types as illustrated in Figure 7.9.

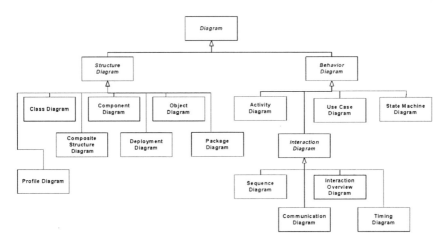

Figure 7.9 UML Diagram Types

It is not necessary to go into detail with UML diagrams here. A separate supplement or book is in preparation to go into UML diagrams in more detail. The UML meta metalanguage is muddled in its differences between metalanguage and meta metalanguage. Far greater separation and clarity are needed. The muddle is that if starting from a meta metalanguage, the derivation of UML would be separate and clean; it isn't.

However, as all diagrams are derived from one source, generating linguistic versions is straight-forward.

The same principle applies to UML diagrams as applies to all diagrammatic forms of representing processes. The diagrams can be helpful to clarify and describe a limited number of processes. However, the very existence of 14 diagram types means that the semantics are not joined up, and the method is fatally flawed in terms of not being scalable beyond relatively trivial situations. Imagine trying to manage 25,000 business processes with UML! In pedagogical terms, training analysts to think in terms of separating out process information into the disparate diagram types is dysfunctional and likely to introduce excessive time into process description or analysis problems.

Data Diagrams

The most widely used data diagram type is the entity relationship attribute (ERA) diagram, of which there are some variants.

An early presentation of data diagrams is that of Bachman (1969). Although Bachman's diagram types have not taken on much in terms of use, that 1969 paper established some key principles of data processing.

Bachman realized, consistently with OPR principles, that 'object' can have multiple levels of use, so he declared explicitly that he would use the term 'entity' at the level of a "...particular object being considered" (p4).

He introduced terms entity class, entity set, and class set. Attributes and relationships are used in his paper. Relations are implemented by way of 'sets'; thus one entity class 'department' may have a set of employees who are assigned to the department. Thus, a set has two or more entity classes in it.

Bachman was a member of the CODASYL Data Base Task Group that produced a definition of the CODASYL Data Definition Language and Data Manipulation Language.

It is worthwhile making an historical diversion at this stage. Bachman's paper sets out how a set class may contain multiple entity classes with the role of owner. This is, in essence, the kind of structure to implement directly n–part relations where there are many-to-many relations between the various parts. In hindsight, it is very regrettable that the Data Base Task Group (Bachman et al., 1969) did not implement this in their Schema Definition Language, specifying: " Each set must be named and must have one owner record and one or more member records declared for it in the schema" (section 2.9, p18). From that point onwards, the reality was that commercial database management systems, whether network or subsequently, relational, only 2-part relations could be defined directly. That had a profound impact on the evolution of commercial database management systems, and indeed led to the subsequent chaos of many data analysis courses and textbooks asserting, incorrectly, that data analysis is generally only necessary to 3rd normal form. It has taken many years for the field of normalization to remedy this by the slow emergence of 4th and 5th normal form, and recent considerations of a 6th normal form. Ironically, the ISDOS project at the University of Michigan spotted this in the early stages, and developed their own database management system that could implement n–part relations directly by permitting set types that had multiple owner record types.

This unfortunate restriction on schema definition stemming from 1969 has made the life of many analysts and database designers much more difficult. The reality for applications in the business and management fields is tough because n-part relations with many-to-many relations are very common. Many analysts and database designers simply haven't been trained to handle this. The implication for BPW analysis is that the analysts need to be ready to handle n-part relations with multiple many-to-many relations.

Following after Bachman's work in the 1960s, and the ISDOS work in the late 1960s and early 1970s, Chen's Entity-Relationship model emerged (Chen, 1976).

Chen sets out entity-relationship diagrams, and these have been used by innumerable analysts.

A simple entity-relationship diagram is shown in Figure 7.10.

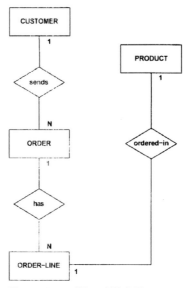

Figure 7.10 Chen ERA Diagram

Creating a metalanguage to use for defining the contents of such a diagram is easy. The boxes are Entities, the diamonds are Relations. The numbers represent the cardinality of the relations.

> **DEFINE ENTITY** customer ;
>   **SENDS** order ;
> **DEFINE ENTITY** order ;
>   **SENT BY** customer ;
>   **HAS** order-line ;
> **DEFINE ENTITY** order-line ;
>   **PART OF** order ;
>   **ORDER FOR** product ;
> **DEFINE ENTITY** product ;
>   **ORDERED-IN** order-line ;

Note that the diagram does not have quite sufficient information about the two directions possible for each relation, therefore the analyst will need to create relations for both directions.

> **DEFINE RELATION** sends ;
>   **LEFT PART IS** customer ;
>   **RIGHT PART IS** order ;
>   **CARDINALITY IS ONE** customer **MANY** order ;

```
DEFINE RELATION sent by ;
  LEFT PART IS order ;
  RIGHT PART IS customer ;
  CARDINALITY IS ONE customer MANY order ;
DEFINE RELATION has ;
  LEFT PART IS order ;
  RIGHT PART IS order-line ;
  CARDINALITY IS ONE order MANY order-line ;
DEFINE RELATION part-of ;
  LEFT PART IS order-line ;
  RIGHT PART IS order ;
  CARDINALITY IS ONE order MANY order-line ;
DEFINE RELATION ordered-in ;
  LEFT PART IS product ;
  RIGHT PART IS order-line ;
  CARDINALITY IS ONE product ONE order-line ;
DEFINE RELATION order-for ;
  LEFT PART IS order-line ;
  RIGHT PART IS product ;
  CARDINALITY IS ONE product ONE order-line ;
```

Clearly, the diagrammatic representation is easy to deal with and will help discussions between various stakeholders. However, when the number of such diagrams becomes very large, it is necessary to reduce the diagrams to some linguistic form defined formally by a metalanguage so that completeness and consistency can be checked. Also, the ERA diagram is not very rich, and so much process information is missing. Eventually, the analyst will need to link all together.

That simple ERA model will require attribute information. It will need at least 25 processes to implement, each of which will implement required business rules.

Diagram consistency and completeness checks

Analysts invariably develop an ability to examine diagrams and assess their completeness and consistency. This may involve observing that various symbols or lines are missing, or noting that a particular line performs a disallowed connection. The existence of formal diagram notations provides the basic completeness and consistency rules for that diagram type.

Analysts are more or less able to detect incompleteness and inconsistency by visual inspection and walkthroughs. This may be enough for simple diagrams but for complex sets of diagrams it becomes increasingly difficult to be certain that manual techniques have sufficient precision. Converting diagrams to formal language form is preferable, entering the statements into an encyclopedia. The contents of the encyclopedia can then be examined for completeness and consistency according to predefined meta models. This technique is completely scalable to cases of hundreds or thousands of objects and connections between objects; it is the kind of task for which computers are well suited.

Concluding remarks

In this chapter an approach was outlined to analyzing the semantics of diagrams by constructing formal language statements that can be checked subsequently for completeness and consistency. The creation of meta models for diagram types was advanced. This will help the analyst to position a diagram technique in terms of what the diagram can help with and where more information is needed for a more complete analysis.

Even where it proves impracticable to follow such a method in totality, the discipline of creating meta models at least highlights the strengths and weaknesses of the diagram techniques under investigation.

When analyzing diagrams, the extreme simplicity of the meta models becomes evident. There is nothing inherently wrong in that, because ultimately it is a question of fitness for purpose—and there is considerable merit in providing good, simple, overall, cognitive models of process ... that, essentially, is what they give. Even for more complex types such as IDEF diagrams, there are serious deficiencies arising from the incompleteness of control mechanisms and imprecise classification of the interfaces. The other main use for diagrams is to start the analysis work and provide a useful communications medium to stimulate discussion.

However, even despite their overall simplicity, diagrams are unwieldy as an analytical medium for anything other than small systems, and very discouraging to maintain as the diagrammatic representations of processes iterate and develop. This leads to the conclusion that *from an analytical point of view* diagrams may be necessary, but are most certainly not sufficient if the purpose is to describe and analyze detailed business processes.

Graphical techniques are understandably popular, and indeed people who express an almost religious fervor that for tools to be used, they must be graphical, are encountered frequently. Meta models provide a more neutral device to help people to know what a diagram can say and what it cannot.

The analyst needs to make an evaluation of audience and purpose and produce appropriate diagrams where it makes sense. The analyst also needs to be able to produce meta models of diagram types, understand the gaps, and find other techniques to fill those gaps, particularly as BPA work moves nearer to the implementation of processes and people require more detail.

Figure 6.2 shows a simple method for identifying business processes from text sources. A similar approach can be adopted where the source material is diagrams. After producing meta models from diagrams, processes can be identified from objects and relationships.

This chapter concludes the journey into techniques to handle primary source material for BPW projects. In the next chapter a search for techniques from other disciplines starts. Firstly, are there any contributions from information systems analysis, which is the origin of most business process analysis methods?

Chapter 8

Analyzing information

An exploration of the possible contributions from information systems analysis techniques to BPW was a very early activity in this book's journey.

There is often an over-emphasis on traditional techniques used in the development of computer-supported information systems, or rather the development of the software components of those systems. Those techniques may be necessary but are certainly not sufficient for the business process engineer.

Some of the approaches offer interesting paradigms for BPW, but more work is needed to test their applicability. For example: are object-oriented approaches useful for BPW?; Does the structured software development goal of functionally cohesive data coupled modules have a useful analogy in organizational design?

An expression such as "analysis techniques for information systems" seems to cover a field that is excessively narrow. There appears to be an horrendous bias in the information systems literature (and this bias is discussed in more detail in Darnton and Giacoletto, 1992)[1]. If corporate expenditure on information work in many enterprises is the most significant source of cost and an order of magnitude greater than the general range of corporate expenditure for information technology (typically 1-8% of total expenditure), then why is it that so many writers see information systems planning as primarily concerned with the development and use of computer-based information systems? At the board level in many enterprises, the IT function costs need to be monitored and kept under control, but they are by no means the major financial concern. Most enterprises have not even bothered to estimate their total expenditure on information work, although they may have some idea of total expenditure on computers and related products and services.

The significance of this last point for the business process analyst is that if information systems and information work encompass a resource consumption an order of magnitude greater than resource consumption by computer-based systems, then are the classical information systems analysis techniques sufficient for a wider definition of information system? Probably, they are not. Of course, there is a variety of subcultures in terms analyzing information, each of which makes some contribution to the business process analyst's toolbox.

1   to be updated in 2012, or shortly thereafter.

Therefore this chapter takes a wide-ranging view of techniques for analyzing information systems.

Information systems analysis and BPW

There are various levels at which information analysis is important for BPW:

- information systems[2] are frequently important components of business processes;
- information is a factor of production for many business processes;
- business process analysis is itself a form of information work and an application of information processing.

Analysis techniques for software development

The term *systems analysis* these days is usually associated with software development, and not really with systems more generally. This is a recent trend, accompanying a general narrowing of the scope of systems analysis.

It is interesting to compare an earlier approach to systems analysis with a very recent approach to structured analysis. Table 8.1 is presented as an illustration of a trend towards divergence between general systems analysis techniques and the techniques which are increasingly presented to computer system analysts. For this purpose Kilgannon (1972) and Yourdon (1989) are compared, with Table 8.1 showing a summary of the different contents. In this table, the more recent approach formalizes the scope of structured analysis to be much narrower than the earlier approach to systems analysis. As discussed in chapter 3, early systems analysis techniques formed a practice generally known as O&M or work study. This practice could be exercised whether the target system had computer-aided activities or not. Conventions emerged to pay specific attention to the computer- aided components, in the distinctions between systems flowcharts, high- level programming flowcharts, and detailed programming flowcharts

There has been a divergence from these earlier analysis techniques towards a separation between modern structured analysis and operational research.

For the purposes of this discussion, the software development analysis techniques are classified as data analysis, process analysis, and object-oriented analysis. This represents the classification implicit in much of the literature.

2 The term "information system" in this kind of context, is problematic, even though it is in common usage. A system has various properties including purpose and viability. Therefore an information system must necessarily include the people involved, but this is often not done. Perhaps a term such as "information technology configuration" may be more appropriate to describe computers, their software, and other related artifacts, or other kinds of information technology (such as paper, printing, and libraries) where computers are not the dominant technology.

Kilgannon (1972)	Yourdon (1989)
Analysis and design techniques:	Modeling tools:
■ basic human relations ■ motivation and training ■ fact finding and averaging ■ probability, matrices, and analysis techniques ■ design, presentation, and control techniques	■ dataflow diagrams ■ the data dictionary ■ process specifications ■ entity-relationship diagrams ■ state-transition diagrams ■ balancing the models ■ additional modeling tools ■ modeling tools for project management

Table 8.1 Systems analysis and modern structured analysis

It is not particularly important to distinguish between these kinds of analysis, since there is a point beyond which data analysis cannot proceed without process analysis, and *vice versa*. Similarly, *at a meta modeling level,* there is not much to distinguish structured from object-oriented analysis. Within each of the classification categories, however, ideas and techniques are helpful to the business process analyst.

Data analysis and modeling

Data modeling techniques started primarily with the construction of files and records from individual items. The concern was with highly structured data that could be formed into well-defined records, this delivering a set of record definitions for data to be stored by a computer. Earlier generations of information technology used forms or books for the storage of data.

Data analysis emerged because of early experience with problems caused by unstructured data. These problems were called "anomalies", for example by Date (1981). They arose because of restrictions arising from computer technology. Traditionally, data was stored on tape or disk and processed using a computer program kept separately from the data. Relationships between data items are "activated" by running a computer program. The data processing anomalies resulted in having to write more complex computer programs.

Consider a very simple example. Customers buy machines from a supplier, therefore each customer may have one or more types of machine. Engineers are trained to service machines, therefore each engineer may be able to service one or more types of machine. Without doing any data analysis, if the data about which customers have which machine types and which engineers could do the servicing are stored in one file, the result (where each line is a record in the file) would resemble Table 8.2.

VISIT

customer	machine-type	engineer
C1	M-I	E1
C1	MI	E2
C1	M1	E3
C1	M2	E3
C1	M2	E4
C2	MI	E1
C2	MI	E2
C2	MI	E3
C3	M2	E3
C3	M2	E4

Table 8.2 Customers, machines, and engineers: 1

Now imagine that these data evolve over time. To take a few specific scenarios, notice that:

- employee E3 leaving the company requires four deletions; E4 then leaving the company requires two deletions, together with loss of information about which customers have machine type M2;
- to store new information that employee E5 can service machine M3 bought by customer C3 requires only one store;
- to store new information that employee E6 can service machine M1requires 2 stores, because two customers own that machine type;
- to update the fact that employee E1 has received training on model M2, we must ADD two records to perform the single logical update;
- to retrieve a single fact, all occurrences should be checked for consistency and "locked against update" before the logical read commences; because of the possibility of inconsistency, reads should be disabled for specific sets while updates are underway.

Thus, the table as structured introduces read, write, modify, and delete "anomalies". Data analysis shows that if the table is simplified by being broken down into two smaller tables, as shown in Table 8.3, the example processing problems become much simpler, and therefore writing and maintaining the associated computer programs is also much simpler.

This approach to de-composing larger data structures into smaller structures is called normalization. Data analysts also use *dependency diagrams* consisting of bubbles and arrows to indicate how one kind of data can be used to find out some other related kind of data. For example, using information about model type to know which customers have that model, and which engineers could service it. There are rules about what can be decomposed, but most importantly, when the smaller data structures are joined back together again, the result is the same as the initial data (in technical terms, the original de-composition was a *non-loss* de-composition). For example, adding dependency diagrams, and joining the two smaller tables by using model type, results in Figure 8.1[3].

HAS-BOUGHT			CAN-SERVICE	
customer	machine-type		machine-type	engineer
C1	M1		M1	E1
C1	M2		M1	E2
C2	M1		M1	E3
C2	M2		M2	E3
			M2	E4

Table 8.3 Customers, machines, and engineers: 2

Chapter 6 describes building an OPR model from text. A refined OPR model then supports the business process analyst because there need to be processes for all operations on the objects, and every relationship needs at least two processes to implement it.

The technique of normalization is very helpful for refining an OPR model. At the high levels of abstraction encountered frequently in business process discussions, there is a tendency to imply a large number of many-to-many relationships (such as customer and product or service) or many-part relationships (such as lecturers, courses, and books, or staff, locations, roles, departments, and resources). In many-part relationships, some combinations may be dependent or independent depending on the business rules. The data analyst learns how to identify dependent and independent relationships, and de-compose many-to-many relationships where possible.

Therefore good data analysis skills are very useful for creating business process models, independently of whether there is also a need to create data models.

The other main contribution from data analysis is in the area of notation. Simple examples of diagrammatic notation from data modeling are given in chapters 4 and 7. Subtle differences exist among the different diagram notations in common use, such as indicating reverse relationships, putting attributes into the entity boxes, or having a common point on which to join multiple entities in one relation (see, for example, the three-part relation illustrated in Figure 4.3).

---

3 In technical terms, this de-composition is in fourth normal form.

ALLOW (cust# model, *emp#)*

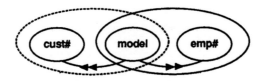

NON-LOSS DECOMPOSE
INTO 2x 4NF PROJECTIONS

cust#	model
C1	M1
C1	M2
C2	M1
C2	M2

model	emp#
M1	E1
M1	E2
M1	E3
M2	E3
M2	E4

ALLOW-C-M (cust#, model)   ALLOW-M-E (model, emp#)

EQUI-JOIN OVER model,

cust#	model	emp#
C1	M1	E1
C1	M1	E2
C1	M1	E3
C1	M2	E3
C1	M2	E4
C2	M1	E1
C2	M1	E2
C2	M1	E3
C3	M2	E3
C3	M2	E4

Figure 8.1 Customers, machines, and engineers: 3

Another form of notation is Pure Entity Type[4] where the name of each object or entity is followed by a list of attributes in parentheses. Where processing in a software system is anticipated, key values can be underlined. For example:

- CUSTOMER (<u>customer#</u>, name, address,)
- ORDER (<u>order#</u>, customer#, date, total)
- ORDER-LINE (<u>order#, part#</u>, quantity, line-total)
- PART (<u>part#</u>, description, unit-price)

Process analysis

Several approaches to the analysis of processes in the software development analysis literature were explored:

- information flow diagrams and analysis;
- control flow diagrams: data flow with real time extensions;
- state transition analysis.

Information flow diagrams (or data flow diagrams) in one form or another have been used for business processes. For example, this is taken to its limit by Born (1994) who presents a quality process language (QPL) based substantially on IDEF0. He addresses the question of business processes

---

4 The term Pure Entity Type appeared in the Open University's course Data Analysis for Information System Design, 1983, as applying to entities, normalized to third normal form.

using a range of resources explicitly, but decides that it is sufficient to use an information modeling technique, saying "Unlike some other approaches—for example, flow process techniques...—QPL models resources as information, rather than as part of the process ... to keep maximum generality and objectivity, I want to treat resources as just another item of information".

For modeling business processes, "pure" data flow diagrams can be substantially unhelpful. They are useful for the production of conceptual models of information flow. However, for business processes, when the flow of materials is added, the semantics of data stores and flows becomes much more difficult. Data flow diagrams are another case of a de-composition technique: high-level diagrams are de-composed until the "right" level of granularity is achieved. At the lowest level, it is the final processes are the things that need to be implemented. However, the meaning of all processes on the intermediate diagrams is not clear, and they are certainly not implemented as such; they are levels of abstraction, not units of implementation.

In contrast, data flow diagrams with real-time extensions can be much more useful, and they raise particularly interesting points with respect to business process analysis.

For many years data flow diagrams were used with no particular attention paid to matters such as timing and sequencing. For example, one process may receive orders and place them in a data store. The next process may read them from the data store, validate them, placing valid and invalid orders in different data stores. The data flow diagram gives no indication of sequencing—order entry may be working on receipt of each order, whereas order validation may perhaps run only once a week.

While there was a batch oriented commercial data processing culture using data flow diagrams, there was another computing culture dealing with process (the word here is not used with the same meaning as business process) control and real-time issues. The two cultures did not really come together until the mid-1980s, with the addition of real-time constructs to data flow constructs. Two classical data flow diagram texts are Gane and Sarson (1979) and De Marco (1978). In both of these texts, the term "structured analysis" really referred to a set of tools: data flow diagrams, data dictionary, and structured English, decision tables, and decision trees. Later, two major texts dealing with real-time issues appeared: Ward and Mellor (1986), and Hatley and Pirbhai (1987). A simple example is shown in Figure 8.2 based on Ward and Mellor's notation. It shows control processes and flows (dotted lines) in addition to work processes and information flows (solid lines).

Another key contributor to business process analysis comes from the structured analysis idea of cohesion. A functionally cohesive module in software is one that performs one function. The business process analogy is that an elementary process performs one function. This implies the factoring of functionality into work and control processes. If a process performs one function and decides what to do next, then it is really performing two functions: the work, and some control. The data flow diagram with real-time extensions shows the separated work and control processes. The intriguing possibility for business process analysts is to perform a similar separation.

Organizational design then includes the allocation of control processes to business functions or other organizational units. At a level of logical analysis, doing this introduces a high degree of flexibility. Software development structured analysis identifies other kinds of cohesion, as summarized in Table 8.4.

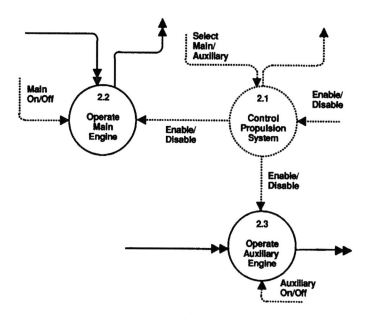

Figure 8.2 Data flow with real-time extensions: example.

In terms of "desirability", Yourdon points out that coincidental, logical, and temporal cohesion "constituted very low and generally unacceptable levels of cohesion", whereas communicational, sequential, and functional cohesion "produced generally acceptable levels of cohesion". The analogy for business processes would be that different ways of combining work and control processes are increasingly undesirable because of greater complexity in process implementation and maintenance.

State transition diagrams and various kinds of corresponding matrices are also useful for the analysis of business processes. Key business processes can be viewed as a sequence of state transitions on key business objects. For example, a sales order proceeds through a series of state transitions such as received, validated, scheduled, manufactured, delivered, and paid for. Processes are needed to effect the state transitions as well as to report on objects in the various states.

State transitions can also be modeled with a requirements language using little more than the Level II process descriptions. More attention needs to be paid to the relationships between Process, Event, and Condition to model state transition diagrams completely. They can be used to model complex combinations of the possible, as well as helping to identify the impossible.

For example, there may be a rule that goods are not delivered to a customer before receipt of a valid order, but this may be broken in cases of urgency for a customer who is well trusted. Conversely, goods could not be shipped out if the necessary components have not yet been received from suppliers.

Type of Cohesion	Description
Coincidental Cohesion	A module has coincidental cohesion if the elements of the module have no real meaningful relationship, that is, it is a "random" module.
Logical Cohesion	A module has logical cohesion if its elements are related "logically" but there is not actual flow of data or control.
Temporal Cohesion	A module has temporal cohesion if it contains elements which are only related to activities performed at the same time.
Procedural Cohesion	A module has procedural cohesion if only control flows from one element to another, and the activities in the module may be different, with no relationship between them.
Communicational Cohesion	A module has communicational cohesion if the elements of the module either use the same input data or are responsible for generating the same outputs.
Sequential Cohesion	A module has sequential cohesion if its elements represent some kind of sequence of activity and data are passed from one element to the next. The output data of one element represent the input to the next.
Functional Cohesion	A module is functionally cohesive if it contains all the elements which are sufficient and necessary for a single problem-related and well-defined function. This form of cohesion is the "ideal".

Table 8.4 Cohesion in software design

The data dictionary aspects of structured analysis are less helpful, because a system encyclopedia that is capable of handling meta data for a very wide range of languages is used, thus implementing OPR modeling requirements.

The decision tables (and related structures such as decision trees) are helpful for clarifying sets of conditions, rules, and actions. They provide a set of completeness and consistency checks for a wide range of decision-making scenarios.

Structured design

The business process analogy from structured design is to design lower level processes that possess certain properties. Under the term software engineering, one key design concept is that of coupling.

Coupling is an indication of the *strength* of interdependence between modules or objects in a system. The strength of coupling can be indicated by the number of other modules or objects which must be considered while changes are being made to any particular module or object.

There are several types of coupling between modules or objects, as described in Table 8.5.

There are several factors that influence the suitability of the different types of coupling. These factors include:

- type of connection: what mechanism is used to couple the modules;
- complexity of interface: what interface is used for the various modules;
- type of information flow: is the information flow simple (for example, part of a record), or complex (for example, a document with many components);
- binding time of connection: at what point procedurally, are the modules connected?

The intriguing question for the business process analyst is the extent to which these ideas of coupling are applicable to coupling between processes. Having applied these contexts in a few real cases, the business process analyst will benefit from remembering these principles of coupling while defining more elementary processes. The business process equivalent of a software module is a unit of work. The way in which these units are coupled together, and the way in which they are controlled and sequenced have a fundamental impact on organizational maintenance, or the ease with which changes to the enterprise can be implemented.

Therefore, the business process analyst will benefit from an understanding of software module coupling, even if the analyst never has to design a piece of software.

The "ideal" design results in data coupling. This means that a controlling module does not decide how a work module is to performs its function. Obviously, business processes and human work are far more complex and it does not make sense to try and reduce them to the level of a mechanistic device. However, the idea of more autonomous work groups as a way to implement work groups needs serious consideration by business process engineers, and there is empirical evidence supporting autonomous professional work. There are important implications for management, if managers are more concerned with higher level planning issues and triggering work activities, rather than detailed, hierarchical control.

Type of coupling	Description
data	Modules have data coupling if the data needed, and only the data needed, are communicated between the modules.
stamp	Modules have stamp coupling if they communicate related data items, but not all the communicated data items are used.
control	Modules have control coupling if they communicate control information from one module to another, i.e. tell another module how to perform an operation.
common	Modules have common coupling if they share data contained in a common area.
content (or pathological)	Modules have content coupling if a module refers to or modifies data contained inside another module without reference to that module, or if one module alters a statement in another.
hybrid	Hybrid coupling occurs when the coupling between two or more modules involves structures and calls that involve more than one kind of coupling.

Table 8.5 Coupling in software

Object-oriented analysis

According to Meyer (1988),

> "Object-oriented design is the method which leads to software architectures based on the objects every system or subsystem manipulates rather than the function it is meant to ensure. Don't ask what the system does: ask WHAT it does it to! Object-oriented design is the construction of software systems as structured collections of abstract data type implementations."

Readers may think they have detected a very strong process-oriented decomposition approach in in this book, although the point was made in chapter 3 that OPR modeling encompasses both structured and systemic views. Why not take an object-oriented approach to business process analysis?— this comment usually comes from software developers who are moving into BPW work! At a simple level, an initial retort is often something to the effect that object-oriented cost accounting has not yet been developed!

Information hiding[5], data abstraction, polymorphism and inheritance are the key concepts of the object-oriented paradigm. Information hiding and data abstraction contribute to decoupling specifications from the actual representation[6] Through the use of polymorphism design flexibility can be increased by creating new classes of objects without changing the existing code, while inheritance reduces the need to specify redundant information.

An *object* can be thought of as a package of data and operations that it suffers. In more general terms an object is the encapsulation of data (state information), operations and their corresponding methods, exceptions, and constants.

Messages are the mechanism for communication between objects. An early task for designers is to understand the kinds of messages needed throughout a system.

In order to defer for as long as possible, binding decisions about the physical implementation of data structures, the specification of data should describe data in terms of the services available on those data.

According to Meyer, the formal specification of an abstract data type involves the following:

- types: the name(s) of the abstract data type;
- functions: the services available on instances of the type;
- preconditions: any preconditions for the use of any of the functions or partial functions;
- axioms: these add the semantics which may be necessary to distinguish one abstract data type from another with similar functions.

As with structured approaches, there are techniques encompassed by object-oriented approaches which are of value to the business process analyst, by analogy at least.

The formation of classes relies on genericity, or collecting together things that are similar at one level of abstraction, and identical at some other level. Hence the identification of common business processes involved recognizing that the types of information and processing are the same for many instances of implementation (for example, call handling systems: the call could be viewed as the object type, with implementation to handle cases such as requests for service engineers, or inquiries for product information).

There is a much higher level of complexity in business processes than in object-oriented software systems. For example, implementation of an object-oriented software design depends in part on the implementation of messages that can pass between objects. In the case of business processes, what would

---

5 Originally, the idea of information hiding introduced by Parnas (1972) was partly concerned with insulating a system design from the consequences of making difficult decisions in complex cases.

6 This is not done by only object-oriented approaches; the mechanism in SADT is designed to be added to or refined as work proceeds.

pass between business objects would be more complex combinations of resources or factors of production, including material goods.

Therefore, for the business analyst, a grounding in object-oriented ideas will be useful, but the strength of the application to business processes by analogy warrants further investigation. It would be intriguing to see an object-oriented implementation of an enterprise. To some extent, this is also the case for object-oriented software development, and there are some useful discussions about the work that is still needed to be done for object-oriented approaches to mature, for example the discussions by Booch (1991), and Rumbaugh *et al* (1991).

Information analysis

Those who are familiar with the computer and software configuration development world will recognize much of the discussion in this chapter so far. However, it is directed at the development of software. The business process analyst is in some difficulty because the most likely kinds of literature to be encountered while investigating the analysis of information are precisely those focussed on the development of software. Are there any other approaches, and if so are there any good reasons why the business process analyst should bother with them?

Earlier in this chapter, the order of magnitude difference between expenditure on information work, and expenditure on computer-related information technology was mentioned. It can be estimated that for every monetary unit spent on the management of IT, 10-30 monetary units will be spent on information work. A more detailed discussion of this point is made by Vincent (1990). If expenditure on IT is in the range of 1-8% of total cost, and expenditure on information work is in the order of 30-80% of total cost, then 10-30 is a reasonable range to cover many cases. Financial institutions may spend 8% on IT and 80% on information work. Whereas manufacturing companies may spend 1-2% on IT and 30-50% on information work.

What is information work? The concept of its scope includes management, administration, design, marketing, education, training, accounting, sales, planning, problem solving, and everything to do with information systems. As an additional point, the concept of a business process is very broad, including beyond 'business'. Therefore information play may be as important sometimes to business process analysis as information work.

Rubin *et al.* (1986) discuss the problem of classifying work as information or knowledge work, explaining that there is primary information work done for other enterprises, and there is secondary information work done in house. In their discussion, they assert that " ... five categories of information activities can be identified: (1) education; (2) media of communication; (3) information machines; (4) information services; and (5) other information activities". They point to a 1977 US Department of Commerce study that reported 25.1% of GNP attributable to the primary information sector, and 21.1% to the secondary information sector. Landauer (1995) attempts to quantify (for the US) expenditure on computer equipment plus associated costs, and concludes that " ... total current expenditures for the United States amount to around 10 percent of GNP". The work by Rubin et al., followed the seminal work about the proportion of GDP attributable to an information or knowledge 'age' by Machlup (1962).

Therefore even in generous macroeconomic terms, expenditure on information work is an order of magnitude greater than expenditure on information technology. This line of reasoning provides both macroeconomic and microeconomic reasons for inquiring about other ways of looking at information.

It is common for BPW projects to take as a starting point the future vision for an enterprise. This is often expressed in terms such as those identified in chapter 5 for strategy exercise. There is a widespread prescription that it is good for enterprises to articulate a strategy.

Phlips (1988) discusses the need for enterprises to understand the information structure of their market situation. He looks at information structure in terms of being (1) complete or incomplete (that is, how much of the possible information is known); and (2) symmetric or asymmetric (that is, the extent to which all players in a market know the possible information). Therefore one market situation could involve complete information, another could involve incomplete symmetric information, and yet another could involve incomplete asymmetric information.

A link between the information structure of an enterprise's market situation and strategic behavior is suggested when Phlips states " ... it is the informational asymmetry which leads to interesting forms of strategic behavior ... ". This has led me to hypothesize that there is an inverse relationship between information symmetry and the need for strategy (the more symmetrical and complete the information structure of an enterprise's market situation, the less the usefulness of strategy).

Hirshleifer and Riley (1992) make a distinction between event un-certainty and market uncertainty. Event uncertainty is concerned with not knowing which events will occur, or the distribution of the events. Process analysts are very concerned about building processes that handle events. Market uncertainty is to do with the absence of information about all players in the markets in which enterprises are operating.

Therefore the business process analyst needs to be concerned with the information structure of an enterprise's market situation. However, the analyst needs to be very wary of assuming that better information is generally a good idea, and will be welcomed. Phlips introduces an intriguing observation drawn from social psychology that in many cases people do not want to be informed better, suggesting that "The theory [cognitive dissonance in economic terms] is supported by experiments showing that (1) groups of persons with the same information have systematically different beliefs so that they interpret a given information differently, (2) groups of persons with different beliefs display differences in receptivity to new information, and (3) persons who justify to themselves some difficult undertaking are likely to have a strong and persistent belief that the undertaking is a good one".

This last comment suggests that the analyst could benefit from some grounding in understanding how beliefs are formed and propagated. Another issue is the applicability of epidemiological theory to the spread of ideas. Many examples of irrationality exist in the information technology and BPW worlds that bear the hallmarks of ideological epidemics; for example the deployment of relational database management systems for inappropriate application types, the adoption of fashionable operating systems, and ISO 900x certification.

Then there is information theory. Approaching information theory from a software development background is a severe cultural shock (and *vice versa)—they* seem to have nothing whatsoever in common. There are two worlds out there deeply involved in information systems but they hardly ever communicate. Is there anything in information theory for the business process analyst?

At a lower level of process, information theory is very much concerned with communications.

Apart from that, many more general applications of information theory have taken into account the model introduced by Shannon and Weaver (1949). Figure 8.3 shows the basic model, identifying the difference between message and signal.

Weaver set out three levels of problem for the transmission of information:

- Level A: how accurately can the symbols of communication be transmitted? (The technical problem.)
- Level B: how precisely do the transmitted symbols convey the desired meaning? (The semantic problem.)
- Level C: how effectively does the received meaning affect conduct in the desired way? (The effectiveness problem.)

Most of the applications of information theory have been at level A.

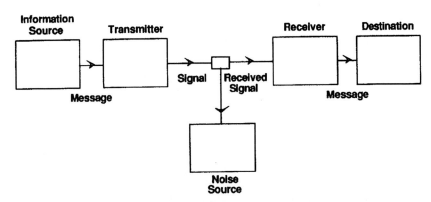

Figure 8.3 Basic communication model.

Figure 8.4 brings the key ideas into a more general form, more applicable to business processes. Ideas, facts, and so forth need to have their meaning represented in some way, then it is necessary to decide how to communicate the meaning, and some kind of signal must be used for the communication mechanism. On the receiving end, the operations are reversed. There are several sources of potential problem in this, including expressing or understanding meaning incorrectly, communicating or receiving messages incorrectly, and errors in the signal transmission and reception.

Information theory may be necessary for certain classes of communication process descriptions. Otherwise, the analyst will benefit primarily from an understanding of the key concepts and ensuring that potential semantic and syntactic problems are handled during process design.

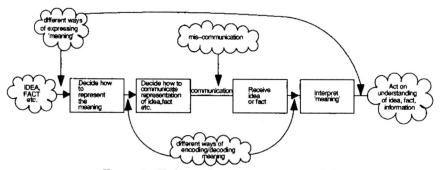

Figure 8.4 Enhanced communication model.

What about information economics? A clear relationship exists between economics and information in the approaches by writers such as Phlips discussed above. There is an important connection between the economists' depiction of markets using terms such as perfect or imperfect competition, and information. The idea of perfect competition is predicated on an assumption of complete and symmetric information structures in the markets. Of course, in reality there is nothing quite like perfect competition. Essentially, the volume of information implied by the idea of complete symmetric information is too much. In part this is because information about markets is generally replicated, rather than being available in one source and accessible to all at will. The sheer volume of information means that for use it must be attenuated in some way. This is often done by participants in a market forming an implicit view of the statistical distribution of parameters such as price and quality. For example, a consumer does not usually telephone every dealer to find out all prices. What is more likely to happen is that the consumer telephones a sample of suppliers, building up a model of the distribution of price against which a buying decision can be made. The search for more price data will stop when the consumer thinks that the extra effort is likely to exceed the value of the new information.

The present "information revolution" is not without its critics, and some of the criticism has profound implications for business processes. The relationship between investment in information technology and increased output or productivity as a result is not the obvious foregone conclusion espoused by many very enthusiastic commentators. For example, Landauer (1995) takes a long look at macroeconomic returns and presents a debate that the serious business process analyst needs to consider. Early in his book he states "The bottom line ... is that while there are exceptions, most business investments in computers have yielded significantly lower returns than investments in bonds at market interest rates. Two analysts dissent ... ". He looks at an overall slowdown in productivity increase since the early 1970s, saying at one point in his analysis, while trying to account for an estimated $30 billion in expected output, "If IT capital yielded an average of 13.3 percent less than other forms of investment, it would have generated $30 billion less output than the normal equations predicted, and thus the shift of investment to IT would account for the missing money".

Another commentator who advises caution is Strassman (1990) in his now famous observation, "The lack of correlation between information technology spending and profitability is contrary to advertised claims. It defies the common belief that investing in electronic processing of information somehow leads to lower costs and results in competitive advantage".

The obvious conundrum is that if IT costs per unit of processing are falling rapidly while performance/price ratios are supposed to be rising, why is it that most enterprises do not take the available advantage of following the cost curve downwards, but choose instead to have a year on year increase in spending on IT? The reality for most enterprises is that their IT costs are rising, not falling.

This is a difficult area for the business process analyst, because clearly there is much more to the decision making than purely rational investments to achieve demonstrable efficiency and effectiveness gains.

A difficult problem for the business process analyst is the provision of supporting evidence and perhaps advice about which parts of business systems should be automated, and which parts should be left to human beings. Wiener (1954), often depicted as the father of cybernetics (and while claiming invention of the term, he acknowledges that others had done so earlier, unknown to him at the time), has a profound discussion about the relationship between machines and humans. The evolution of technology is in part the evolution of the mechanization of routinized work. He points out, "Let us remember that the automatic machine, whatever we think of any feelings it may have or may not have, is the precise economic equivalent of slave labor. Any labor which competes with slave labor must accept the economic conditions of slave labor". In a similar vein, Roszak (1986) reminds us that "The burden of my argument is to insist that there is a vital distinction between what machines do when they process information and what minds do when they think".

In the design of systems, the business process analyst needs to understand those parts of the target system which are not susceptible to routinization or automation; for example, difficult problem solving, deciding priorities, and human goals.

Finally, various writers have touched on the relationship between information and decision theory or decision making. Where the business process analyst is working in the context of an enterprise that is attempting to arrange its processes with a view to gaining competitive advantage, a grounding in game theory and decision theory may be required. According to Wiener, "The theory of games is, in its essence, based on an arrangement of players or coalitions of players each of whom is bent on developing a strategy for accomplishing its purposes".

Hirshleiffer and Riley (1992) present a synthesis of several approaches to decision making, information, and economics. They discuss a case where individuals make decisions based on the information available to them at the time and the actions that can be taken. Market structures are based on the aggregation of the decisions of individuals. They then turn to the question, "supposing you could get additional information before having to make a terminal decision, how ought you to decide whether and how much information to collect?". This problem is central to those aspects of business processes concerned with monitoring the enterprise's environment and context.

There are some very detailed theoretical books about information theory, such as Cover and Thomas (1991), which will give the analyst substantial grounding in information theory. For the purposes of business process analysis and information system design, it is useful to convert information theory into some practical suggestions, such as only provide information if it is able to affect a decision, information systems need to pay as much attention to information amplification as they do to information attenuation, and attempt to calculate the maximum value of information.

Much information theory, game theory, and decision theory is virtually inaccessible to the practitioner because of a high level of dependence on mathematical reasoning (and the presentation of that reasoning). Very few BPW practitioners have the mathematical background to be able to apply that work, and this is one reason why many business process analysts are unfamiliar with even basic ideas from those fields. A useful book for practitioners is by Rivett (1994), who gives many down-to-earth examples (in contrast with highly mathematical approaches), and he commences with the observation that " ... in the paddy fields down on the plains, the labourers are concerned with more earthy matters".

Concluding remarks

Information must be considered to be a factor of production in addition to the more traditional economic factors of land, labor, capital, and enterprise (some people would prefer to treat it as a subset of one of these traditional categories).

A broad view of the term "information system" is needed in that its scope is far wider than the prevailing association of the term with computers and related technology. The idea of system needs to include all the human beings involved, as without them the system would, in reality, be devoid of purpose (and hence not really a system).

The most common approaches to the analysis of information are based on variants of analysis employed during the specification and design of software. Several very important concepts are included in these approaches, at least by analogy, if not by the direct applicability of the techniques to business processes.

Some additional areas of information analysis are not found so readily in mainstream business process analysis literature. However, depending on the nature of the problem being addressed, they can provide the analyst with additional and powerful tools. These additional areas are information economics, information theory, cybernetics, decision theory, and game theory. For the practitioner, the value is in the practical application rather than the theoretical content.

The processing of information by machines is substantially different from the processing of information by human beings. Both kinds of information processing are required in most business processes. Therefore the analyst needs to be prepared to handle the problems associated with identifying the information processing aspects of business processes to be handled by machines or by people.

Chapter 9

Analyzing costs

It does not take long to recognize that perhaps the most common motivation for BPW projects is to reduce cost. However, depending on the BPW culture of the analyst, this may be at the forefront of concerns, or it may not even enter into the debate. For example: the term "cost" (or, costs) appears in the index of Harrington (1991), Davenport (1993) and Johansson *et al (1993);* Hammer and Champy (1993) have weaker references ("cost reductions at Bell Atlantic Corp" and "costs of inaction, in cases for action"); the term does not appear in the index for Born (1994), Ould (1995), or Holt (2009). Hegedus (2008) has many index entries for cost. Patig and Casanova-Brito (2012) do not indicate money in their question 21 about what resources respondents wish to include in models or descriptions of processes. The discussion of process costs in UML is astonishingly conspicuous by its absence, notwithstanding the number of organizations moving towards UML for describing business processes.

Readers of business process literature can be forgiven for thinking that for many writers, process cost is just not an issue. That is an astonishing state of affairs given the importance of cost in business! This book takes an opposite view: the business process engineer must consider process costs.

At a superficial level, cash can be seen as one input for processes, perhaps because of the economist's recognition of capital as a factor of production. However, it is not as easy as that. In another sense, cost is one dimension of the measurement of inputs and outputs. As discussed in chapter 12, the difference between the technical efficiency and the allocative efficiency of a process arises when the costs of inputs (or the values of outputs) are taken into account.

Surprisingly, it may prove to be very difficult to decide how much a process costs. This is because of the classical dilemma for cost accountants in deciding how to allocate costs that have arisen from performing multiple processes. Infrastructure, or overhead, is the major problem. Infrastructure may be in place to support many different kinds of process, or it may be in place to support one process that runs many times. Ultimately, enterprises must recover all of their costs from somewhere. Therefore there is frequently a major difficulty in deciding the actual cost of one unit of output, and there may be several perfectly reasonable answers.

Having said that, it is also important for the analyst to appreciate that ultimately, the argument is not only about costs; it is also about *margin,* or profit. It is too simplistic to assume that lowering costs automatically leads to increased profits. The relationships between cost, revenue, and margin are empirical questions that need good models based on actual performance.

There are many good texts available about costs, therefore this book will not try to replicate this material, but concentrate instead on a summary of the issues, and move on to relevance from a business process perspective.

This chapter starts by looking at a simple example, then reasons for assigning costs. This is followed by a summary of different approaches to cost allocation. Further discussion of this is also available in Maddison and Darnton (1996).

A simple example

Consider the following scenario, which is a realistic simple example (albeit slightly dated now, but still very useful to exemplify several key points) that have been repeated in many enterprises round the world:

> At present, all major documents are produced within a pool of copy typists who are using conventional electric typewriters. The finance department has calculated that the cost of employment for one copy typist is 20,000 MUs [monetary units] after the allocation of all overheads. The management team is thinking about replacing the typewriters with computers performing word processing.
>
> After carrying out a study of work practices, it looks as though each document is typed on average 2.1 times between original and final draft. Copy typists generate 6,000 A4[1] pages per working year. The level of final document output is 2,400 A4 pages per year.
>
> Quotations have been received from computer suppliers who can supply the computers and word-processing packages, give initial training, and provide on-site maintenance of the equipment. The whole package for 50 copy typists will be supplied at a cost of 300,000 MUs including three years of maintenance.
>
> Senior management decide that they will use a period of three years to write off the equipment.

What level of output will be required from the copy typists to break even with such an investment?

The total additional cost per typist will be 6,000 MUs, or 2,000 MUs per year for the three-year period assuming zero value for the equipment at the end of the period. As the current cost of employment is 20,000 MUs, this means increasing costs by 10%. Therefore, finished output per typist needs to rise to 2,640 A4 pages per year to break even. Any higher levels of output are then contributing to a positive return on investment.

---

1 There is very little difference between A4 pages (almost 96.94 square inches) and US letter pages (96.25 square inches).

In this case, the senior management team decided to make the change. The final outcome was that the number of finished pages rose to an average of 2,850 A4 pages per copy typist per year. The other surprising result was that the number of document iterations rose very substantially from 2.1 to 5.8. The typists themselves knew the minimum necessary to produce basic documents, but it took about two years of elapsed time to learn about all the available features of the word-processing package, and the basics of the computer operating system required by users.

On paper this project is either a modest or a spectacular success. There are different ways of doing the arithmetic, but the positive gain, after discounting the cost of investment, can be calculated as 2,850/2,640, or almost 8%—within the range of many industrial returns on investment. It is not spectacular, and there will probably have been several alternative investment opportunities available which would have yielded more than 8%. However, the number of document iterations increased by 5.8/2.1, or 176%—a spectacular return on investment that is bound to impress any financial controller!

This appears to be a trivial example, but it exposes some very fundamental issues. Is the right figure to use for return on investment (RoI) 8 % or 176%? What was the productivity gain? Even if people do work a document many more times because the technology is now available to enable them to do so, what are the correct measures of output and productivity? Is document quality improved because it is printed out more times during its development, or is it primarily a cognitive aid to the writer?

There are other matters that have not yet been taken into account. In costing the transfer from typewriters to word processors, no allowance was made for the management costs of considering the idea and managing the transition. In terms of operations, no account was taken of hidden support costs caused by interruption when typists needed to inquire about operating system or word-processing package features (this may not have mattered among themselves as total output could be calculated in any event, therefore much of the impact was already discounted).

There are several "correct" answers to the problems posed (whether or not to make the investment, and how to calculate RoI). The problem even suggests an extension to the familiar condemnation of statistics: *there are lies, damned lies, statistics, and IT investment cost—benefit analyses!*

The business process analyst will benefit enormously from a literacy at least in key aspects of cost analysis, and a team of such analysts should have someone available who is fluent.

Types of cost: collection and classification

In business process analysis, cost should be considered as one dimension of the measurement of process inputs and outputs.

There are questions about the possible technical combinations of input resources that can be used to produce the desired outputs. In practice, these different combinations of inputs are weighted according to their costs, as the dominant approach to decision making about which combinations of factor inputs to use.

Different costs are the usual driver for factor substitutability. For example, countries with higher labor costs tend to make more extensive use of capital; countries with very low labor costs are generally much slower to introduce automation. In the developed countries, a PC is likely to cost a fraction of the annual cost of employing someone, whereas in some developing countries, the cost of a PC may be a multiple of the annual cost of employing someone.

In this way, it may be very difficult to define business processes that are standard in all operating countries of an enterprise, because there may be substantial differences in relative costs. Some multinational corporations may want to roll out the same processes world-wide, but before this can be done, it is necessary to know whether there are major differences in cost structure or culture that could affect the way processes are performed.

Classically, the costs of producing goods or services are divided into variable and fixed costs. The assumption is that variable costs relate to those costs that are incurred directly for the production. The acid test is that if output is zero, then variable costs will also be zero. These costs are sometimes referred to as direct costs.

Fixed costs are those costs that will arise, certainly in the short term, even if output is zero. Thus, the costs of resources such as land, machinery, administration, and so forth, are considered as fixed costs, at least in the short term, because ultimately, for all enterprises, if output remains at zero, eventually all costs can be dispensed with.

There are many kinds of costs that appear in the costing literature, such as period costs, product costs, unexpired costs, expired costs, prime costs, job costs, relevant costs, irrelevant costs, sunk costs, avoidable costs, unavoidable costs, opportunity costs, average costs, marginal costs, variable costs, fixed costs, and total costs.

Cost information needs to be collected in some way, and then classified so that it can be used in conjunction with specific cost objectives. The *collection* of cost information involves recording cash and liabilities as the business is in progress. The *classification* of cost information poses greater complexity. Cost information is needed by a business to know whether it is making a profit, breaking even, or making a loss. For other enterprises that are not pursuing profit, cost is important to know whether a cost budget is being followed. Beyond these simple reasons, there may be very complex cost objectives to be achieved by a cost measurement system. Cost collection and classification are dealt with in most major accounting texts, for example, Drury (1992) and Horngren and Sundem (1987).

The basic collection of cost information is essentially a matter of self-discipline and organization. In furtherance of a business, or the objectives of an enterprise, every time an item is purchased, or obtained with a promise to pay, cost is incurred. It is a matter of recording the costs as the first part of cost collection. Failure to collect cost information is usually a matter of records of expenditure being lost, or not being made available for some reason. For example, it is possible for employees not to claim business expenses for some period of time, therefore there is no visibility to the business of those costs until the claims are made. Similarly, some transactions may occur without formal records at the time, in which case someone must make a note to ensure the recording of costs.

The classification of cost information is usually done by means of a *chart of accounts*. The chart of accounts sets out how all financial transactions will be classified and grouped together in order to produce summaries such as a balance sheet or an income and expenditure statement. Process analysts are not usually concerned with the chart of accounts.

However, an analyst may need to support the examination of different ways of allocating costs. For this reason, some information warehouses in the early 1980s developed out of a need to retain a high degree of granularity in financial information. Many accounting systems journal transactions, typically monthly, to the accounts related to the chart of accounts. In order to simulate alternative cost allocation decisions, a chart of accounts should be seen as only one view of the transaction data warehouse. Simulation would then involve creating alternative charts of accounts and rejournaling the underlying transactions to investigate what would happen if costs were treated differently. This is a very powerful way to test alternative cost allocation structures against historical data.

There are several simple ways to classify costs. Some of the common categories are employment expenses, employee travel and subsistence, property occupancy costs, utilities, goods purchased to make into final goods for sale, advertising and marketing, equipment, buildings, repairs, office supplies, postage, and delivery. In designing a system for classifying costs it is necessary to know the purpose for which the consolidated cost information will be used.

Some costs are related directly to the production and delivery of goods and services, whereas others are only related indirectly because they are incurred while providing some kind of infrastructure to support the production and delivery of goods and services. For example, some managers may be responsible only for a service delivery activity which could not be delivered without operations management support. Such costs could reasonably be allocated to the service itself. However, some managers may have a range of responsibilities that cannot be attributed to particular goods or services.

Infrastructure is used extensively by business processes. One motive in the design of business processes is to identify opportunities for cost savings by the provision of common services from infrastructure. For example, it would be very unusual indeed for a company to ask the local telephone provider to supply a direct line to every desk; usually, an infrastructure of telephone exchange, telephone extension cabling, and a smaller number of external telephone lines, is provided. Similar economies of scale can be obtained across a large corporation. In many large organizations, different departments set up their own communications networks, which may lead to difficulties because different standards are selected by each department. Substantial economies of scale may be obtained by installing a common communications infrastructure.

Cost objectives

Before starting on an exercise to examine costs, the business process analyst needs to be aware of the reasons for the task, referred to as *cost objectives*.

Important cost objectives for the business process analyst are the costs of an overall process and the costs of smaller component processes. The client of the analyst is likely to be very interested in potential cost savings either from reengineering a process, or by the most cost-efficient way of designing a new process.

A cost objective refers to some kind of decision or category of information required with respect to cost. It is, according to Drury (1992), " ... any activity for which a separate measurement of costs is desired". At an aggregate level, a key cost objective is to compare total costs with total revenue to determine gross profit. A marketing cost objective could be to compare marketing costs with revenues to understand the level of expenditure needed for marketing. Other reasons for knowing the costs of a process are to compare with:

- other ways of performing the process;
- taking decisions about which processes could be outsourced;
- attributable revenue to establish the added value of a process;
- alternatives to the process;
- budgeted costs for the process;
- competitors' costs for performing similar processes.

A very common question that arises for the business process analyst is "how much does a particular process cost?" Table 9.1 shows four examples of cost objectives, along with suggestions for corresponding cost schemas.

A major problem with estimating the "real" costs of an activity or acquisition is that many of the costs may not be realized explicitly. A typical example of this occurs when new equipment is made available. Explicit costs include categories such as acquisition, installation, and training costs. Implicit costs can arise from incomplete training leading to informal training delivered by interrupting the normal flow of work to deal with inquiries from other people about the new equipment. For example, what are the costs of PC ownership and use in an enterprise? One approach to this question is shown in Table 9.2.

An interesting example of defining cost objectives is in project management, where costs may be required at an activity level of granularity, rather than at a product or service level of granularity. Slemaker (1985) describes a cost account manager who is responsible for a single task, which lies at the intersection of organizational structure and project work breakdown structure. There is an analogy here with the business process, where components of the process are likely to lie at the intersection of process responsibility and functional responsibility.

Cost objective	Sample cost schema
What is the cost, over a determined period of time, to provide a product support telephone service?	Number of calls per period; average time duration per call; costs per person answering calls (labor, employment costs, occupancy, overheads); useful person days per year; hours per day.
What does it cost to deliver a particular professional service?	labor; overheads; materials
How much does it cost per transaction for a service to provide a transactional environment?	Number of transactions; person time per transaction; machine time per transaction; fully loaded labor costs.
How much does it cost to provide an IS infrastructure service?	Equipment costs; acquisition and maintenance; operational costs occupancy costs; communications costs; support costs; software acquisition, software development.

Table 9.1 Business process sample cost objectives

Direct costs	Indirect costs
hardware ancillary equipment communications equipment software acquisition license fees installation support costs: formal support	time to become familiar with functionality support costs: informal support from colleagues (for example, time spent on interruptions) time spent on version control time spent on integrity and security maintenance contracts

Table 9.2 Costs of PC ownership

Conventional allocation of overhead costs

Overhead costs are those costs incurred to support the production and delivery of more than one good or service. Because they are effectively part of infrastructure costs, there are usually many possible ways to allocate them to the costs of delivered goods and services. According to Drury (1992), "overheads are those costs that cannot be directly assigned to cost objectives such as a product, process, sales territory, or customer group".

Should overhead costs be allocated to the production of goods and services? This is usually more straightforward in a manufacturing system where manufacturing overheads are allocated to goods produced, but nonmanufacturing costs are deducted from gross profit in the calculation of net profit (I will not be discussing the construction of balance sheets or income and expenditure statements). The need to do this is more apparent when valuing stock and work in progress. In the case of services and business processes, there is far less need to value stocks because there are few valid cases of holding services in stock.

Table 9.3 shows some particular scenarios along with different ways in which the overhead costs could be allocated, ways which are in common use.

There is an obvious connection between volume of output and cost because of the need to recover costs somehow. Therefore Horngren and Sundem (1987) and Arnold and Hope (1990) refer to "cost-volume-profit analysis". The relationship between technology and economies of scale means that the process analyst must understand the relevant range over which any fixed cost assumptions are valid.

In each of these examples, the suggestion of a different way of allocating overheads is based on the recognition of an overall cost driver for the business, and the cost objective can be expressed in terms of understanding metrics such as profit per person, profit per machine hour, or profit per square meter of retail space.

Opportunity costs

The performance of a process involves the use of resources. A simple view of the cost of the process is to add up the cash costs of the resources used.

A much more sophisticated approach to the cost of a process is to consider the nearest alternatives to the decision to do the process. Could the resources used for a process be used instead for a different process? Would the different process lead to higher revenue or higher added value? Could the process be done by someone else at a lower cost? According to Arnold and Hope (1990), " ... the opportunity cost ... of using a scarce resource may be greater than the incremental cash flow directly associated with its purchase". For Horngren and Sundem (1987), "An opportunity cost is defined as the *maximum* available contribution to profit forgone by using scarce resources for a particular purpose. It is measured by examining the *best* forsaken alternative; it is not an outlay cost because cash is neither received nor disbursed".

Hence the opportunity cost of a process can be measured by the alternatives foregone by the decision to do the process rather than by the cash cost of the process.

The question of opportunity costing explains in part why many enterprises restructure their activities to concentrate on *core competencies*—doing some processes is less efficient with respect to business objectives than using the resources for processes that the company is actually better at doing.

Allocation method	Scenario	Example
Overhead per person	A service organization sells consulting services. The consultants use an infrastructure that includes building facilities, information systems, and secretarial support. There are central management services to cover human resources and finance	The various overheads are grouped into categories of expense (e.g. facilities, IS and telecom, secretarial support, HRO, finance) and the total costs in each category are divided by the number of consultants to give an average overhead cost per consultant
Overhead per machine hour	A manufacturing company has extensive mass-production factories. Labor costs are only 17% of total costs. The main overheads relate to buildings and production machinery.	Overheads are added together and divided by the average number of machine hours available for production. Product costs are built up from direct labor costs, material costs, and overheads obtained by multiplying the number of machine hours to produce an item by the overhead rate per machine hour.
Overhead per square meter	A retailing organization has a substantial amount of retail floor space and some separate office accommodation. The main *direct costs of sales are the* costs of buying in the products. The biggest overhead costs are rent and the cost of sales staff.	Overheads are added together and divided by the total number of square meters of retail area. Goods are considered for sale in the shops depending on the profit *per sale, number of sales per year,* and area of sales space needed to handle the volume

Table 9.3 Traditional overhead allocation criteria

Cost drivers

One major contributor to the difficulty in either allocating overheads, or even simulating alternative scenarios, is the absence of good operational data about those activities that determine the overheads. For example, the cost of the accounting function is determined in part by the total number of transactions that need to be recorded and handled.

Hope and Hope (1995) propose a "transformation diamond" at the top of which they say, "understand the causes of costs by measuring work". One of their goals is to measure non-value-adding work and change processes to eliminate it, as a major contributor to reducing costs.

Cost drivers can be identified from relatively low-level process analysis. The first step toward implementing activity-based costing is to identify the activities performed—this is the same as identifying the components of business processes.

For each activity, the resources used are calculated, along with their costs. As suggested in chapter 3, every process should be characterized by at least one type of event. Every process will also process inputs in response to those events. The events and inputs are the most likely *cost drivers* of the activities, and examples are shown in Table 9.4.

The establishment of activities and associated cost drivers is an essential preliminary to the implementation of activity-based costing, according to writers including Innes and Mitchell (1990, 1991) and Drury (1992).

There is a very useful cross-check before activity-based cost allocation is done. The work done by all people involved in overhead activities should be classified by activity. Total overheads should then be allocated to the different activities that are classified as overheads. Thus the overheads are accounted for by all the activities.

The volumes of the events and inputs for each of the goods and services produced should be calculated. The next step is to identify the cost drivers of the activities (as illustrated in Table 9.4). Then the costs can be allocated to goods and services based on their contribution to the cost drivers.

Process or activity	Resources used	Cost driver(s)
Receive and enter orders	labor; real estate; computer systems	orders received
Material handling	labor; warehousing; vehicles; goods handling equipment	goods received, dispatched, or moved
Accounting	labor; real estate; computer systems	financial transactions; management report requests
Management meetings	labor; travel	number of organizational structures
Machinery	labor; real estate; energy; depreciation	labor hours

Table 9.4 Example cost drivers

Activity-based costing

One of the reasons cited frequently for business process engineering and reengineering is to do with achieving greater competitive advantage by more effective control of costs. This can only be done by more "accurate" costing to support decision making about which processes to do and which to outsource.

Enterprises are becoming integrated more extensively, partly as a result of supporting information systems. One consequence of this is the increase in the size of infrastructure. Earlier overhead cost allocation systems were developed when nonproduct or nonmanufacturing overheads were a relatively small proportion of total costs. Today, when knowledge work can absorb 50% of cost and most knowledge work is overhead in some way, the allocation of costs has become a more complex problem. In some modern manufacturing plants with high levels of automation, labor costs may account for less than 15% of total costs. This makes the allocation of building and equipment costs more difficult.

It is against this kind of background that activity-based costing (ABC) has emerged in recent years. There are even some ardent supporters, such as Turney (1996) who states: "Conventional costing not only *does not* work well, it is positively dangerous. The consequences of conventional costing— such as selling the wrong products, mispricing products, or improving the wrong things—are not acceptable in today's competitive world".

There is an additional reason why a recent emphasis on business processes may be more appropriate to activity-based costing for the allocation of overheads. Traditional overhead allocation is based on allocating overhead costs to different departments (or responsibility centers) according to some volume-based formula (such as number of people employed, number of machine hours, or space occupancy). Activity-based costing is concerned with identifying those activities (processes) that contribute the most to the emergence of the overhead costs.

ABC is not practiced universally. There is a lively debate in the accounting and management literature about its advantages and disadvantages. Useful discussions about the issues, along with example case studies, can be found in Innes and Mitchell (1990, 1991). The process analyst should take note of the controversy, but ultimately, should be sure that:

- the main activities performed have been identified;
- appropriate metrics for the process/activities have been defined and data obtained for those metrics;
- whether the process engineer uses traditional cost allocation or activity-based cost allocation, all relevant overheads must be accounted for and allocated;
- the cost allocation procedures adopted should provide the most suitable information for the appropriate cost objectives.

Hence, although the process analyst is likely not to be a professional accountant, the analyst should be able to establish a set of cost objectives based on the decisions needed about the various processes and their costs. A professional accountant can always be used to help with defining the relevant collection and classification schemes, and making sure that they can be mapped to other objective such as financial reporting requirements.

There is substantial agreement between Innes and Mitchell (1990) and Drury (1992) about the steps required to implement ABC:

- establish a set of overhead cost pools based on the activities that cause overhead costs;
- decide which cost drivers to use;
- calculate activity driver allocation rates;
- allocate overheads according to the calculated rates.

Following on from setting up a collection of allocation rates, it is necessary to maintain the measurement of the underlying cost drivers by appropriate operational metrics.

The practitioner needs to be aware that there are many practical problems to be resolved in implementing activity-based costing systems, and that not all attempts have been successful. Cobb *et al.* (1992) discuss several practical problems in some detail and give examples. They state that "The most common problem ... was the amount of work involved in installing an ABC system ... the four other most common problems were ... the organization had other competing uses for resources ... the lack of suitable accounting staff ... scarce computer resources ... difficulties of selecting suitable cost drivers".

Activity-based costing: a simple example

A company sells two products, A and B, each of which requires the use of production machinery and direct labor. Purchase orders are raised to buy material for the manufacture of the products. The finished products are sold to distributors, which involves raising invoices for the sales. The work involved for each purchase order is about the same as the work involved for each invoice. The products are manufactured with the help of the same flexible manufacturing system (FMS) that has to be set up for each production run. The company batches production to keep down the inventory of finished goods. Basic data are presented in Table 9.5.

Direct labor costs 12 monetary units (MUs) per hour. There is an accounting department that costs 200,000 MUs per year. A team of six people, each working 2,000 hours per year, performs all machine set-ups. All other overheads cost 625,000 MUs per year. Total overheads are (200,000 + 6 x 2,000 x 12 + 625,000) = 969,000 MUs. Therefore total production costs are 969,000 + 64,000 x 12 = 1.737 million MUs per year.

What is the cost per unit of output? This is where the difference arises between more traditional cost allocation and activity-based costing.

Total overheads are slightly more than 25% above direct labor costs. Direct labor hours and FMS hours per year are similar. In cases of traditional overhead cost allocation, there is a choice between allocating overheads by labor hours, and allocating overheads by FMS machine hours.

If all overheads are allocated by labor hours, the overhead cost per direct labor hour is 969,000/64,000 = 15.141 MUs per labor hour. Therefore the overhead cost for each unit of A would be 8 x 15.141 = 121.128. The overhead cost for each unit of B would be 3 x 15.141 = 45.423.

Alternatively, if all costs are allocated by FMS machine hours, the overhead cost per machine hour is 969,000/62,500 = 15.50. Each unit of A would cost 5 x 15.50 = 77.5 for overheads. Each unit of B would cost 3 x 15.5 = 46.5 for overheads. (There is slight rounding of these results.)

This change in the basis of allocating overheads produces a small change in the costs of B, but quite a substantial change in the costs of A.

Product	Labor hours per unit of output	FMS hours per unt of production	Annual Output	Total direct labour	Total FMS hours	Purchase Orders	Sales Invoices	FMS reconfigurations
A	8	5	500	4,000	2,500	250	200	5
B	3	3	20,000	60,000	60,000	4,000	200	200
				64,000	62,500	4,250	400	205

Table 9.5 Activity-based costing example: basic data

To apply activity-based costing, it is necessary to identify cost drivers. From the data supplied, it can be seen that the machine reconfiguration overhead costs are driven by the number of reconfigurations.

Obviously product B accounts for most of this overhead cost. The data identified the overhead costs of the accounting department, an obvious cost driver for which is the number of documents generated (purchase orders and invoices). The other less specific overheads can only be assumed to be related to the volume of output in some way. Let us take machine hours as the volume-related driver.

Reconfiguration overheads are 144,000 for 205 re-configurations. Therefore the overhead cost per re-configuration is 144,000/205 = 702.439. Accounting overheads are 200,000 for 4,650 documents, therefore the overhead cost per document is 200,000/4,650 = 43.01. The remaining overheads, 625,000, are allocated by machine hours, therefore the overhead per FMS hour is 625,000/ 62,500 = 10.

Therefore overhead costs per unit of product A are (702.439 x 5 + 43.01 x 450 + 10 x 2,500)/500 = 95.733 MUs. Overhead costs per unit of product B are (702.439 x 200 + 43.01 x 4,200 + 10 x 60,000)/ 20,000 = 46.06.

These results are summarized in Table 9.6. It can be seen that selecting a different basis for allocating overheads has a substantial impact on the costs of A, but very little impact on the costs of product B. This is because the volume of production of B is 40 times that for A. If, instead of using machine hours as the basis for allocating the general overheads, units of output are used as the cost driver for general overheads, the results are different yet again, as shown in the last line of Table 9.6.

Basis for allocating overheads	Product A	Product B
Labor hours	121.128	45.423
Machine hours	77.500	46.500
ABC (machine hours)	95.733	46.060
ABC (units of output)	76.220	46.550

Table 9.6 Activity-based costing example: comparison

Business process costs

In process costing, as opposed to job costing, the flow of costs follows the flow of work. In other words, production overheads are allocated to the processes in a process chain[2]. As goods and services pass from one process to the next , the costs associated with the flow are brought forward into the next process. This is illustrated in Figure 9.1, which shows a simple process flow that follows a linear sequence. Of course, a process is likely to be a more complex network flow where the output of one process could go to more than one subsequent process. One major advantage of arranging work by process cost centers is that many costs that would otherwise be general overheads can be assigned specifically to different processes (for example, management or administrative costs). The flow of costs following the simple process flow is illustrated in Table 9.7.

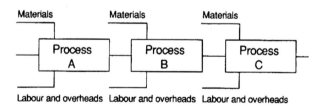

Figure 9.1 Process costs and process flows.

---

2 On a job costing basis, overheads would be allocated in some traditional way such as labor hours or machine hours.

Cost category	Process A	Process B	Process C
Brought forward	0	21,000	36,000
Material	10,000	2000	6000
Labor	5000	5000	2000
Overheads	6000	8000	7000
Carried forward	21,000	36,000	51,000

Table 9.7 Process costing: linear example

Concluding remarks

The business process analyst needs at least a literacy in costing techniques, and many practitioners will have specialized in the area.

There are usually several valid views of costs. Often, the weakness in simulating alternative ways to allocate costs is caused by the absence of good operational data that are needed to back up the various approaches. In my experience, costing techniques are frequently a weakness in practitioners who move into BPW from the information systems world.

In this chapter there has been an emphasis on cost allocation and its principal approaches: traditional techniques, activity-based costing, and process costing. The analyst may also need to take into account the capital investment requirements of alternative ways to perform a process. It may also be necessary to include financial measures of process performance when putting together proposals for monitoring the enterprise's processes. This is likely to require an understanding of variance analysis that would be used to understand changes in costs over time, or deviations from expected values. In any event, I believe it is important for the professional business process analyst to include financial techniques in the toolbox and library.

The next chapter moves away from costs to investigate enterprise organization.

Chapter 10

Analyzing organization

BPW high-level projects consider (or, rather, some people associated with the projects)the possible need for radical *organizational change*. Of course, radical change may not be needed and only incremental change would help. The motivation for such change could be "merely" to implement redesigned processes. Alternatively, there may be deep-seated reasons for change based on the possibilities of reorganization in itself. For example, there are important themes in current literature about "learning organizations", "knowledge-based enterprises", and harnessing the intellectual creativity of employees, all of which have been depicted in the literature as benefits available from new organizational structures.

Management over long distances is a relatively new phenomenon in terms of commercial enterprises (in the sense of exercising control and communication during an activity). Some of the earliest examples of enterprise organization, coordination, and control over vast distances are for military enterprises in contemporary accounts from Ancient Greece, Rome, and Byzantium (examples of which are described by James and Thorpe, 1994). More recent commercial examples are described by Yates (1989), and are also discussed in chapter 3.

The business process analyst is likely to find this subject matter more difficult due to an absence of relatively "hard" techniques. However, literacy is important, because there are several recurring themes. There are also many claims in the organizational literature which are difficult to verify, and some consulting enterprises base their approach on one or more organizational paradigms, about organizational behavior and design, and teams. The business process analyst is certainly advised to have access to some key literature in this area.

Several texts about organizational behavior, organizational design, and teams have been consulted while forming the ideas in this chapter.. The business process analyst is certainly advised to have access to some key literature in this area. For example, Beardshaw and Palfreman (1986), Buchanan and Huczynski (1985), Child (1984), Handy (1985), Katzenbach and Smith (1993), Morgan (1986, 1989, 1993), Scarbrough and Corbett (1992), Wilson and Rosenfeld (1990), and Wilson (1992), in addition to the other specific references made here.

A defined business process often implies the routinization of some work.

The automation of work is the extreme of routinization and dependent on technological capabilities. Therefore some routine work cannot be automated because of economic or technological infeasibility; conversely, some work is not routine, therefore defining a process is extremely difficult if not impossible.

At the level of groups, most computer-based technology that requires human interface is based primarily on a paradigm of leveraging the work of individuals. It is probably no accident that several writers describe personal computers as "personal productivity tools". The support for collective work appears as mainly at the level of aggregating the work of individuals. For this reason, computer support for collaborative work is still in its infancy. There is not yet a clear vision of what technology able to support collective work actually looks like.

One key to successful organizational design is locating system points of control in the "right" place. The significance is the hypothesis that if points of control are located in the "wrong" place, then the system is likely to cost more in resources to build and more to operate. A potential trap in this line of reasoning lies in an implicit assumption that the primary goal of system design is the minimization of *financial* cost, therefore it is necessary to produce an organizational structure that minimizes enterprise costs. The trick is to understand the human goals and values involved, and recognize the significance of aesthetics and ethics. For example, some senior managers may feel much more comfortable with centralized decision making and are willing to put in place the bureaucratic structures to make it happen. It may be possible to run such an enterprise at a lower financial cost, but with less comfort to senior managers—which way is "correct"? Direct links between business processes and corporate ethics are discussed by Adams *et al* (1991) who report a survey of a number of large companies with respect to a wide range of specific ethical criteria.

There is a bias in organizational literature towards questions of organizational *design* and organizational *behavior*. This poses some problems for us as business process *analysts*, because it is more difficult to find literature about how to *analyze* organizational and human factors from a perspective of enterprise processes.

Given the widespread commentary that computer-based information technology is the enabling technology for BPW, is there a link between organization and IT?

Are there any objects and relationships that are helpful for an analysis of human and organizational issues?

Organizational models

The 20th century saw the promotion of a wide range of organizational models. These include hierarchical models (for example, Fayol, 1916), matrix models (for example, Galbraith, 1973, 1977), and more modern ideas such as webs, orchestras, and so forth (for example, Savage, 1990).

The tasks of the analyst with reference to these models are:

- be able to recognize many of the possible forms of organizational structure and dynamics;
- be aware of the key issues related to the different organizational possibilities;
- be able to make recommendations concerning appropriate organizational structures for the various business processes to be implemented;
- help with modeling the behavior of different organizational forms.

Organizations are highly complex, and probably too complex for the analyst to portray a "complete" or a "correct" view. Simple hierarchical models are discussed later in the chapter, and although they do not represent much of the real world of work, nevertheless they convey useful concepts for some purposes. Similarly, some writers claim that alternative views of organization are more correct, or nearer the reality of something. An interesting and helpful approach is the set of metaphors described by Morgan (1986). He explains his approach thus: "The basic premise on which the book builds is that our theories and explanations of organizational life are based on metaphors that lead us to see and understand organizations in distinctive yet partial ways".

Many critiques of traditional hierarchical views of organization are based on:

- real flows of information and materials do not follow the lines of authority on the organization charts;
- the real world of work involves many informal structures in addition to the formal;
- large organizations need to be broken into smaller units because of diseconomies of scale arising from the excessive bureaucracy needed for very large hierarchical structures implied by the hierarchical management of huge enterprises;
- more agile and responsive enterprises require smaller, quasi-autonomous units.

In addition to Morgan, there are other ideas about flow in organizations. Davis and Olson, (1984) talk about a "workflow pervasiveness" in organizations. Mintzberg (1979) describes *The Organization as a System of Flows*. He asserts that organizations have five parts: operating core, strategic apex, middle line, technostructure, and support staff; and that these parts are joined together by different flows: authority, work material, information, and decision processes. This can lead to seeing an organization as a "system of work constellations" (to use Mintzberg's term) with work flowing from one work constellation to another. At a meta-modeling level, such an approach can accommodate workflow in terms of flow between work constellations, flow between functional units, and the more recent idea of flow between "business objects" (in an object-oriented sense as applied to business processes). Many writers have an implicit manufacturing metaphor of work flowing from one unit to another. Of course there are situations when organizational units flow to the work (for example, creating a building).

One important change in paradigm in recent years is that agricultural and manufacturing work usually require people to move to where the work is, whereas information technology offers the opportunity for much information work to flow to where the people are.

The significance for the analyst is the need to classify the different kinds and directions of flow. A system of work constellations is at a sufficiently high level of abstraction to be applicable to many kinds of organizational structure.

For example, perhaps the most traditional form of organizational structure is to see an enterprise as divided into a collection of departments, which are de-composed hierarchically into smaller organizational units.

The essence of this traditional enterprise departmental model is that it is the flow of authority and decision processes which is organized hierarchically. The emergence of BPW can be attributed in part to the inherent contradiction that arises from the widespread depiction that although the flow of authority and decision processes is hierarchical, the flow of materials and much of the information will be directly from one organizational unit to another, and not hierarchically through the established management chains.

The work constellations in some cases can be seen as the various enterprise departments, and in other cases as the smaller organizational units. Different collaboration is needed to coordinate authority and decision making with the work material processes. In an hierarchical organizational structure, the ability of the lower organizational units to interact directly with other units is restricted by the flow of authority and decision making. The direct material flows will usually be subject to rules and procedures authorized in the context of the hierarchical structures.

One of the greatest dilemmas for the business process analyst and designer is to design an organizational structure that is able to achieve an optimum overall use of resources. In a traditional hierarchical model, the different enterprise departments have goals to meet, which are often expressed in maximizing or minimizing terms. However, overall business processes frequently require some optimizing strategy, rather than maximizing or minimizing. For example, a department may be required to minimize its costs, therefore it enters the market and buys its own PCs and communications facilities. However, on an enterprise-wide basis, economies of scale may be achievable by implementing an infrastructure for communications, which may imply reducing the autonomy and decision making of individual departments.

Organization and information technology

Computers need not be used merely to automate certain tasks, but can instead enhance skills and "empower" people. There are many levels at which the effects can be felt, from the individual, to the company, to the wider virtual enterprises and virtual communities.

It is conventional BPW wisdom that the key benefits of information technology may not arise primarily from the automation of tasks performed previously by other means. Rather, they could arise from a redefinition of fundamental processes and the ways in which they are performed, along with the use of IT as a means to increase the skills of people in the enterprise. This is often a major work issue for business process engineers.

There has been some fear that the automation of many tasks by information technology will lead to significantly greater unemployment, and undoubtedly there have been cases where this has happened. However, as explained in some Organization for Economic Cooperation and Development (OECD) sources (1986-1989), the real long-term change will be more in the quality and nature of work, with far greater opportunities for people to use technology to enhance their skills and level of effort. In order to look explicitly at the ways in which organization and IT interact, it is useful to speculate about what IT can give to an enterprise.

Information technology adds organizational possibilities in some fundamental ways, which are summarized in Table 10.1. The use of these properties is presumably what enterprises hope to take advantage of; enterprises alter their organizational structures to make increasing use of these properties. For example, virtual teams do not need to be in the same place because IT mitigates many of the effects of time and space, and key enterprise processes can be redesigned because of the possibility of linking tightly interdependent sequences of events.

Every employee in an enterprise, as well as every employee of trading partners, can be considered in part as an information processor. Some of the information processes can be very simple, whereas others can be very complex. In the past, with the traditional division of labor, only a very few people in a company, the managers, had complicated tasks. By definition, they were information processors, since their job was to gather, collate, and analyze information, and use it to give direction. The traditional view is that as enterprises evolve, these tasks regarded as simple (in terms of economic and technical feasibility) are automated and middle management is squeezed out. A less traditional view is that complete business processes are overhauled or redesigned, resulting in different ways of organizing enterprises in which traditional management roles are no longer needed.

In the latter view, alternative styles of working, along with a greater information component in all jobs, shifts the means of gaining power from controlling information to using it for added-value activities. More and more professionals make autonomous decisions based on information that they receive directly. Eventually an enterprise will comprise a network of professionals using sophisticated information technology to enhance their own information-processing capability.

In such an environment traditional management control no longer works. Pure top-down, central planning is not effective because of the increasing complexity and size of the information-processing task. This is analogous to the failure of centrally planned economies, which cannot overcome the enormity of controlling everything.

Property	Added value
Space	The effect of space can be reduced dramatically so that many activities can be performed in spite of the geographical distance between them.
Time	Barriers of time can be reduced dramatically, and many activities can be performed with very small time gaps between their different components.
Event sequences	Partly as a result of reduced need for time and space, it is possible to put together tightly dependent sequences of events.
Complexity	Some calculations are simply not an option without computer support.
Knowledge	The knowledge of several experts can be combined to provide an accessible pool of knowledge beyond the scope of any individual.

Table 10.1 IT added value

For any particular enterprise the extent of an observable powershift depends on the questions of how far managers manage and how much autonomy the individual has in achieving enterprise objectives. If managers "manage", then they must be able to make some decisions that cannot be made by others, and these decisions must be based on additional information. Such decision making needs the support of information-processing facilities.

A much broader concept than simply empowering managers is empowering all employees. Individuals, in order to have more autonomy, must have access to the kind of information that supports their activities. The evolution of autonomous entrepreneurial teams, and the increased "informating" of the people performing different tasks, requires new ways of organizing. Organization is independent of management, insofar as it brings added value that is unobtainable without it, as is illustrated in Table 10.2. The information given in this table is optimistic, and for every "added value" there may exist specific disadvantages as well. The business process analyst needs to look for both benefits and disadvantages.

Building up a picture of the properties of IT and organization, independently of each other to begin with, provides a theoretical foundation from which it can be hypothesized that any IT that comes to depend on any of the properties of organization described in Table 10.2, or *vice versa*, contributes to an enterprise that is dependent on the interactions between IT and organization.

This is an important way in which information technology is an enabling technology for the design of processes which would not be possible without such an interaction between IT and organization. There are many alternative ways of looking at this interaction.

Lee *et al.* (1995) discuss the interaction between these two in terms of synergy. They conclude that "Top managers no longer have to settle for a centralized or decentralized structure. The hybrid structure has the potential to deliver the best of both worlds of centralization and decentralization. However, the strategical success is contingent on the synergistic deployment of IT within a matching organizational structure". Stebbins *et al.* (1995) survey several theories and ideas about organization and IT, propose a model for the subject matter, and present an *"eclectic design process"* that has six steps (very much like a traditional waterfall). They observe that "Both conventional and unconventional organizations will increasingly depend on information technology for learning and integration". Eason (1988) has an interesting contribution to the discussion of IT and organization.

Property	Added value
Cohesiveness[1]	An enterprise probably could not survive and achieve its objectives if its components simply interacted in random ways.
Specialization	Organization enables different people to specialize in different skills and activities.
Inter-dependence	Almost a corollary of specialization; when people are specialized, interdependencies build up and organization provides a mechanism to implement these interdependencies.
Mechanization	Organization brings together specialized parts, and so is a way of achieving the mechanization of certain tasks and activities.
Rationalism	Planning and organization to implement planning are very powerful paradigms. They lead to a rationalized view of achieving objectives.
Implemented determinism	Organization arises as part of a process to achieve an objective; hence, it is a way of implementing a deterministic approach to goals and objectives.
Power	Power generally arises from organizing specialists and by manipulating the resulting interdependencies.

[1] This is offered by Beer (1979) who states that *"Cohesiveness* is the primary characteristic of organization. This fact derives from the very purpose of organization which ... exists to contain the variety proliferation that arises from the uninhibited interaction of the elements of a system".

Table 10.2 Organization added value

Individuals, too, experience resulting changes in the underlying distribution of power. There is a major shift in paradigms of power away from achieving power by keeping information, towards achieving power by making information available, and away from achieving authority by position, as more and more people obtain authority by the application of knowledge and acquisition of respect.

Authority no longer comes exclusively from the number of people controlled or from budget size, but increasingly from the leadership provided, from personal value added, and from the manager's ability to set the direction for a team of professionals. As Zuboff (1988) states, "Managers who must prove and defend their own legitimacy do not easily share knowledge or engage in inquiry. Workers who feel the requirements of subordination are not enthusiastic learners".

The business process engineer needs, at a minimum, a literacy in business structures that contribute to leadership, such as Rath (2007) and, Rath and Conchie (2008).

Traditionally, many middle managers have been information processors, creating and passing on summaries of information, passing on policies and decisions further down the enterprise, or attempting to handle unexpected events[1]. Layers of management can now be skipped for both communication and decision making; there is much horizontal and vertical communication across many layers. As a result, the value added that was provided by pure information gathering and distribution is no longer needed. Perhaps the middle manager can only survive in the future by providing personal added value, and to do that, the manager must be an expert at something. More managers must "coach" people, not merely direct and coordinate them. They

---

1 In more formal terms traditional middle management performs the roles of information attenuation, information amplification, and variety attenuation—tasks that information technology can support, and often performs very well.

cannot afford to be independent of the technical requirements of what is being managed.

All of this takes away even more power from line managers, who simply no longer have the ability to understand what is going on but must trust professionals such as project managers, account managers, engineers, and team leaders to do the work. Thus, the impacts on the enterprise include changes to the traditional chain of command and traditional lines of authority.

Toffler's (1990) essential thesis, that knowledge now provides the key raw material for creating wealth, is echoed by writers such as Stewart (1991). One of the enterprise's greatest challenges is to move away from being driven by the interests of its organizational units, toward taking direction from customer needs and the entrepreneurial realization of new opportunities (see, for example, Dumaine, 1991, who explores ways in which traditional organization charts are replaced by ever-changing flexible teams). These shifts in power and traditional organization are inextricably linked with the application of information technology and the existence of both information and IT infrastructures. Toffler makes the point that "Just as owners became dependent on managers for knowledge, managers are becoming dependent on their employees for knowledge". Solutions to needs and problems rely increasingly on knowledge. It is becoming irrelevant to know only what a product will do, but it is critical to know the kinds of situations in which products can add some value, when to use them, and when not to use them.

Collaborative work

All around us we see many examples of people cooperating at work. There are many important reasons why people need the help and cooperation of others if they are to achieve their objectives (personal or professional). Organizations are being set up to perform tasks of increasing novelty and complexity. There has been a very long evolution of different ways of achieving a division of labour which leads to a need for interdependent and collaborative working methods to do work that cannot be done by one person alone.

In addition to cooperative working in order to meet work objectives, most people enjoy a satisfying psychological and social environment that should be taken into account when designing organizations or organizing work. It is all too easy for activities such as business process reengineering (or innovation or improvement) to place a great deal of emphasis on things like process and information flows, without paying proper attention to the social organization of work or the social needs of people at work.

All of these forms of cooperative working have elements of specialization or differences in interests. They are all examples of work that cannot be done by an individual alone, therefore the work must be organized in some way.

Work on one project (Darnton, 1995), proposed the following five different ways in which people work together:

- ■ Common task: this category covers people working together in a group to produce some product or service, or perform some activity. This kind of collaborative situation is sometimes referred to as a *work-group*—a group of people put together for a specific set of objectives.

- Sequences of tasks: people may need to collaborate together in a "chain" of activities. One person or group finishes one phase of work, and then the work passes to another individual or group, until the whole product or service is finished. This kind of collaborative situation is sometimes referred to as *workflow*—in part, it is a contemporary positioning of transactional systems.
- Problem solving: multidisciplinary teams and multiskilled teams work together to solve many different kinds of problem.
- Command and control: formal structures of command and control to coordinate a complex set of activities.
- Mutual aid: people come together to cooperate for various reasons, often in an *ad hoc* way, but with the common element being mutual self-interest.

The challenge for the business process analyst is to represent that collaborative work in process models. Returning to OPR modeling, a network of PROCESSOR objects can model the people (or mechanisms) involved in collaborative teams.

A rich literature for CSCW is emerging, along with early products to support collaborative work. Case studies, discussions, and pointers to additional literature can be found in works such as Ackroyd *et al.* (1992), Bentley *et al. (1992),* Bowers and Benford (1991), and Hughes et *al. (1991).*

Goals, values, and cultures

Some themes of profound importance to the business process analyst are difficult to handle using formal models of the kinds described in earlier chapters, and they will provide analytical challenges to be addressed in the coming years.

Enterprises and organization involve some difficult paradoxes. People do work for a variety of reasons. Those who establish and own enterprises are usually a subset of the people involved. Those who do not own the enterprises are usually employees. The traditional contract of employment is an evolution of earlier ideas of the master-servant relationship. This even appears in modern court judgments. For example, Crump (1976) cites one case where the judge[2] said: "A contract of service exists if the following three conditions are fulfilled: (i) The servant agrees that in consideration of a wage or other remuneration he will provide his own work and skill in the performance of some service for his master. (ii) He agrees, expressly or implicitly, that in the performance of that service he will be subject to the other's control in a

---

2 Mackenna, J. in the case of Ready Mixed Concrete (South East), Ltd v. Minister of Pensions and National Insurance, [1968] 1 All E.R. 433, p. 439.

sufficient degree to make that other master. (iii) The other provisions of the contract are consistent with its being a contract of service".

The fact that most people doing work in exchange for money or goods do so under a master-servant contract has an important impact on motivation, and this has been a recurring theme in organizational literature. There is a lot of evidence (such as Maslow, 1954, 1968, and 1971; Kohn, 1993; Herzberg, 1968) that beyond a certain point, money is not the most important motivator for many people. This is one reason for alerting the analyst earlier to the problem of anthropomorphism when managers talk about enterprise strategies and objectives. A modern paradox in organizational design is how to create the most suitable context for the servants to develop the skills of being creative, innovative, and entrepreneurial. Of course, some people do have a serious 'clinical' addiction to money!

Therefore, the business process analyst may need to add techniques to handle the variety of motivators that may explain why some processes are more successful than others.

Processes that involve human beings involve taking many different actions. Modeling complex business processes warns us about the potentially serious differences between describing processes in an abstract way and the real world of work. Action is "situated" and context dependent. According to Suchman (1987), " ... plans are best viewed as a weak resource for what is primarily *ad hoc* activity. It is only when we are pressed to account for the rationality of our actions, given the biases of European culture, that we invoke the guidance of a plan. Stated in advance, plans are necessarily vague, insofar as they must accommodate the unforseeable contingencies of particular situations. Reconstructed in retrospect, plans systematically filter out precisely the particularity of detail that characterizes situated actions, in favour of those aspects of the actions that can be seen to accord with the plan". Hammer (1994) also makes the point that business process design must take human factors into account.

Of course, there are some processes that are substantially routinized, and process descriptions (which can be construed as plans for what to do when certain events happen) can be produced which are valid for much of the time. The significance of action being situated is likely to be more relevant for processes that have higher degrees of complexity or novelty, or whenever the unexpected happens.

Thus the business process analyst may need to pay attention to identifying the boundaries within which a system can be considered viable and ongoing.

Organization and practical analysis

Consider the part of a simple organization chart[3] shown in Figure 10.1(a). It is a very typical example of an hierarchical chart for the top levels of an

3 CEO = chief executive officer, CFO = chief finance officer, HRM = human resources manager, CIO = chief information officer. The diagram does not imply that the management lines shown are the only ones that exist—there are others, not shown for reasons of space.

enterprise. What does the chart mean? Vertical spacing usually distinguishes job level. Functions at the same horizontal level are presumably at similar job levels. The connecting lines indicate, for instance reporting and authority relationships. The different boxes indicate enterprise functions. Such a diagram can usually be de-composed further to lower levels of management and eventually to operations. Figure 10.1(b) shows a smaller part of an organizational structure, but this time multiple connections are included, indicating matrix management rather than hierarchical management.

An organization chart can be constructed to a level of detail where every employee in the enterprise can be located. This can be very useful to describe reporting, functional, line[4] and management responsibilities.

(a)   **(b)**

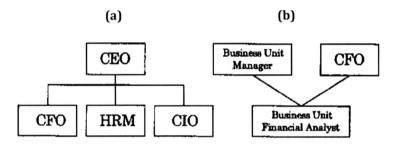

Figure 10.1 Simple organization chart.

The chart does not indicate core business processes. It may or may not indicate formal lines of communication, and almost certainly does not indicate informal lines of communication. Indeed, a recurring theme is that business processes cross functional boundaries. Formal teams consisting of people from different business units or functions may be set up for specific purposes. Informal teams may be established by people who need to communicate with others for the solution of various problems.

Chapter 6 begins with a sample of ethnographic field notes from a study in a financial institution. To quote from Darnton (1995), "Ethnography is concerned with observing the real world of work, how it is actually done rather than how it is described in manuals, rule books or other abstractions. It tries to capture the 'workaday' character of work in all its richness and variety".

Another (unpublished) project, conducted an evaluation of the usefulness of the Software Engineering Institute's (SEI) (at Carnegie-Mellon University) questionnaire that is used to help in assessing the "maturity" of software development organizations. The questionnaire was tested for reliability and validity. One part of that project was fascinating. There was a strong difference in reported opinions about the use of software

---

4 A line is used to show responsibility for some deliverable of the enterprise (goods or services) and a function is used to show responsibility for the application of some core competence. Thus a financial analyst may have line responsibility to a particular business unit, and functional responsibility to the CFO.

development methods depending on the role of the person who was being asked. Put simply, software development managers generally stated quite strong beliefs that defined software development methods were followed in practice. However, consultants and practitioners in the same enterprises tended to say in response to the same questions that although they generally *stated* that they followed the prescribed method (because it may have been a disciplinary matter to state that the methods were not followed), in reality, many workarounds and fixes were needed to deal with deficiencies in the prescribed methods. When the results of those investigations were combined with an inability to identity data that related quality of software delivered with computed maturity level, there was no option but to deliver the opinion that the questionnaire failed essential tests of reliability and validity ... and yet despite the absence of such demonstrable data, many enterprises continue to take decisions based on similar assessments of maturity. This issue has now appeared by the emergence of a Business Process Maturity Model (OMG, 2008).

Lessons drawn from experiences such as CSCW projects and International Organization for Standardization (ISO)900x or SEI type evaluations center around potentially serious disconnections between how people *believe* processes are working, state how they are working, and how they are actually working in practice.

The same is true with respect to many assertions about how organizations work. The formal organization charts and procedure manuals depict idealized versions of how someone thought the processes "should" work. The necessity for informal communications and virtual teams to ensure that the work actually gets done is often not identified by formal techniques, and this is where approaches based on ethnography or social anthropology[5] have been found to be helpful.

What is the analyst to make of such overt inconsistency? A word is required for this kind of problem, and such a word would complement anthropomorphism as part of the analyst's quagmire.

One OPR approach to this kind of problem has been to add an ASSERTS relation to many of the objects defined by the analyst. For example, imagine that there are two methods: methodX and distorted-methodX, where methodX is the official version. The analyst then needs to define both methods (probably by defining them as PROCESSES) and add the relation to the effect that methodX is asserted by *managers* to be the process for problemX whereas distorted-methodX is asserted by *practitioners* to be the process for problemX.

Then, an assertion consistency check can be performed on the system encyclopedia. In this way, the analyst can present in the model all the various views, whether they be belief or reality, and highlight discrepancies.

Organization places individual and collaborative work in a broader context. Work is allocated to formally defined organizational units. Materials and information flow from one organizational unit to another, at least in terms of who is doing the work[6].

A traditional view of people in enterprises is that they do jobs. Certainly, many enterprises prepare, issue, and evaluate against job descriptions. An enterprise can assess its capabilities by adding up the number of people employed according to the various job descriptions.

However, harnessing the creative abilities of people often implies that the innovating people may be working outside their job description. Similarly, the emergence of self-regulating virtual teams may happen such that the people concerned are working outside their formal job descriptions. Thus the analyst needs to disentangle a range of objects and relationships that are often bundled together in formal ideas about people and organization.

Key objects and relationships are set out in Table 10.3, showing the different objects or relationships found to be useful.

So far, this discussion has focussed on the analysis of organizational structure, rather than the dynamics. A radically different approach is to model organization itself as a process. Reasons for doing this stem from the emergence of a contingency approach to organizational design in response to a recognition that different kinds of organization may be appropriate for

5 For example, one topic in social anthropology is the study of belief systems. This helps in the understanding of phenomena such as the application of relational database management systems in inappropriate problem situations, or the classification of overtly proprietary systems as "open". Another contribution from social anthropology is the study of ritual—for example, why do projects still go wrong after extensive sign-off of analysis and design documents by many professionals; is sign-off principally a ritual when clearly the review processes failed to identify infeasibility?

6 For example, in processing a mortgage application, the associated paperwork (or electronic equivalents) may move from one group to another; however, in building a house, the flow of work is more logical in that it is the different kinds of labor which "flow" in and out of the house, and materials that flow in, depending on the stages of work—it would be misleading to portray the house as flowing!

different forms of task. The business process analyst can make some progress with this. For example, Lorsch (1987) indicates a relationship between process linkages and the degree of coordination needed. This is analogous to understanding the degree of coupling (as discussed in chapter 8) between processes. Galbraith (1977) relates the degree of uncertainty in tasks to be performed with the capacity of organizations to process information and to provide satisfaction extrinsically or intrinsically.

Galbraith (1987) goes even further by suggesting that " ... we should see organizing as a continuous management task like scheduling, budgeting, and so on. As managers plan their tasks and strategies, they should plan their organizations". This would mean that rather than treating organizational units as objects (as in Table 10.3), organization could be treated as a process.

Object or relationship	Explanation
PERSON	Usually, a person "does" many things in an enterprise—if each of these things is a role, then a person can be modeled as a processor which has a structure of being composed of several other processors (the roles).
ROLE	A role really means being a PROCESSOR for a process—a person performing a role.
JOB	This means a unit of personnel—typically a person is employed because there is an explicit or implicit job requisition.
ORGANIZATIONAL UNIT	Could be formal or informal—therefore there needs to be an attribute to cover that.
SKILL	An ability to perform a task—usually in a many-to-many relationship with person or processor.
TASK	As discussed earlier in the book, the term task is usually part of a structural de-composition of process—I treat them as synonyms.
MESSAGE	A flow of information.
PROCESS	Modeling organization as a process.

Table 10.3 Objects and relationships for people and organization

Concluding remarks

This part of the book's journey was particularly difficult because there is not a wealth of analytical techniques that the analyst can use.

In terms of understanding business processes, it is necessary to separate process and business function, while understanding how they are linked. Therefore, the earlier OPR models can be extended to include new objects and relationships that can be used to describe organization and some of the connections between components.

It seems that often, proposals about organizational design are often prescriptive and normative, rather than being based on any analytical foundation that can predict consequences accurately. Therefore the least the analyst can do is to describe. The next thing the analyst can do is to try to understand the volumes of work involved in testing the viability of organizational structures to handle the expected activity levels.

In the next chapter, the subject of organization and business process is continued, but with an emphasis on IT as an enabler of process.

Chapter 11

Information technology and business processes

A recurring theme in the BPW literature is that computer-based information technology is the current great enabler of new business processes.

There are two traditional ways in which there is an intimate connection between BPW and new information technology:

- IT is the technology that enables different ways of performing business processes which are not possible without IT;
- interactive computers are an essential part of the toolkit for those doing BPW because various forms of analysis and presentation are either enhanced or can be performed at lower cost.

In addition to these two classical views of the relationship between BPW and IT, there are two more emergent relationships:

- there are many writers who proclaim an information age in which computer-based systems will be embedded in wider systems in a way so ubiquitously that many aspects of life will become increasingly dependent on that new information technology—the idea is that this will also become increasingly so for business processes;
- there is increasing pressure to consider information as an asset: this implies added value from the ownership of information, and future streams of revenue from the exploitation of those information assets— the connection between information assets and IT arises because of the volume of information to be managed as well as the extensive processing required.

The business process analyst needs an understanding of these connections in addition to a literacy in modern information technology. These connections are becoming more complex, leading to an increasing requirement for the analyst to be multidisciplinary. Recent years have seen increasing specialization and divergence of various subjects, while at the same time human-made systems have become more complex as a result of an increasing convergence of technologies (requiring an accompanying convergence of methods).

This chapter starts by examining the two more classical ways in which BPW and IT are connected. Then the idea of an information age is investigated to see whether there are any implications for the business process analyst. Finally, the concept of information as an asset is discussed to understand the implications for BPW and IT.

Information technology and business processes

One of the strongest statements of the importance of information technology for BPW work is by Davenport (1993): "By virtue of its power and popularity, no single business resource is better positioned than information technology to bring about radical improvement in business processes". Other statements occur frequently in the BPW literature emphasizing that information technology is the principal enabling technology for BPW. For example, Venkatraman (1994) states, "IT has become a fundamental enabler in creating and maintaining a flexible business network". There is an important debate expressing doubts about the returns on investment in IT (e.g. Landauer, 1995; Strassman, 1990, as noted in Chapter 8) but this section of the book comments on IT as an enabler of additional *technical* capability.

A major study by MIT's Management in the 1990s Research Program represents a major collaborative effort between industry and academics to examine the interrelationships between IT and organizations. A summary is provided by Scott Morton (1991) in a compilation of Program papers. In a contribution by Davenport and Short *(The Networked Organization and the Management of Interdependence)* four major classes of ways in which IT enables organizational forms are suggested: internal structure, team-based work groups, disintegrated (but interconnected) organizations, and systems integration.

In another contribution to Scott Morton's book, Venkatraman *(IT- induced Business Reconfiguration)* suggests five levels of IT-induced reconfiguration: localized exploitation, internal integration, business process redesign, business network redesign, and business scope redefinition. Each of these levels is positioned with increasing values of range of potential benefits and degree of business transformation. The levels are then discussed and exemplified in more detail. Below, information is discussed as an asset, but Venkatraman also details IT infrastructure as a strategic resource, categorizing its treatment as independent, reactive, or interdependent with respect to the enterprise's strategic context.

In a later article, Venkatraman (1994) declares that the original framework of levels (described in Scott Morton, 1991) was a preliminary version that has been applied in the subsequent five years. He states his central thesis as " ... the benefits from IT deployment are marginal if only superimposed on existing organizational conditions (especially strategies, structures, processes, and culture). Thus the benefits accrue in those cases where investments in IT functionality accompany corresponding changes in organizational characteristics".

Of course, consieering the discussion in Chapter 3 about the very long term relationbetween business processes and technology, and the observations by Landauer and Strassman discussed in Chapter 8, Venkatraman's observation could be extended to 'Thus, the benefits accrue in those cases where investments in IT functionality accompany corresponding changes in organizational characteristics, *and other forms of technology*'.

Is there a basis on which it is reasonable to assert an interdependence between information technology and business process? Clearly, for an interdependence to exist, there must be some inseparable combination of properties of information technology and business processes. To explore this, a theme started in chapter 10 is continued.

In Table 10.1 several properties of information technology are presented, while in chapter 8 there are several examples of information work[1] Table 11.1 presents a summary the most common operations performed on information while doing information work.

It is also helpful for the analyst to monitor short-and long-term trends in technology. For computer technology Anderla and Dunning (1987) and Cutaia (1990) provide paradigms (still appropriate today) for the evolution of computer hardware. In terms of more general technology trends there are publications such as the annual IEEE Spectrum issue that looks specifically at technology trends.

The principal roles of the analyst are seen here as understanding requirements, analyzing requirements to understand their implications, and presenting results in ways that support design.

Because this book takes a broad view of information technology, analysis should not make any presumptions about design unless there are explicit constraints or nonfunctional requirements. For example, in an accounts receivable department, before recommending a technical solution (lever-arch files, filing cabinets, electronic storage, CD-ROM jukeboxes ...) the analyst should understand the information to be handled, the operations to be performed, the associated quantitative details, and any nonfunctional requirements such as security, the legal burden of proof in disputed cases, or prejudices. Then alternative designs can be proposed and the analyst can support an assessment of each proposed design in terms of its ability to meet the technical needs of the task.

Information technology provides "leverage" to enhance human effort. For example, there have been several comments in recent years that software developers are becoming more productive (that is, they deliver more software per unit time of effort). Generally, improvements in the productivity of software developers come about not because they are typing more quickly, but because the available hardware and software provide increased leverage. Overall typing speeds have not increased for the past 100 years or so, therefore the characters typed are "amplified" in some way by the available technology. It would be possible to employ and train people to memorize the details of invoices with great accuracy, and pass the information from one person to another, but the use of filing technology can enhance greatly the ability of humans to manage larger numbers of invoices.

[1] There is a more detailed discussion of operations on information in Darnton and Giacoletto (1992).

Operation	Description	Example
Knowledge	application of information for problem solving	medical or other problem diagnosis
Origination	initial identification of information	forms, documents, instruments
Collection	creating sets of related information	files, databases
Organization	classifying information	indexes, knowledge and rule bases, bibliographies, abstracts
Storage	permanent copies of information	databases, magnetic media, CD-ROMs, filing cabinets, microform, libraries, video recorders
Processing	computations and transformations	arithmetical and mathematical operations, list processing
Interpretation	putting information into a specific context	data conversion, dictionaries, dials and gauges, diagrams, charts, graphs
Application	manipulation or use of information	data processing systems, documentation for meetings and operations, valves and switches
Retrieval	bringing information out of storage	database management systems, data manipulation languages, microfiche, microform, instrumentation
Communication	sending information from one place to another	Communications hardware and software, telephones, faxes, pipes, wires, information display boards, TV, radio
Dissemination	multiple copies and broadcasting	electronic mail, reports, books, newspapers, overhead projectors, printing and print handling
Decision making	using information to support control choices	spreadsheets, simulation, statistical and mathematical calculations, formulae, models, support for meetings, theories, case studies

Table 11.1 Information operations

The application of computers and laser storage can support even larger volumes of documents. Obviously a computer and CD-ROM technology can be employed even if only one invoice needs to be stored and retrieved. The final design deployed will be some optimization of microeconomic factors, technical feasibility, and the preferences and prejudices of those involved in the decision making. There are many cases where computers are not *necessary*, but they are deployed in any case because that is what people want to do (and even if it costs more than noncomputer designs)—after all, many aspects of computers and management can be seen as fashions[2]

A dependency between business process and information technology will exist whenever the process needs to perform an operation such as those illustrated in Table 11.1, while obtaining one or more advantages as outlined in Table 10.1, and which cannot be achieved without the technology. The most frequent constraint likely to result in a need for computer-based systems is time—that is, the requirement for results to be available within a stated period of time. For example, when making airline reservations for a journey, confirmation of bookings may be required within minutes. For a simple journey involving one airline, this may be possible using a telephone. However, for a more complex journey involving several airlines and destinations, telephones may be too cumbersome and would involve a lot of manual locking until a complete and acceptable itinerary could be constructed, which would then have to be confirmed.

It should be noted that this book is not claiming that information technology is the only technology to handle the properties required in a system design as shown in Table 10.1. For example, transportation technology is deployed particularly to overcome some restrictions of time and space: it is feasible to set up face-to-face meetings from people from around the globe within 24 hours or so. One hundred years ago this was not feasible. Today, meetings can also be held electronically, either synchronously or asynchronously. Manufacturing technology is able to support many cases of complex sequences of events.

---

2 This is not intended as a statement criticizing the choice to deploy computers when they are not necessary. The analyst should recognize the importance of human factors such as preferences and wants, and not view system design in merely functional terms.

There are many examples where information technology has enabled new processes. A sample of these is listed in Table 11.2, along with explanations of the relevance of information technology.

Process type	Description
Just-in-time	Inventory is maintained at the lowest possible level commensurate with meeting customer orders and obtaining new stock from suppliers as shortly before the required time as possible. IT enables continuous monitoring of inventory levels, production requirements, and lead times, and is able to initiate orders automatically.
Flexible manufacturing systems	General-purpose, adaptable machines are used instead of dedicated machines. Computer programs are used to change the machine configurations for different output.
Mass customization	Products or services are produced in volume but it is possible to change some of the characteristics of individual products or services.
Teleworking	It is no longer necessary for many people doing information work to have to work in the same location. Communications and computer technology can distribute work, and coordinate results, thus enabling people to be located in different places.
Span of control	Traditionally, managers have performed the roles of information attenuation and information amplification. Information technology has replaced some of these roles, and enabled managers to increase their spans of control, leading to "flatter" organizational structures.
Integrated systems	Localized, departmental systems that originally operated on a stand-alone basis can be linked together to give smooth process flow.
Capital markets	Cash is increasingly replaced by information about cash. Modern capital markets are dependent on the ability to move information about cash around the globe almost instantaneously.

Table 11.2 IT-enabled processes: examples

Much of the development of computers used by people has been directed at enhancing the work of individuals. There is increasing effort to develop information technology applications to support the collaborative work of many people. This is known by terms such as computer-supported collaborative work

(CSCW), and is discussed in more detail in chapter 10. A useful collation of several projects in this area is available in Chapman (1996) who explains that "We look here at typical changes in working methods and the way in which IT developments are keeping pace with, and facilitating them".

Information technology and business process analysis

Information technology is used extensively in business process analysis work. The activities for which IT is useful are:

- recording information about processes;
- producing high-level representations of processes;
- maintaining a business process encyclopedia;
- checking the syntax of process descriptions;
- checking the completeness and consistency of process descriptions;
- performing different kinds of analysis on process descriptions;
- defining standards for the presentation of information about processes;
- producing process specifications;
- preparing reports about business process analysis;
- document processing.

There is a virtual business process analysis workbench, the functionality of which is described in more detail in chapter 15. The required functionality is divided into front-end (for the capture of information), analysis, and back-end (for the presentation of results).

In constructing the workbench it has not yet been able to have a set of functionality with seamless interfaces. Some of the interfaces are very awkward. This is reminiscent of the many years of discussion and development of computer-aided software engineering (CASE) environments. Despite the many millions spent on such environments, the automation of software generation always remained an elusive goal. The existence of software maintenance problems is itself symptomatic of the failure to produce environments that are able to hold software requirements specifications in sufficient detail to be able to generate the necessary software on demand (in other words, what needs to be maintained are the statements of requirements rather than the software sources). Today, with the advent of rapid application development, there is still a failure to build environments that are capable of documenting adequately the software systems produced by means of modern rapid application development tools.

The generation of business processes is more complex than the development of software, if only because software is likely to be only one type of business process component. It is not possible to automate the generation of enterprise organizational structures or manufacturing systems. Therefore the more modest and more realistic goal is to be able to automate the generation of business process descriptions and specifications.

There are some activities where the result can be either obtained manually or be computer aided; for example, the production of high-level process diagrams. Previously these were drafted by analysts using flow-chart templates, and final results produced by an art department. There are several good flowcharting software products available which can help to produce high-quality charts. Similarly, word- and document-processing software is available to produce high-quality process documentation.

When it is necessary to analyze process descriptions, the volume of information may make it impossible to do manually, as discussed in chapter 2.

If an enterprise can be described by 10-30 processes, the volume of information and its presentation can be managed either manually, or by supporting software with modest tools such as graphical editors, word processors, and document processors. However, if it is necessary to deal with 10,000-30,000 processes then there is a quantum leap in the order of magnitude of the management and analysis problems to be handled. That number of processes cannot be maintained manually and requires the support of tools that are scalable to such a magnitude simple graphical, word, and document processors are hopelessly inadequate for the job. It is a recurring theme throughout this book that the principal modeling technique (OPR) is scalable to many thousands of objects and relationships. An environment has been produced, which is capable of performing completeness and consistency checks on such a number, and automating the production of process specifications.

Other areas of analysis where software are tools particularly helpful (which are discussed in other chapters) are costing (chapter 9), statistics, simulation, and data envelopment analysis (chapter 12). The performance of these kinds of analysis on an enterprise-wide process model would be effectively impossible without computer-aided tools.

There are many different views about what information technology can do for BPW projects. In recent articles, Thé (1995) presented his views of the contents of an analyst's BPR toolkit. The functionality and features that he looks for are:

- BPR program planning;
- organization entity analysis;
- modeling analysis;
- activity-based costing;
- graphical simulation modeling;
- business metrics;
- benchmark analysis;
- visual modeling;
- templates;
- business logic;
- what-if analysis;
- time and resource management;
- budget analysis;
- links to application development tools.

An alternative and simpler view is presented by Vacca and Andrews (1994) who focus on process mapping tools. These generate flowcharts and support the addition of other information about timing, frequency, resources, and so forth. Process reports and charts can then be produced. They see these tools as the first step in a BPR project.

The information ages

There have been many recent commentaries about modern economies having a service sector as dominant, where earlier or less developed economies are based on agriculture or manufacturing being dominant[3].

Rather than portray the modern world as a new information age, perhaps it is more as the third information age, following two earlier significant information ages.

The first information age involved the development of systematic ways to assimilate, learn, and disseminate information using oral traditions. There were people who specialized in learning and transmitting information, and who made a living of sorts from that activity. Several cultures and religions have myths and beliefs from the mists of history transmitted orally from generation to generation, and scholar to scholar. Today, a substantial proportion of the world's population is affected in some way, perhaps the most significant being various behavioral tendencies, by information from this first information age. Indeed, until recently, rhetoric was an important part of many academic curricula. Certain institutions such as the House of Commons in England were designed in anticipation of oral presentation and rhetoric being the dominant medium, with the chamber of the House designed without provision for people bringing printed material, or writing. There seems to be almost no information technology associated with this age.

A second information age is suggested based on written and printed material. As with the first information age, the second has left a profound legacy. There is substantial technology involved in this second information age—writing instruments, inks, paper, printing, and binding.

The present information age sees the addition of the use of electrical and electronic engineering to support the storage and processing of information. Information technology has a major role including artifacts such as telephones, televisions, videos recorders, computers, and electronic communications.

My thoughts about information ages are summarized in Table 11.3. The information ages are cumulative in that the skills and technologies of the second include those of the first, and those of the third include those of the first and second. Having said that, some commentaries suggest that the transition from the first to the second information age may have lowered skill levels in memory and rhetoric. Similarly, a move to the third age may involve a lower level of average literacy and conversational ability. If this is the case, then the skills and technologies are not quite cumulative.

The business process analyst should recognize the potential interactions

---

3 Some of these macroeconomic ideas are discussed in chapter 8.

between technology and skills in information processing while looking at business processes[4]. All the skills identified for the different ages are likely to be needed in various business processes. The analyst needs to take a broad view of information technology rather than a narrow computer-centric view..

Information age	Description	Dominant skills	Characteristics
First	oral	speech, memory, rhetoric	myths, beliefs, experience; learning and transmission by oral tradition
Second	printing	reading, writing, epistemology	paper, printing, libraries, newspapers and tracts; learning and transmission supported by printed materials
Third	computer and communication	keyboard, applications, machine control	computers, magnetic and laser storage, electrical communication; learning and transmission supported by electronics.

Table 11.3 Information ages

Perhaps the real significance for the business process analyst of appreciating the characteristics of different information ages is to avoid a modern-day fixation on computer-based technological issues, and focus on the real meaning and application of information in terms of human goals and aspirations.

Much of today's discussion about IT and BPW focusses on computer-

---

4 For example, an attempt to automate the checking of prices on transactions that had been recorded in handwriting on small pieces of paper. Experienced clerical staff could validate the prices of up to 300 items without the need to check a price list. On examining the error rate in the clerical staff doing the job manually, the cost of providing computer support for the task would have been substantial, there were new errors introduced at the data input stage, and there was no demonstrable benefit from the computer-based process. Human beings could use their mental faculties to do the job more efficiently. Therefore the advice had to be that there would be no benefit in terms of cost reductions on a scale sufficient to justify the cost of the new process. However, the people concerned really wanted a computer system in any case, so they went ahead with the project even though it would cost more!

based IT, but information technology more generally is of fundamental importance to business processes.

Information as an asset

There is a tension between organizing an enterprise by function and organizing by process: where emphasis is placed on function, processes that cross functional boundaries are more difficult to organize for smooth performance; where emphasis is placed on process, it is more difficult to organize for functional excellence.

In a similar way, there is another tension between infrastructure and business unit: infrastructure provides an opportunity to realize economies of scale and commonality across a wide range of functions and processes; business units understand their business responsibilities and may require a lot of persuasion to contribute to infrastructure.

These tensions can come to the fore with respect to the management of information. Many texts portray the essential role of information systems planning as the identification and deployment of those information systems needed to support the strategy and operations of the enterprise. Many enterprises have a systems, IS, IT, or MIS department to provide information technology infrastructure.

An asset is something that either has intrinsic value in its own right, or can contribute to the future cash flow of the enterprise. Accounting practices have well-developed approaches to the valuation of physical assets such as building and machinery. Intangible assets are more problematic from an accounting point of view. If information is to be considered as an asset, it is really an intangible asset.

Business processes are very much concerned with the utilization of enterprise assets to provide maximum added value. The management of cash, people, and tangible assets is well understood, whereas the management of information assets is not so well understood—it requires identification, valuation, protection, and exploitation. The responsibility to exploit information assets must rest with business units in the same way that responsibility for the exploitation of other assets lies.

An enterprise decision to recognize, manage, and exploit information assets has a profound impact on information systems planning (ISP). ISP then moves away from being MIS-centric to being more business process-centric. One frequently cited core business process is product or service development, which is required to put in place the exploitation of information assets.

In traditional economic texts assets were given as land, labor, and capital. Capital remains an asset, of course, but over the past hundred years or so, automation has reduced the need for physical space and labor per unit of output. More recently time has become more significant to the enterprise. The optimization of activities within available time definitely contributes to future cash flow[5]. Although time may not yet be a recognized asset according to strict definition requirements, there is no doubt that an enterprise should behave as though time is an asset.

The value of information to the enterprise has begun to be recognized only in the past few years. It has now become one of an enterprise's essential assets, along with cash, time, people, and resources. These four are well understood, but we need to explore information in more detail.

Horngren and Sundem (1987) define assets as "economic resources that are expected to benefit future activities". It is traditional for accountants to distinguish tangible from intangible assets, a distinction Horngren and Sundem explain as: "*Tangible assets* can be physically observed. In contrast *intangible assets* are a class of *long-lived assets* that are not physical in nature. They are rights to expected future benefits deriving from their acquisition and continued possession. Examples are goodwill, franchises, patents, trademarks, and copyrights".

The essence of intangible assets is their likely contribution to future cash flow, but they are difficult to measure, and in general there is much debate in the accounting profession over how to treat them[6]

Vincent (1990) explains the principle of an asset laid down by the

---

5 Davis (1987) states that "We are talking about *instantaneous* products and services, those that are offered within the blink of an eye of their conception. If you can imagine this occurring, then the product is in research, in development, in manufacture, and being consumed *virtually* all at the same time. This is a truly holistic conception of the product". Keen (1988) gives many examples of organizing enterprise activities that would probably not be possible without the tele-communications part of IT platforms, and he illustrates the significance of using time to obtain competitive advantage.

6 For example, in the United States the Financial Accounting Standards Board has been wrestling with this issue.

Financial Accounting Standards Board as including probable future benefit directly or indirectly to future cash flow, the ability to control access to the asset, and that the investment in the asset has already occurred. He defines four physical properties of information: it is not consumable, it can be copied, it is indivisible, and it is accumulative.

According to the OECD, the trend of enterprises separating their service activity from their manufacturing activity has created the illusion of a shift from a manufacturing to an information economy. The illusion notwithstanding, there has been an increase in the number of enterprises dealing substantially with information, and Vincent identifies these as banking and finance, insurance and security, most government agencies, marketing and sales, accounting and auditing, software development, and investment. He calls these information-driven companies. An outstanding example is *the replacement of cash by information about cash*.

As discussed earlier in the book, for many enterprises information handling accounts for a significant proportion of total cost. The problem for the accountant is to separate total cost into current expenditure, which should be written off immediately, and expenditure on information, which is a true asset that can be valued and reported as such.

Vincent offers observations showing the ratio of average information investment to IT annual expense as 18:1 in information-driven industries and 36:1 in manufacturing industries. He also points to other studies that show similar ratios of 88:1 and 53:1. These ratios do not reconcile easily with the Datamation data in David (1989)[7] but that does not alter the fundamental observation that *enterprises spend considerably more on information than they do on IT.* For this reason the enterprise must establish clear responsibilities for information investment, expenditure, and asset management or, as Vincent says, "The business community must recognize information, not the data-processing hardware and software used to make it available, as its major resource". In the opinion of Strassman *et al.* (1988), "Perhaps the most imaginative of all taxonomies for identifying the value of information is the Critical Success Factors (CSF) method". He then continues with a critique of an executive planning for data processing (EPDP) method, which he says " ... implies a view of the world in which: all gains are attributable to computer technology; all value is calculated based on the costs of the most obsolete technology available, that is, manual methods". He draws the amusing analogy that such a method would "price all existing automobiles in terms of the equivalent market cost of horses", so that the owner of a truck could report a payback on the investment in only 20 days.

Meyer and Boone (1987) report returns on investment from IT that are so high they deserve careful attention. For example, when they attribute an 830,000% return substantially to database search results, Strassman *et al.*, in

---

7 The 1989 Datamation *Industry by Industry Spending Survey Special Report* (Davis, 1989), estimates IS spending overall at 2.3% of corporate revenue, with telecommunications, electronics, automotive, and industrial businesses among the most IS intensive, and retailers, food and beverage producers, and oil companies among the least. Companies in the banking and finance sector may spend up to 75% of profits as IS investments.

a review (1988), ask "does it make any sense to assign almost all of the total value gained to a few computerized database searches? ... this does not allow much for the providers of capital, the sources of technology, the employee teams ...".

It can be concluded that information is an intangible asset, represented strictly by the difference in the value of an enterprise with it and without it and by contribution to future cash flow arising from its exploitation. Recounting an all too familiar scenario of someone with wonderful knowledge and ideas but no tangible assets trying to borrow money from a bank, Stewart (1995, 1996) starts a discussion of the practical difficulties in putting a value on information assets. He observes that "A corporate metaphysician can argue, for example, that Visa International, though it processes financial transactions worth two-thirds of a trillion dollars a year, doesn't exist".

He cites an NCI Research project where "the group borrowed a method to evaluate brand equity". This follows from the observation that the market value of a company reflects both tangible and intangible assets. The method is based on finding a calculated intangible value (CIV) of the intangible assets as the net present value of the amount by which the after-tax earnings exceed average returns on investment (that is, returns on *tangible* assets) for companies in the same industrial sector. He also points out that "A nice feature of CIV is that private companies can use it, comparing themselves with their publicly held brethren; so can divisions or business units ... a weak or falling CIV might be a tip-off that your investments in intangibles aren't paying off or that you spend too much on bricks and mortar".

Stewart's later article (1996) describes the idea of the "knowledge bank" which is attributed to Alan Benjamin who developed it for a three-year study conducted by the Royal Society for the Encouragement of Arts, Manufactures, and Commerce. It shows a modified income statement assuming that the main measurements were creation of knowledge and cash. Capital spending is treated as an expense, and labor costs are divided into current year and future "seeding". Year-end surpluses are expressed as cash and banked knowledge.

The current trend toward considering knowledge and intellectual capital as assets poses great challenges for the business process analyst. The absence of generally agreed accounting practices that are also accepted by taxation authorities and investors means that it will probably be necessary to define standard accounting procedures along with alternative accounting procedures to give management the information to value information assets and assess the extent to which they are being exploited (and to know whether greater returns are being obtained from tangible or intangible assets).

The challenge is similar to that posed by information warehouses where it may be necessary to retain fine granularity of transactional information so that the formal balance sheet and income and expenditure statements are seen only as particular views of those transactions, with alternative views that can be generated to evaluate intangibles, or to support simulation of alternative business scenarios or cost classifications.

It is in areas such as information warehouses and valuing information assets that the business process analyst can make a substantial contribution to business process flexibility by decoupling underlying information models from current views and implementations of those models (for example, by analyzing requirements for charts of accounts and transaction journaling but retaining the multidimensional values associated with every transaction and not losing the detail on journaling).

Key paradigms

The relationships between information technology and business processes imply some fundamental paradigm shifts:

- the first industrial revolution saw movement of people to where the work is located; the current industrial revolution (or third information age) is seeing the movement of work to where the people are;
- many of the traditional roles of management are being replaced by information technology;
- flatter organizational structures are possible through increased spans of control and management by metrics rather than policies;
- enterprises can be much more responsive to their customer needs rather than blindly adhering to an established strategy.

These are at the heart of many new business processes.

Concluding remarks

Following investigations, there are certainly many new ways to organize business processes which are enabled by information technology, and some useful frameworks have been developed to examine such interdependence. This applies in terms of the *technical* construction of business processes, while at the same time recognizing that there are serious and unresolved questions at the microeconomic and macroeconomic levels about the returns obtained from information technology investments.

The business process analyst needs a literacy in information technology capabilities, but what is probably more important is an understanding and fluency in the ways in which information technology, business process, and organization interact with each other.

The business process analyst needs to take a broad view of information technology while examining its applications and avoiding unwarranted emphasis on contemporary computer-based technology. One important lesson from history is that it is the more general use of information which has resulted in radical business process changes over a period of hundreds or thousands of years, and although modern technological innovations have undoubtedly produced an acceleration in the number of alternatives available, it is a continuation of a much longer trend.

The set of business processes for an enterprise will require all the skills identified for the various information ages.

The next chapter looks at performance measurement. This provides a benchmarking foundation to test ideas about redesigning processes to take advantage of new organizational forms or information technology.

Chapter 12

Measuring process performance

The need for quantification is introduced in the Level II process descriptions described in chapter 4, and in chapter 9 it is explained that cost reduction is a frequent motivation for BPW work.

Whether the goal is process improvement or radical new process innovation, it is necessary to establish some basis to assess process performance. An important part of our journey was to explore ways of approaching this assessment.

The result of completing a BPW project is usually a new or modified business system. It is a real-world system working to achieve real-world objectives. As such, a major challenge for business process analysts and designers is that it is usually not realistic to experiment with alternatives, or even to split activity into work done by the old and new processes to evaluate the effects of changes. The best that can be done is to take decisions about new processes based on the best available effort to estimate performance. There is therefore an important role for simulation in predicting process performance.

Performance measurement involves presenting a number of quantitative dimensions of business processes which apply to different aspects of a process (such as the volume of inputs, or statistical distribution of events). Similarly, there is a need for comparison of process performance against targets (this is the essence of what is meant by benchmarking—having some independent basis against which to compare).

This chapter starts with a general discussion of process and performance measurement. The key points are linked to the earlier discussions about OPR models and activity-based costing. This helps the analyst to understand how the various substantive techniques are linked to each other

The chapter then explores data envelopment analysis as a technique for the empirical calculation of the most effective combination of resources that can be used to perform a process that is performed in many different places.

An approach helpful in the rationalization of business processes involves a combination of managerial cybernetics and applied linear programming expressed in terms of data envelopment analysis. This is discussed in the chapter.

Quantification of business processes

An important reason for a business process analysis project is often either to support a report on proposals for improvements to processes, or to support proposals for new processes.

Presumably, the objective is to support recommendations for processes that are "better" in some way (that is, better than an existing process), or to help in the selection from a range of available alternatives according to some criteria that are used to judge whether one choice is "better" than another (that is, between a range of alternative ways to implement a new process).

Many approaches to BPW are intuitive. Where a choice between alternatives is made on an intuitive basis, there is the question of how to measure the resulting performance to know whether there is an improvement or not.

Judgments about the performance of a process may be either *qualitative* or *quantitative*. For example, one process may be perceived as better, although no explicit metrics are available; a new approach may simply be more comfortable than an old one; a new process may be 35% more efficient in terms of the utilization of some input resource.

Thus, there are *levels of judgment* as listed in Table 12.1. Although measures may be qualitative or quantitative, the analyst needs to try and achieve some appropriate level of measurement for performance.

For example, a word-processing system may be considered "better" than a typewriter, initially because the results look nicer. Having the results look nicer is of course a qualitative judgment, but from a measurement point of view, document processing output scores higher than typewriter output according to some arbitrary scale of "niceness". It is not possible to say by how much, or that one document is twice as nice as another, but a comparison is possible. The first measure is classifying the output as either document processing output or typewriter output. Classification is considered by many writers to be the lowest level of measurement, and is referred to as a nominal level of measurement. Ordering categories according to some arbitrary measure (say, "niceness") is what is referred to as an ordinal level of measurement. There are many examples where it is possible to rank categories, but not necessarily have meaningful *comparative* measures (for example, one document is better than another, but it is not meaningful to say that one is three times as good as the other).

Table 12.2 provides a list of all the levels of measurement, along with descriptions and examples. The analyst needs to be aware of these levels in formulating performance measures for business processes.

The other fundamental problem of which the analyst needs to be conscious is that of units of measurement. Every time a scheme of measurement is identified, it is also necessary to identify the units of measurement involved. This will help the analyst to avoid the fundamental error of performing comparative, arithmetical, or statistical operations under conditions of incommensurability[1] One notorious example of this is encountered in a well-known procedure to assess the maturity level of software development processes. The assessor collects data on a range of attributes of the software development process. These attributes involve very different implied measures. Arithmetic is then performed to produce an aggregate score of maturity level, for example 2.7. This is of course a totally invalid procedure that fails an elementary test of commensurability, and is a common mistake with surveys based on questionnaires and interviews.

Level	Explanation	Example
satisficing	there are no specific metrics available for the process, but in overall business terms, the performance and resource costs of the process are considered satisfactory and acceptable	it is not possible to quantify the costs and benefits of the IT infrastructure, but we are satisfied that overall costs are acceptable, and we feel that the support given by the available IT really helps the business
maximizing	some variable in a business process is maximized	some activities (such as delivery to customers) are outsourced because the resources used (vehicles and logistics systems) can be utilized to give higher added value (by supporting service engineers)
minimizing	some variable in a business process is minimized	electronic messaging is employed to exchange project information—this reduces the need for travel to times when team building is necessary
optimizing	there is an optimum combination of variable levels in a business process	varying combinations of labor and capital
possible	a particular goal is not being achieved at the moment, but could be	There are no definite metrics, but the process is possible
essential	a certain level of performance from some process is critical for the success, or to prevent failure, of the enterprise	customer satisfaction
desirable	a particular process would be nice to have	customer delight

Table 12.1 Levels of judgment

---

1 Incommensurability refers to variables that have different units of measure, so arithmetic operations result in meaningless measures. For example, an apple weighs 100 g, a hat has a diameter of 40 cm, therefore the hat plus apple has a combined measure of 140!

Level	Description	Example
Nominal	classification or binary	red, yellow, blue; true, false
Ordinal	ranked	very poor, poor, average, good, very good, excellent
Interval	exact and meaningful differences between measures	temperature (in °C or °F: 70°C is not twice as hot as 35°C)
Ratio	exact and meaningful differences between measures; absolute or non-arbitrary zero	length (100 cm is twice as long as 50 cm)

Table 12.2 Levels of measurement

Following on from levels of judgment and levels of measurement, the process analyst may need to identify appropriate distributions for all quantifiable aspects of business processes (for example, inputs, outputs, events, and the invoking of processes). We have found that traditional statistics provides the foundations to do much of this.

There are many excellent statistics textbooks available, a range of which should be included in the professional analyst's library. Use appropriate measures of central tendency (such as means, mode, and median) and dispersion (such as variance, and range). Where a good fit can be identified, it is very helpful to identify appropriate distributions.

There are some interesting detailed statistical approaches to process design. For example, Brinkley *et al.* (1996) show one case of optimizing the production of circuit boards where initially speed of output was the major concern, but it was necessary to arbitrate between speed and quality. This should bring home to the analyst the potential dangers of minimizing time or maximizing speed. Sometimes it is necessary to ask whether a process is being done *slowly* enough!

In many cases of business processes there are seasonal or similar variation because the occurrence of business events will often be driven by some external factor. For example, in a tax office, the arrival of repayment claims tends to be bunched soon after the date when claims can be entered, whereas the arrival of payments tends to be bunched shortly before payment deadlines. Many consumer-facing enterprises experience increased activity during the lunch time. Stores that open all weekend often find that Sunday is their busiest day. More ice creams are sold on warm days than cold days. Therefore the analyst will also need to develop models of time series to show such process variations.

The other area of statistics used frequently is basic queuing theory. Many business processes depend on the arrival of people and materials that need to be dealt with in some way. The implementation of business processes requires making provision for an appropriate number of servers to deal with the people or materials. This requires an understanding of the arrival, queue and server characteristics. The availability of servers will impact the ability to deal with the queues. Therefore the operational characteristics of servers need to be known. Business process management needs to understand when it is possible to vary the number of servers to deal with variation in queue arrivals.

Efficiency

Judgments of efficiency are based on some idea of "wastage". A relatively efficient process either requires fewer inputs or produces more outputs than another process, to achieve the objectives of the process.

There are serious problems to be resolved about the level of abstraction[2] which is used to measure efficiency, but let's start by setting out the basics.

In its simplest form, efficiency is an indicator of the level of output achieved by a process relative to the input factors of production. Greater efficiency is obtained (i) by using fewer inputs than other processes, to achieve the same outputs, or (ii) by achieving greater outputs than other processes, given the same levels of inputs. This is called *technical efficiency* because it is based on the actual quantities of inputs and outputs.

For a process with a single output and a single input, efficiency is shown by the simple ratio:

$$Technical\ efficiency = \frac{Output\ quantity}{Input\ quantity}$$

Different business units performing the same process can be compared by calculating the efficiency of each unit (giving a set of measures of *absolute efficiency* and comparing the results). More efficient units may produce more for a given level of input, or may require less input for a given level of output. By doing this, it is possible to compute the *relative efficiency* of different business units (examples follow shortly).

It should also be noted that a comparison of the relative efficiencies of several business units performing the same process provides a set of *empirical efficiency* measures. It may be possible to calculate *theoretical efficiencies* against which the performance of particular business units can be compared. Similarly, it is possible to calculate the *average efficiency* of a set of processes, and any business units could be compared against the average.

An important variant of efficiency is *allocative efficiency*, sometimes called *price efficiency*. This involves weighting the inputs and outputs by their monetary values. Thus

$$Allocative\ efficiency = \frac{Value\ of\ outputs}{Cost\ of\ inputs}$$

2 For example, are the efficiency measures for a high-level process such as order fulfillment, or are they for a lower level process such as order entry?

Effectiveness

Effectiveness is very similar to efficiency, but the measure is related to some enterprise objective rather than the technical quantity of output.

For example, one common indicator of effectiveness is related to customer satisfaction rather than output. Therefore the effectiveness measure of a business process can be indicated by the resource inputs needed to produce a level of an enterprise objective.

One measure of effectiveness is given by:

$$Effectiveness = \frac{Enterprise\ objective}{Input\ quantity}$$

Performance measurement

Enterprises set objectives, goals, targets, and similar aims all of which are achieved by processes. We see the following fundamental performance questions arising from this:

1. How is it possible to know whether the various objectives and targets are being achieved?
2. How is it possible to know whether the objectives, goals, targets, strategies, and so forth, set previously remain valid?

Therefore, in addition to measures such as efficiency and effectiveness, the business process analyst needs to address questions of the extent to which processes are succeeding in their objectives.

Whenever there exists (or is created) a relevant strategy study for a BPW project, appropriate performance measures or business metrics are sought, against which every strategy can be evaluated. In doing this it is important to keep in mind the points made in chapter 5 that strategies must be linked formally to other strategy elements such as critical factors, strengths, weaknesses, opportunities, and threats along with the vision of where the enterprise should be so many years from now.

Many required metrics are obvious, such as percentage market share, volume, return on capital, employee turnover, resource utilization, and so forth. These are reasonably easy to specify, although identifying where the necessary data will come from may not be so straightforward.

Other strategies may be more problematic for defining metrics. For example, a strategy may be to create a more flexible manufacturing environment. This would need to be expressed in terms such as time to re-tool for a new product, cost of re-tooling for a new product proportion of output that is mass customized, and time lag between order and delivery. The point is to identify relevant metrics in terms of the service levels to be achieved.

Every critical factor, SWOT, or strategy should eventually be covered in some way by relevant metrics.

What is more difficult for the analyst is to define metrics that will monitor the continuing relevance of the direction set for the enterprise. For example, there may be a strategy to achieve a minimum level of market share Usually market share targets are set because of other factors such as relationships between market share, costs of penetration, brand added value, selling costs, and economies of scale. It is therefore necessary for the analyst to identify the *reasons* for the enterprise direction and define corresponding metrics and ways of collecting data for subsequent measurement and monitoring. Some new technology may arrive that has a fundamental impact on economies of scale requiring a reevaluation of current objectives and strategies.

The definition of metrics and performance measures is really a matter of the careful selection of measurement units that are suitable for the measurement objectives. Juran (1988) exemplifies this succinctly with his chapter 5, *Establish Units of Measure*, followed by his chapter 6, *Establish Measurement*. A feedback loop to establish measures of the continued relevance of the prior measures, should be added.

Some help can be obtained from the literature. Almost all books about operational management use some performance measures. There is a well-developed area of study for statistical quality control which has evolved over a long period to give tools that can be used to know whether a process is producing results of an acceptable quality, or whether some variation is setting in which may need corrective action. Key words for the analyst to look for in the literature are control charts, warning lines, and action lines. Even if such control charts are not used formally for business process metrics, the metaphors of warning and action lines are important for management to focus on performance levels where some important decisions may need to be made.

One survey of performance measurement has been prepared by Fitzgerald *et al.* (1991). They propose six generic performance dimensions: "competitive performance; financial performance; quality of service; flexibility; resource utilization; innovation". They then give specific examples of measures that fall into each of these categories. They propose a framework for monitoring competitive advantage incorporating competitor centered and customer-focussed approaches. Constructing such frameworks is relatively straightforward, but in practice the problem is identifying suitable sources of high-quality data for the desired performance measures along with appropriate models to analyze the data. The problem arises because in reality most firms are working in circumstances where the information structure of their market situation is asymmetrical, therefore by definition the required data are difficult to find or indeed may be misleading.

Eccles (1991) presents several illustrations of where emphasis on measures of financial performance is either inappropriate or can be enhanced significantly by other performance measures. He makes an important point, that "More dangerously, the numbers these systems [accrual-based performance measures] generate often fail to support the investments in new technologies and markets that are essential for successful performance in global markets".

Chapter 8 indicates the serious difficulty involved in evaluating returns on IT investments at both microeconomic and macroeconomic levels. In chapter 11, ways are set out in which business processes and information technology are interdependent in *technical* terms. One point made by Eccles, is that if financial performance measures are dominant, decision making may exclude investments that are necessary to enable alternative technically feasible ways of performing business processes, and the need for the alternatives may be required on technical rather than financial grounds. Therefore performance measures must go far beyond financial metrics. Of course matters of cash flow, profitability, and returns to stakeholders are paramount but this implies interconnections between financial and other metrics.

The kinds of performance measures discussed by Eccles in relationship to specific cases include customer satisfaction, quality, market share, human resources, manufacturing effectiveness, innovation, productivity, employee attitudes, public responsibility, and balance between short-term and long-term goals.

The quality and TQM literature is rich with examples of quality metrics. Many writers, such as Oakland (1991), link quality metrics to cost, recognizing that the quality of goods and services is usually an optimization between technical and microeconomic issues.

Fitzgerald *et al.* (1991) explain a distinction between control and performance measurement in manufacturing, and services, in terms of four qualities: intangibility, heterogeneity, simultaneity, and perishability. They argue for a range of measures that is balanced, stating: "In choosing a range of performance measures it will be necessary to balance them to ensure that one dimension of performance is not stressed to the excessive detriment of another".

One of the unfulfilled dreams associated with putting IT on the desktop is the ability of senior management to control the enterprise (or part of the enterprise) using a computer-based control panel. The panel would supply a range of gauges to show current status and trends, with switches and knobs to take decisions. Clearly such a panel is heavily dependent on appropriate enterprise performance measures.

One elaborate attempt to network many enterprises with an exchange of information to help with subsequent planning and decision making is the work of Beer in Chile in the early 1970s, and described in Beer (1981-1st edition was 1972). One of his chapters *(Corporate structure and its quantification)* outlines the concepts of actuality, capability, and potentiality. These concepts have proved immensely useful in business process analysis work.

Kaplan and Norton (1992) start by stating "What you measure is what you get". They set out to describe their *balanced scorecard* which is "a set of measures that gives top managers a fast but comprehensive view of the business". They make an explicit link to the "dream" when they ask readers to "Think of the balanced scorecard as the dials and indicators in an airplane cockpit". They draw the analogy that a pilot is dependent on various combinations of states, and that reliance on one instrument alone could be fatal. We would add that the dream implies not only the dials and indicators, but the controls as well. A very strong bias in traditional information systems planning is to focus on information *attenuation* (that is, information reporting), neglecting problems of information *amplification* (that is, implementing decisions taken on the basis of the information supplied). So many database management systems and management information systems are focussed on collecting and reporting information, but there is much less help for the amplification of decisions[3]

One project involved a combination of balanced and personal scorecards in a way that provided an information amplification capability to support decision making. Alternative distributions of responsibility to meet corporate goals could be simulated, followed by the negotiation of commitments. A similar approach can be used to help with the consequences of organizational change.

Kaplan and Norton's scorecard includes measures of financial perspective, customer perspective, internal business perspective, and innovation and learning perspective. Goals and measures are established for each perspective. The initial balanced scorecard encourages the identification of goals and measures for the four perspectives, but with rather weak links between the perspectives. Additional measures that are built explicitly from ratios between measures of each perspective, in order to be able to measure interdependencies, can be helpful. For example, they give an illustration of an electronics company with cash flow as one measure of the financial perspective goal "survive", and ranking by key accounts as one measure of the customer perspective "preferred supplier". One part of implementing the link between financial and customer perspectives could be an additional measure that shows the contribution (positive or detrimental) of the various key accounts to cash flow.

In subsequent articles, Kaplan and Norton (1993, 1996) strengthen their initial approach with explicit links between measurements and strategy via critical success factors (1993) and move some way towards meeting the needs for information amplification by describing a personal scorecard that came from a large oil company (1996). They raise the issue of linking rewards to performance measures, but on that point we would caution in terms of all the issues raised by Kohn *(Punished by Rewards,* 1993) which are discussed in chapter 10. The practitioner can strengthen this approach even further by paying particular attention to additional measurements that handle interdependencies between the perspectives.

An interesting project to define a *Business Flight Simulator* (BFS) is described by Holtham (1996) (in Chapman, 1996). It is "concerned with how to improve the performance of groups of managers when they have available an intensely computer supported work environment". Holtham includes a brief but succinct summary of how much computer support today is directed

---

3 Amplification does not mean mere broadcasting – a decision to increase revenue by 10 million next year will not be implemented by just broadcasting the wish; it will need to be amplified by assigning enough realistic commitments throughout the enterprise to have a good level of confidence that the goal can be achieved.

at supporting the work of the individual, rather than supporting collaborative work. Management of enterprises requires collaborative work, hence BFS is considered as a CSCW project. The simulator was a research project. Holtham points out that whereas aviation flight simulators are model based, the simulation of enterprise management is a human interaction simulation with computer support.

Such a distinction is important for the business process analyst. There is a danger in techniques such as balanced scorecard being implemented by means of new management information systems that support the generation of the performance measures needed to check that the enterprise is on target to meet its various goals. The management of an enterprise is a collaborative activity, therefore in addition to the functionality of management information systems (MIS) driven by the need for performance measures, it must also be driven by the need for collaboration between decision makers and decision implementers.

Data envelopment analysis

A fundamental problem for the business process analyst is that a process (or indeed any organizational unit) usually involves multiple inputs and outputs. Alternative ways to perform a process arise because of possible input factor substitutability.

Assuming that a process is performed in several places with some variation in the input factors to produce the same standardized output, the interesting question to answer is, "what is the most efficient way to produce the required outputs?"

According to Dyson et al. (1990), "Data envelopment analysis (DEA) is a linear programming based technique for measuring the relative performance of organizational units where the presence of multiple inputs and outputs makes comparisons difficulty". Several writers attribute the starting point of DEA foundations to a paper by Farrell (1957). Charnes, et al. (1994—based on a 1989 conference) explain the introduction of the term data envelopment analysis to Charnes et al. (1978) as a generalization of Farrell's work to multiple input and multiple output cases. Charnes et al. (1994) provide a collection of case studies in the use of the technique.

The use of DEA requires a definition of process outputs, in a standard way, so that different combinations of inputs to produce the same outputs can be examined. In an interesting paper, Barrow and Wagstaff (1989) point out that one problem with performance indicators occurs when emphasis is placed on measurements of processes and inputs, neglecting outputs and objectives. One example they use is in health care, where performance measures may be developed to indicate resource usage (such as the number of patients per doctor) and process throughput (such as time spent waiting, or number of days per hospital stay). However, the fundamental objective of hospital health care is improvement in the health of patients. Therefore overall performance metrics need to relate input factors to the improvement of patient health. This is similar to the distinction that we make between measures of efficiency and measures of effectiveness.

Barrow and Wagstaff classify efficiency as either allocative or technical. Where the costs of a process exceed their feasible minimum level because input factors are employed in the wrong proportion (given the existing state of prices and productivity), there is *allocative* inefficiency. For example, highly qualified and highly paid staff are used to perform tasks that could be performed by lower paid people. Where the level of output is lower than the feasible maximum given the input factors, there is *technical* inefficiency. For example, there is too much wastage in a process because of poor maintenance scheduling.

At this point the analyst needs some basic concepts from economic analysis. Economists have the idea of a production function. Usually (because the relevant diagrams are usually printed on paper), a production function is shown with two factor inputs used to produce one output. A line is then drawn on the graph to connect all the combinations of the factor inputs which yield the same output. Such a line is called an *isoquant* (same quantity). The particular combination to be used usually depends on the relative costs of the factor inputs. Another line represents the combinations of factor inputs which have the same cost. Such a line is an *isocost* line. The isocost line is moved until part of it is just at a tangent to the isoquant curve. That point gives the most cost-effective combination of factor inputs to produce the level of output. Examples of isoquants and isocost are shown in Figure 12.1. The curves AB and $A'B'$ are example isoquants and the line CD is an example isocost. For this particular example, the relative costs of input factors X and Y mean that for a quantity represented by A', the optimum combination is at Z.

The graphs shown in Figure 12.1 are over-simplistic in showing only two input factors and one output factor. In reality, a business process will probably require an analysis of multiple inputs and outputs. Therefore some computer assistance is needed with the analysis.

In the literature there are three important cases described in the course of building up a general DEA model:

1. one input factor, several outputs;
2. several input factors, one output;
3. multiple input factors and multiple outputs.

There is a substantial literature about different approaches to efficiency measurement. Barrow and Wagstaff characterize the evolution of approaches as starting with performance indicators. Then more research was done using statistical techniques such as multiple regression. They then summarize the position at the time of writing as, "The result has been the development of a large number of new methods for measuring efficiency. All of these have in common the concept of the *frontier* efficient organizations are those operating on the cost or production frontier, whilst inefficient organizations operate either below the frontier (in the case of the production frontier) or above the frontier (in the case of the cost frontier)".

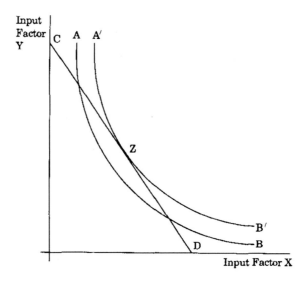

Figure 12.1 Example isoquant and isocost lines.

It is this concept of a frontier which provides the envelope in data envelopment analysis. In the second case listed above in a simple form (two input factors, X and Y, one output, 0), the result is an envelope such as shown in Figure 12.2.

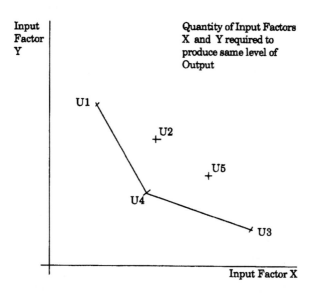

Figure 12.2 Data envelope example.

In this example, there are several points, Ul U5, showing the combinations of X and Y used by the production units UI to U5 to produce the same level of output. Units Ul, U4, and U3 lie on the efficiency envelope, whereas U2 and U5 are relatively inefficient (they both need higher levels of X and Y to produce the same output).

So far, the examples have been simple because they have to be printed on paper (and relatively small pieces of paper!). In real cases, a computer DEA tool must be used.

Table 12.3 shows a relatively simple example of an educational process *repeated in 15 different* ways. The *process is* school *teaching.* The model has been set up with three inputs (number of teachers, number of supporting staff, and monetary capitation per pupil) and three outputs (number of pupils taught, a computed average examination result, and pupil average annual earnings three years after leaving school). In choosing outputs, the number of pupils taught, and average exam results, are examples of efficiency, whereas average earnings three years after leaving school is more of a measurement of effectiveness. A comparison of relative efficiencies even in such a simple case is complex, which is why a data envelopment software package is used[4]

School	Inputs			Outputs		
	Teachers	Support staff	Capitation per pupil	Pupils	Average exams	Average earnings after three years
1	27	27	239.4	784	3.232	9726
2	30	29	202.5	852	3.317	8486
3	25	23	154.7	809	3.231	7211
4	39	37	193.8	1193	2.814	6074
5	42	44	216.8	1390	3.501	8934
6	38	39	183.8	1145	2.237	8445
7	36	35	250.0	1049	2.994	9227
8	36	34	162.4	907	3.122	8735
9	41	40	157.3	1221	3.219	7787
10	66	63	229.4	1995	2.291	9428
11	56	59	230.9	1528	3.919	7386
12	43	39	200.4	1141	2.801	7608
13	43	44	182.9	1029	2.651	8708
14	27	29	175.5	813	3.254	7668
15	60	63	237.9	1943	4 338	7962

Table 12.3 DEA example school data

---

4 The Data Envelopment Analysis package from Warwick University Business School, which implements models from Charnes *et al.* (1978), was used.

The first pass of the data computes a table of relative efficiencies for the different schools. The result is shown in Table 12.4, listing the schools in increasing order of efficiency (from top to bottom, left to right). Schools 1, 10, 15, 3, 5, 8, and 9 are all shown as 100% efficient. This means that those schools are on the efficiency boundary, which is why the technique is called data envelopment analysis; the efficient business units provide an envelope for all the units.

The next problem is to compute the efficiency improvements that could be made by each school. There are possible improvements for all schools that are not 100% efficient. Table 12.5 shows the calculated target values for the least efficient schools (11, 12, and 7).

87-93%		95-100%		100%	
School	Efficiency	School	Efficiency	School	Efficiency
12	87.68	4	96.71	3	100.00
7	89.95	6	97.07	5	100.00
13	90.59	1	100.00	8	100.00
2	93.20	10	100.00	9	100.00

Table 12.4 DEA example: school efficiencies

Variable	Actual	Target	To Gain	Achieved
Targets for SCHOOL11 (efficiency = 87.17%)				
CAPITATION	230.9	201.3	12.8%	87.2%
SUPPORT	59.00	49.15	16.7%	83.3%
TEACHERS	56.00	48.81	12.8%	87.2%
EARNINGS	7386.0	8356.9	13.1%	88.4%
EXAMS	3.919	3.919	0.0%	100.0%
PUPILS	1528.0	1528.0	0.0%	100.0%
Targets for SCHOOL12 (efficiency = 87.68%)				
CAPITATION	200.4	175.7	12.3%	87.7%
SUPPORT	39.00	34.19	12.3%	87.7%
TEACHERS	43.00	36.47	15.2%	84.8%
EARNINGS	7608.0	7836.6	3.0%	97.1%
EXAMS	2.801	2.971	6.1%	94.3%
PUPILS	1141.0	1141.0	0.0%	100.0%
Targets for SCHOOL7 (efficiency = 89.95%)				
CAPITATION	250.0	198.8	20.5%	79.5%
SUPPORT	35.00	29.98	14.3%	85.7%
TEACHERS	36.00	32.38	10.0%	90.0%
EARNINGS	9227.0	9227.0	0.0%	100.0%
EXAMS	2.994	4.116	37.5%	72.7%
PUPILS	1049.0	1049.0	0.0%	100.0%

Table 12.5 DEA example: school efficiency improvements

Data envelopment analysis also enables the generation of tables to show the values of peer groups for each business unit so that the analyst can understand possible improvements in terms of the actual performance of other units.

Actuality, capability, and potentiality

Techniques that are particularly helpful in the rationalization of business processes involve a combination of ideas from managerial cybernetics and data envelopment analysis. The managerial cybernetics approach takes some simple ideas presented by Beer (1979, 1981); his concepts of actuality, capability, and potentiality are shown in Table 12.6. It is important to find quantitative measures for the activities that are expressed in terms of actuality, capability, and potentiality. This may not be easy. When exploring capability and potentiality the scope of the business process involved may need to be altered.

Take, for example, the field repair of laser printers. Customers purchase laser printers to attach to their computer configurations. Some break down each year, and service engineers go to the customers to effect repairs. One possible metric could be the number of repairs per service engineer per week. Say, for one enterprise, that the average is 15 repairs per service engineer per week. That would be expressed as a measure of actuality. Imagine that the procedure is for the engineer to attend the customer, diagnose the problem, order spare parts, and return to the customer to finish the repair when the spare parts are available. Jobs are allocated to engineers on the basis of first-in first-out (FIFO). Spare parts are held in a central warehouse.

Analysis of the key components of this process (the geographical and statistical distribution of service calls, time to respond to requisitions of spare parts, and scheduling of engineer calls) shows that if engineers carry in their vehicles the most commonly used parts, and if calls are scheduled and routed to minimize journey times, rather than FIFO, the capability is 25 repairs per service engineer per week. That is a significant improvement.

Phase	Meaning
Actuality	What the enterprise is doing at present given existing resources and constraints
Capability	What the enterprise could be doing at present given existing resources and constraints
Potentiality	What the enterprise could be doing by dealing with existing constraints and working with other alternatives that are feasible

Table 12.6 Actuality, capability, and potentiality-meanings

Potentiality may require more lateral thinking, and even different metrics. For example, it may be discovered that printer service calls can be reduced in absolute terms by reducing the number of moving parts per printer thus increasing the mean time between failure. Perhaps a more appropriate metric would be total service engineer hours, or even total person hours per printer life-cycle (from manufacture, through use and maintenance, to scrapping). Changing metric would result in metrics that are also appropriate for both actuality and capability. What is important is to have metrics for all three, which use the same units of measurement.

Beer develops the use of these metrics further by suggesting three ratios:

$$Productivity = \frac{Actuality}{Capability}$$

$$Latency = \frac{Capability}{Potentiality}$$

$$Performance = \frac{Actuality}{Potentiality}$$

This is a very powerful way to define process improvement based on some empirical reality.

Many enterprises perform the same process in different places and some variation in the performance of the process in those different places. For example: (i) a petrol retailing company will use different combinations of resources (people, pumps, queues, forecourt space, and so forth) to retail, say, 5000 liters of petrol (ii) a bank will use different combinations of resources (clerks, staff, office space, equipment, and so forth) to manage, say, 1000 personal customer cheque accounts. The fundamental process engineering question is whether the same process can be performed in different places in the same most efficient way. Thus the present process measures become statistical distributions that express actuality. DEA is an application of linear programming, which can be used to compute the most effective way to perform the process (according to predefined optimization criteria). This becomes a measure of capability. Potential resource savings can then be calculated by measuring current resource usage based on actuality, resource usage that would be required based on capability, and working out the difference.

The next step is a reevaluation of the overall process to establish feasible alternatives (that is, potentiality) that can be used as a basis for calculating the resource costs of potentiality. A difference analysis will then indicate the scope for further resource savings. Computing the above ratios will give summaries that are easy to understand.

To summarize, a method for combining DEA and these concepts from managerial cybernetics is:

- calculate inputs and outputs for observed business units: actuality;
- compute relative efficiency boundary: capability;

- identify inefficient units and work out the possible changes;
- identify an absolute efficiency boundary: potentiality.

In the case of the schools outlined above, the measures of what the schools are doing at the moment can be considered as actuality. The exercise of computing changes that can be made in some of the schools to improve efficiency yields measures of capability. Where the costs of the resources used are known, and the costs of a change management program can be computed, it is possible to give good estimates of the cost savings available from efficiency improvements.

Potentiality requires the identification of radically different ways of performing the processes. For example, the schools could move to a more extensive use of information technology to replace or supplement some of the teaching.

Units, resources, and resource consumption in OPR models

The analyst needs to understand the resource requirements of the various business processes in order to provide advice on how to implement processes that can handle the required work.

This can be done by extending the Level II process descriptions outlined in chapter 3. In that chapter we mention the need to define UNITs and add a relationship such as HAPPENS ... TIMES PER UNIT.

Other objects and relationships are also needed. The basic additional model components are:

- an object RESOURCE to be able to define all the different resources used by a process;
- a MEASURED BY ... relation to link RESOURCE to UNIT so that the measurement of each resource is defined;
- a CONSUMED BY ... AT A RATE OF ... PER ... relation to link resource consumption to processes depending on things such as events, inputs, outputs, and so forth;
- a DURATION IS ... relation to link processes to units.

In practice, the analyst will need to express a distribution, time series, or queue by means of a range of units (for example week, summer peak hour, winter quiet hour, and so forth) and then express the different rates of resource usage under different circumstances by linking process, resource, and unit using something like the CONSUMES relation.

There is not yet a seamless interface between OPR modeling tools and statistical analysis tools. On many occasions statistical analysis needs to be carried out independently of other kinds of modeling.

Therefore the suggested approach is to use statistical tools to analyze the available quantitative information, and then design a set of units that accounts for as much of the quantification and resource use requirements as possible. This usually works reasonably well.

Operational metrics and activity-based costing

Cost drivers are introduced in chapter 9. They represent another area for which performance measures and metrics are required.

The main weakness in implementing activity based costing (ABC) is the absence of high-quality data to identify cost drivers and support an alternative allocation of fixed costs. Cost drivers are usually lower level measures than those associated with enterprise objectives.

However, when higher level performance measures are de-composed to identify the components from which they are constructed, many of the metrics needed for the ABC cost drivers will be identified. This provides a complex network of performance and operational measures that satisfy both needs for cost driver information and components of enterprise performance measures.

For example, orders received is a cost driver for the overhead functions of receiving, entering, and processing orders. The dimensions of data for orders received are also components in constructing measures of customer satisfaction in terms of timely delivery of orders or measures of internal flexibility in terms of rearranging production processes. Goods received provides cost driver information for materials handling, but it also contributes to performance metrics related to stock turns and wastage.

Concluding remarks

An important part of the business process analyst's toolkit is the various ways to establish business process performance measures and metrics.

The analyst needs to establish measures of efficiency and effectiveness. Measures are also needed for objectives, goals, and strategies to determine whether they are on target, and to monitor their continued relevance.

It is preferable to establish a range of performance measures. These need to be balanced by the development of measures that are based on the ratios of metrics targeted at specific goals.

The complexity of measures means that the analyst needs computer-based tools for statistics and techniques such as linear programming and data envelopment analysis.

There is a high risk that the implementation of performance measures is biased towards performing information attenuation by providing values to management of the various performance measures. The analyst must also pay attention to the more difficult task of putting in place appropriate mechanisms to support the information amplification needed to implement decisions taken on the strength of the values of various performance measures. This extends the scope of performance measurement from corporate to group and individual.

In the next chapter, the topics of experimentation and simulation are considered. These are quantitative topics that complement performance measurement well, and they should help the analyst to understand the performance that can be expected from processes.

Chapter 13

Business process simulation

There are so many possible ways to organize business processes that it would be wonderful to have a method by which the "best" could be identified before building the organization.

In reality, many processes are put in place in the belief that the way they are organized is better than the alternatives available. The inherent problem is that it is usually unrealistic to experiment with real-world processes, therefore techniques are needed to do the best at predicting how processes are likely to operate in the real world.

Many enterprises have purchased or developed tools to help with the analysis of existing and proposed business processes. The great majority fall into two categories: (i) flowcharting tools; and (ii) simulation tools. Flowcharting is discussed in earlier chapters[1].

Simulation presents a way to play with a *model* of part of the real world, without having to play with the real thing. The essence is that the real-world situation is not being manipulated; usually a representation of part of the real world has been produced in a computer-based model, and it is that representation that is being used for experimentation purposes.

This chapter presents an exploration of the world of simulation. It starts by discussing several general points about simulation, and then goes on to look at important technical considerations from the point of view of the analyst.

Simulation models

There are several strategies to the field of simulation, and broadly they fall into the same categories as those for calculating probabilities in the field of statistics. These are set out in Table 13.1.

Games and experiments

Simulation offers a way to carry out experiments without changing the real thing. It is a way to provide a basis for answering " ... what if ... ?" questions.

---

1 In reality, for many BPW projects, the most frequently used tool is a word processor. Most business process engineers will recognize the extremely limited analytical capability of word processors.

The key lies in constructing a model of part of the real world, and then using that model to predict the consequences of some new process. The value of simulation is dependent on the "fitness for purpose" of the models, and the likelihood that the effects of experiments with the models would be replicated in the real world if the same things were done there as in the model.

For example, the traditional model of banking for individuals and small businesses is that of the local bank, or the local branch of the bank. At the local bank, money is deposited and withdrawn, and assistance is given with the investment of surplus funds belonging to individuals or businesses. The bank maintains the customer accounts in a ledger, and the ledgers are maintained by posting the various transactions that take place. It is common to refer to the cashier and customer interface parts of the bank as front-end or front-office operations, whereas the accounts and ledger operations are referred to as the back-end or back-office operations. In recent years there has been consolidation of banks by merger, and an increase in the volume of transactions involving other banks farther afield. Real estate costs in town centers have been escalating. For reasons of cost and efficiency, many banks have decided to consolidate their operations in regional centers by moving much of the back-office operations from local branches. This involves a radical reorganization and change of business processes. This is also one case where simulation can be used to model the flow of transactions and help to understand the organizational structures and technological support needed to handle the communications and control for such changes to work.

According to Pidd (1992), there are three key phases in computer simulation: modeling, computing, and experimentation. Modeling requires the development of a formal representation of process behavior.

Computing is generally required to be done by computers (in some cases, computation can be done manually, for example with sets of equations).

The relevance of experiments to business process analysis depends very much on the nature of the processes under investigation. Some processes (for example payroll calculations) can be designed with good predictors of the effort needed given the size of the payroll, and nature of documents and other outputs that need to be produced from it. Other processes, for example writing software or assessing risk, are much more difficult to design because there is so much more variation in the factors involved, and indeed not all factors may even be known or understood.

For well-understood, deterministic processes, experimentation is mainly required to demonstrate the feasibility of proposed designs. Thus, given the banking changes described, different levels of transactions can be assumed, and processes can be checked to see that they have adequate communications and control mechanisms.

For other processes that are not so well determined, there are likely to be more random sources of variation which need to be catered for. For example, in some experiments on people writing software for well-defined problems, it appears that more variation is attributable to differences between programmers than to differences between the algorithms to be programmed.

Basis of simulation	Explanation	Example
Empirical	Models of a system can be built on the basis of historical experience and empirical estimates for parameters used in equations which describe relevant relationships. Such a model can be very useful for stable environments, but because parameters are estimated empirically, unless the limits within which the established relationships hold are known, such models can be subject to a "shock" effect if the basic model assumptions change substantially. However, such models may be very useful for investigating alternative decisions which do not change fundamental assumptions.	Models of document production by copy-typists using typewriters—these models can be used as the basis of cost-benefit analysis for proposed computer-based word-processing systems, but after a change, the model may change substantially (for example, increased iterations of documents, rather than increased document productivity).
Theoretical	Models are built from expected relationships. These relationships are usually accepted on the basis of analogy with similar known systems, or abstract theoretical models. They can be very useful in "what if" investigations	Econometric models of national economies—these are notoriously poor for predicting the effects of a change (such as rates of interest), even though they may be based on complex sets of equations.
Experimental	Where there is insufficient empirical data, and where there are insufficient theoretical models, some kind of experiment can be constructed to study the behavior of some process model.	Predicting the effects on communication, control, and collaboration of consolidating bank back-office operations from individual branches into regional centers.
Isomorphism	There may be insufficient data or theory from the immediate field of investigation, but some other field has developed models that prove to be a good fit—in some cases the other field may appear very obscure indeed. This is one major premise of General Systems Theory (see Bertalanffy, 1968) which sees part of its mission as seeking out isomorphisms between models from very different disciplines.	The use of epidemiological theory to study the spread of rumors and fashion.

Table 13.1 Simulation strategies

This makes the definition of processes much more difficult because accurate effort and resource estimates cannot be attached to different parts of such processes.

There is a world of difference between analyzing processes that handle well-defined transactions and analyzing processes to improve client satisfaction.

For a good experiment it is necessary to understand the different ways in which a process could be performed, know what is being measured, and decide how the processes are to be observed.

Where it is possible to play with the real world in some way, by having some groups pursue their objectives using one process, and other groups doing so using an alternative process, the situation is appropriate for formal experimental design.

Formal experimental design is appropriate where there is a number of alternative ways of performing the same process, one of which is applied to each experimental organizational unit performing the process. Measurable (according to one of the levels of measurement in Table 12.2) observations are made for each organizational unit performing an alternative way of doing the process. The objective is to separate out the differences between alternative ways of doing the process from uncontrolled variation (inspired in part by Cox, 1958).

There are also some important rules to follow in constructing such experiments:

- there should be no systematic differences between the organizational units selected for performing the process in different ways;
- random error should be small;
- the experiment should be design to include a range of conditions such that conclusions are valid for the anticipated range of organizational units;
- the experiment should be as simple as possible;
- a proper statistical analysis should be possible without making any assumptions that are not based on realistic enterprise business rules.

For example, in one large multinational corporation involved in consulting, there was a recognition that complex problem solving was often enhanced by a more genial atmosphere (good coffee, comfortable seats, areas to meet for less formal discussions, plenty of plants, a highly aesthetic environment) than by traditional real-estate plans (open-plan offices, individual booths with limited space, meeting rooms to be booked for formal meetings). The corporation then redesigned the office space in some European countries to be able to compare results with those countries that did not redesign.

Such an experiment would give some useful indicators, but of course it violated the above rules for experimental design in that by selecting certain countries, systematic variation (such as different cultures) was introduced.

There are many opportunities for experimental design in the proposal of business processes. There are usually some constraints concerning fundamental business activity and integrity.

Cochran and Cox (1957) suggest a simple structure for draft experiment proposals: "This draft will in general have three parts: (i) a statement of the objectives; (ii) a description of the experiment, covering such matters as the experimental treatments, the size of the experiment, and the experimental material; and (iii) an outline of the method of analysis of the results".

For example, in designing a fast-food chain, there may be uncertainty in how to handle the initial order fulfillment processes when a customer enters the premises—should there be a welcoming person, should the customer be given some time and space before interacting with staff, should information be large and visible from a distance or should it be small and require early interaction close up with a menu? These questions can be explored by some experimentation as long as the business fundamentals of supplying food and being paid for it are met. Adverse reactions to the least favored approach can often be handled by canvassing customers for their opinions and suggestions.

In one bank, which cannot be named for commercial reasons, there was an experimental branch that was able to try out new processes, subject of course to maintaining satisfactory basic banking standards.

Kinds of simulation

There are several different kinds of simulation. This means that the analyst has some choice over the approach—the choice will depend on an understanding of the kinds of processes being investigated and what kind of experimentation and understanding are required. The key characteristics involved are set out in Table 13.2.

In choosing to classify a process, it is important to note that it may be possible to use alternative approaches depending on the objectives. For example, an order fulfillment process could be characterized as a series of discrete events and the handling of those events; alternatively it could be seen as a set of flows. This is similar to the physicist who finds that sometimes a wave model of light is useful analytically, but at other times, a particle model of light is preferable.

From the ideas in Table 13.2, the most common approach is that most business processes are generally modeled as discrete, stochastic, event-driven processes. However, although at a high-level, business processes are often seen as discrete processes, many also contain some continuous systems as components after some degree of process decomposition. Hence journey fulfillment may be a core business process for many transportation enterprises, but the journey fulfillment process includes lower level processes such as vehicle or plane operation.

Why simulate?

There are many reasons for simulation, but given that the essence is experimenting with a model of part of the real world, then the key reasons center around why the same experiments are not carried out on the real-world situation:

- some changes may not be reversible: a new business process may involve the substitution of capital resources for human resources, and performing such a change in real life may be extremely difficult to reverse;
- it is too expensive to experiment with the real world: a major theme in the BPW literature is, as we have mentioned, the radical transformation of the whole of an enterprise and its processes—taking such a step is likely to be very expensive (and perhaps irreversible) so simulation is a much safer and less expensive way to test the ideas;
- it is dangerous to experiment with the real world: many processes involve the destruction or complete transformation of resources;
- the variables involved are not yet well understood: simulation involves experimentation which involves model-building—it may well be the case that equations or models that describe the problem process cannot be defined because the variables or interactions between them are insufficiently understood (for

example, models of a country's economy to support decisions about interest rates);

- the limits within which a model remains valid may not be known: in many examples, as the volumes handled by a business process increase, the resources required may change in nonlinear ways that are not well understood—for example the management of a computer network of 65,000 computers requires a completely different approach from managing a network of 10 computers, and the approaches to manage 10 are not scalable to the management of 65,000.

Characteristics compared	Description
Discrete vs. continuous	A process is either *discrete* or *continuous* depending on how it changes from one state to another. An order fulfillment process will usually be considered discrete because the state of an order is usually expressed as only one of several possibilities; the aircraft used to deliver an order can be seen as a continuous system because variables such as height, position, wind-speed, engine-power, and so forth, can all take an infinite number of possible values.
Stochastic vs. deterministic	For a *deterministic* process, the output of the process will always depend on the inputs and the initial state of the system. A *stochastic* process will respond to inputs depending on the state of the system—the outputs of the process, given a set of inputs, will depend on the state of the system. So the output of a chemical process will depend on the input chemicals and initial states such as temperature and pressure. However, the outputs of an order fulfillment process will depend in part on process states such as which part-finished goods are in stock, and who is sick.
Critical event vs. time-slice	A *critical event* view of a process is one which starts to work in response to an event, and has been completed after a sequence of events. A *time-slice* view of a process, is concerned with all activities taking place (and their interactions) during a particular period of time.
Machine vs. human-machine	Some processes can be modeled entirely by means of a *machine simulation,* where the simulation is set up and run, but some processes involve, say, human decisions, and hence need to be studied by means of a *human-machine simulation.* One of the most difficult decisions for a process designer can be when to leave human beings in system loops, and when to take them out.

Table 13.2 Process characteristics that affect simulation

Advantages and disadvantages of simulation

The advantages and disadvantages of simulations can be double-edged. This means that there are various properties of simulation which in some circumstances can be seen as advantages but in other cases may be disadvantages.

Property of simulation	Advantages	Disadvantages
Cost	Some proposed processes can be simulated at substantially lower cost than doing the real thing.	The simulation of large-scale real processes is very costly.
Skills	Simulations can be very effective ways to improve skills ranging from technical to decision making.	Preparing good simulations is a very skilled activity.
Isomorphism	An appropriate simulation gives a good representation of the real world.	In some cases, a badly designed computer-based simulation may lead to people believing that the way in which the simulation behaves is a good indicator of real behavior.
Complexity	A computer-based simulation may be the only way to model complexity, as manual methods are too slow for the work involved.	Models of complex systems are developed, with major assumptions made to complete the gaps in well-founded empirical induction.
Paradigm representation	Simulations can be constructed to overcome limitations in the usual way that humans do their reasoning.	Simulation may convey unjustified confidence in defective models.
Accuracy	Good models can lead to replicable results, where assumptions are explicit.	Simulation may require excessive precision before the models can be exercised.

Table 13.3 Advantages and disadvantages of simulation

Table 13.3 sets out a range of analytical properties and shows for each how simulation could be either an advantage or a disadvantage. There is no clear-cut position on this, so the analyst needs to balance costs and benefits carefully.

Choice of simulation approaches

How can simulation help the business process analyst?

The most common OPR language was PSL/PSA. In many cases, that is sufficient for the purposes of describing processes, events, process chains, and conditions. The language is also able to define resources and resource consumption for activities (as discussed in chapter 12), so OPR already gives a good foundation for the fundamental model that we have identified.

The late 1950s and 1960s saw the development of a wide range of simulation languages and packages, with several surveys appearing in the mid-1960s. The fundamentals were set down during that period and, since then, evolution has been more by way of refinement and improvements in user interfaces (and, of course, computational power has increased dramatically).

One survey by Teichroew and Lubin (1966) discusses general characteristics of simulation languages and presents a detailed comparison of different packages that were available at the time (some of which are still available on the market, albeit evolved from those early days). They state that "It is convenient to classify simulation models into two major types: continuous change models and discrete change models. Some problems are clearly best described by one type or the other; for some problems either type might be used".

Continuous change models " ... are usually represented mathematically by differential or difference equations that describe rates of change of the variables over time". They were in use before computers because in many cases systems of equations could be managed manually. In addition to differential and difference equations, the authors list calculus of variations and maximum principle as analytical techniques for continuous change models.

For discrete change models they list queuing theory and stochastic processes as analytical techniques. For this kind of model, "Systems are idealized as network flow systems and are characterized by the following:

- the system contains 'components' (or 'elements' or 'subsystems') each of which performs definite and prescribed functions;
- items flow through the system, from one component to another, requiring the performance of a function at a component before the item can move on to the next component;
- components have finite capacity to process the items and therefore, items may have to wait in 'waiting lines' or 'queues' before reaching a particular component".

More recently, Pidd (1992) structured his book to present simulation fundamentals followed by two principal types of model: discrete event simulation, and system dynamics simulation.

Whereas many continuous change models can be used manually because they are represented by a set of equations, this is much more difficult to do for discrete change models. This is because the states of the components need to be known in addition to the state and position of whatever is flowing through the system. This means that there are usually many separate *pieces* of information to track and no devices such as equations to attenuate the volume of information. Therefore computers are generally needed to manage nontrivial discrete change models.

For the business process analyst, because so many business processes are de-composed into smaller components with those components being the responsibility of different enterprise organizational units, and because most transactions can be defined in terms of state transitions, the most common approach to simulation is discrete, stochastic, event-based simulation. That corresponds well to the way in which Teichroew and Lubin characterize systems from a discrete change model perspective.

Discrete, stochastic, event-driven simulation

Many approaches to business processes convey an impression that the enterprise can be defined as a set of processes, each of which represents a range of capabilities that are triggered by some event.

Typically, key business events are linked to some essential transaction such as purchase, sale, hiring, payment, or call. There are likely to be other core business processes that are not so clearly linked to specific events (for example, new product development).

The OPR approach introduced in chapter 4 is well suited to specifying models for discrete event-driven simulation. For the analyst to develop such a model, the major objects are PROCESS, EVENT, and CONDITION. The model is a network (in the sense described above by Teichroew and Lubin) of PROCESSes. Each PROCESS is triggered by one or more EVENTs. The PROCESSes may be subject to various CONDITIONs, and it may be the setting of or change in a CONDITION that triggers the PROCESS. The items that flow through the network, whether they be information or materials, are various INPUTs and OUTPUTs for the different PROCESSes. It is the PROCESSes that perform definite and prescribed functions on the INPUTs to produce the OUTPUTs. The functioning of a PROCESS determines what happens when it terminates for some reason, and PROCESS termination will usually lead to some other PROCESS being triggered either directly or indirectly (such as via EVENTs or CONDITIONs).

There are no tools yet with a direct link between OPR modeling tools and event-driven simulation tools other than using common source material for both. The OPR models provide static definitions of the network, but simulation tools are needed to add animation. Some simulation can be done with the OPR models, but this is by way of RESOURCE analysis, as described in chapter 12.

Pidd (1992) states that "There are at least four widely used approaches to modeling for discrete simulation ... the event approach; the activity approach; the process interaction approach; ... the three-phase approach ... ". For his event approach, the primary object of the modeling is the events affecting the functions performed on an entity (for example, the arrival of a customer and the end of customer service). The activity approach requires a "description of the actions that will always be immediately triggered by a state change in the system". He then gives an example where instead of events customer arrival and end of service, there are three activities, arrival of customer, begin service, and end of service[2] The process interaction approach considers "the sequence of operations through which an entity must pass during its life within the system". It seems as though the three-phase approach recognizes that some events are synchronous, and some are asynchronous.

The depiction of a model as a sequence of events and processes portrays a system as quiet until a business-critical event occurs. Then the processes are activated in turn to process the material or information, and when all state transitions are completed, the system returns to waiting for the next event.

In reality, an enterprise consists of many processes, several of which will be working simultaneously operating on different entities that are in different states passing through the system. Therefore in the literature there is a distinction drawn between these two scenarios. For example, Maisel and Gnugnoli (1972) state "A discrete stochastic system ordinarily is modeled using either a critical-event or a time-slice approach. In the critical-event approach the system is viewed as proceeding from one event to another until a prescribed sequence of events is completed. In the time- slice approach, the system is viewed as changing in all of its aspects over time ... ",

To deal with this kind of simulation, the analyst needs to collect some basic information in order to construct a model:

- information about the PROCESSes, EVENTs, and CONDITIONs as outlined above;
- information about INPUTs, OUTPUTs and flows between PRO-CESSes;
- the different states that each PROCESS can assume (and in practice, we have found that it is helpful to define states by means of a network of CONDITIONs);
- information about permitted state transitions;
- performance characteristics for each PROCESS;
- distributions of each input, output, and flow;
- queue characteristics.

The analyst needs a foundation in queuing theory because discrete event-based stochastic systems are described well by specifying the relevant queuing system characteristics.

According to Gross and Harris (1985), "A queueing system can be described as customers arriving for service, waiting for service if it is not immediate, and if having waited for service, leaving the system after being served".

Therefore there are several separate characteristics that need to be identified:

---

2 This seems to introduce a confusion between event and activity. Teichroew and Lubin (1966) avoid this confusion by their definition: " ... event is usually thought of as occurring instantaneously and taking no time ... activity—represents an occurrence in the simulated world which takes time".

- population: the people or goods which arrive for operations to be carried out;
- queue: the principal characteristic of any queues;
- service: the characteristics of the service facilities that deal with members of queues.

The characteristics of populations of interest to the analyst include size of the population likely to arrive for service, arrival characteristics (for example, whether members of queues arrive randomly or in a known sequence), and whether the population is ordered (that is, are the members of the population ordered or disorderly, and are any goods perishable?).

The analyst will require basic information about queues, such as: are the sizes of queues limited or unlimited? What is the "queue discipline" (that is, questions such as is the queue preemptive priority, nonpreemptive priority, first-come-first-served, or a combination)? How do members of the population leave the queue [for example, some give up after a period of waiting, first-in first-out (FIFO), last-in first-out (LIFO)?

Then it is necessary to know about the pattern of servers to handle members of the queues. Is the system single- or multichannel? How many different servers are there, and if more than one, can they work in serial or parallel? What is the system capacity? What are the distributions of service times? Books are available that describe the details of creating computer-based queue systems, such as Solomon (1983).

At a BPR conference and exhibition a number of tools was available to provide support for discrete event-based simulation. This seemed to be the main focal point for tools development, when a far wider range of required functionality is required.

It is the graphical capabilities of the PC/workstation that have been exploited. Several tools presented computer-based versions of the older layout diagrams (showing rooms, workplaces, counters, machines, and so forth). While others presented block diagrams of processes. Several tools gave some kind of animated output to view processes and queues in "real time".

System dynamics simulation

System dynamics simulations implement continuous change models. The origin of such models is generally stated to be Forrester (1961), although Teichroew and Lubin (1966) cite some earlier work, and Roberts *et al.* (1983) point out that some computer-based simulation work was conducted during the Second World War.

Roberts *et al.*, outline six phases in modeling systems in system dynamics terms: problem definition, system conceptualization, model representation, model behavior, model evaluation, and policy analysis and model use.

Problem definition requires expressing models in terms of quantities that vary over time and causal explanations of the variation. The model will contain a set of causal and feedback loops, and an understanding of the key variables over time.

Ideally the models of causation will eventually be represented by means of differential or difference equations, although it may take quite an effort in model building to produce them.

A major problem for the analyst in constructing system dynamics models lies in the arbitrary nature of choosing some variables. Consider the well-described problem of modeling population. The size of a population is a level, which can go up or down depending on births, deaths, and migration. The population at the beginning of 2016 is the population at the beginning of 2015 plus births during 2015 minus deaths during 2015 plus immigrants during 2015 minus emigrants during 2015. Births, deaths, immigrants and emigrants are all considered as "rates".

One confusing point of terminology in system dynamics modeling is in the use of the term "rate". In common usage, a birth rate is a number which when multiplied by the existing population will give the number of births in a period of time. For example, if the birth rate is 1.4% per year, then the number of births in the coming year is 0.014 multiplied by the size of the population (so for a population of 100 million, there would be 1,400,000 births). In system dynamics terminology, a birth rate is the 1,400,000 rather than the 0.014. The 0.014 is modeled as a coefficient (called something such as "birth rate normal").

Potential problems from arbitrary variables are well illustrated in Forrester (1971) where, in his model of world dynamics, the number of births in a year depends on population level, normal birth rate, birth rate from material multiplier, birth rate from crowding multiplier, birth rate from pollution multiplier, and birth rate from food multiplier. For example, there is no multiplier in the model based on illness or violent conflict. This is not an inherent defect in the modeling *technique*, although it may indicate potential defects in any actual model developed.

As with any analysis and modeling exercise, it is important to determine its purpose, after which relevant variables can be selected. It is also important not to select only those variables that *appear* to be relevant because it suits the purpose of the analyst, but also to select those variables that have statistical significance.

The question for the analyst to evaluate the potential usefulness of system dynamics simulation for examining business processes, may be "can an enterprise be viewed as a continuous process?"

Analysts (and others) have no cognitive problem viewing business processes as discrete event-driven situations. The transition from that scenario to a continuous process can be achieved by seeing what happens to an enterprise as more and more events happen and the capacity of the enterprise is increasingly utilized. More and more orders arrive, the production of goods and services becomes more continuous than just driven in response to new orders, goods and services arrive and are delivered, and so forth. Over time, the enterprise becomes a hive of continuous activity with many processes going on in parallel. This may be less so with very small enterprises, but for an enterprise of any greater size, if most people are doing something useful most of the time, then it can be visualized as many flows taking place simultaneously with feedback and feedforward occurring in many places. Statistical analysis can help to identify whether events such as the arrival of orders can be described reasonably accurately by means of distributions for which the equations can be specified.

For these reasons, system dynamics simulation is indeed appropriate. In fact, it is more than appropriate because investigating business processes by means of trying to set up a system dynamics simulation often leads to a very different set of questions from those needed to establish a discrete event-based simulation.

There are deeper reasons for exploring enterprises as collections of continuous processes interacting with each other. The *analysis* of business processes usually yields future plans of how processes should be or will be performed, frequently based on a retrospective analysis of how things have worked in the past. At the time of performing an action, what is actually done will depend very much on the situation and context at the time. Hence Suchman (1987) observes, "One kind of activity is an essentially situated and *ad hoc* improvisation—the part of us, so to speak, that actually acts ... Plans and accounts are distinguished from action as such by the fact that, to represent our actions, we must in some way make an object of them. Consequently, our descriptions of our actions come always before or after the fact, in the form of imagined projections and recollected reconstructions".

Working with ethnographers on some projects, brings out the importance of situation and context for the outcome of a process, and the extreme difficulty in producing models of this. Six people tackling the same problem will produce different results in different settings for the problem solving, and it is difficult to establish reasonable deterministic models that have predictive value.

At the heart of a system dynamics simulation are "levels" that represent the major system variables. For example, in modeling an enterprise, levels may be cash, inventory, real-estate, orders, employees, customers, and so forth. A level can be envisaged as a tank and is usually represented on a diagram as a rectangle. Therefore a useful starting point for the analyst is to identify the key levels of concern for the BPW work.

Following on from an identification of levels, the analyst should identify flows to and from each level. Each flow will be determined by a "rate". As each level may rise and fall, there must be a flow to increase the level, and another to decrease it, so if there is a level for Orders, the value of the level will indicate something such as backlog. There will be a flow of new orders into the level and a corresponding rate at which new orders arrive. Similarly, there will be a flow of orders from the level as they are completed or sent on to another stage with a corresponding rate at which orders are leaving the level. Obviously, if there is not a balance between the flows, there will be an increase or decrease in the backlog. Cash is a level that will have flows in and out. Generally, levels operate with a true zero and there is no operational concept of a negative level. For example, although an enterprise balance sheet may show borrowing, the level of cash cannot be negative as borrowing must be represented by a flow of cash in.

The flows in and out of the levels according to the corresponding rates are assumed to come from and go to a source or sink, respectively. Therefore for cash, there will be the corresponding cash flows in and out of the level plus one rate for cash generation and another rate for cash utilization. A typical equation for the level of cash would be:

$$CASH.K = CASH.J + \partial T(CASHG.JK - CASHU.JK)$$

This equation means that cash at time K is equal to cash at time J plus the difference between cash generated and cash utilized during the period from time J to time K.

Having identified the levels, flows, and rates, the analyst needs to identify the main factors that affect the rates. This can involve a lot of careful consideration of the points of greatest importance. In the case of cash, what affects cash generation? The answer will include factors such as sales, borrowing, rate of bad debts, interest on prior investments, and so forth, some of which can be modeled as constants, whereas others will themselves be multipliers dependent on other factors. For example, sales will be dependent on order completion and rate of bad debts may be dependent on some macroeconomic factors. Similar questions need to be raised for cash utilization and answers will include factors such as levels of investment, purchases, time lags between fulfilling purchase orders and sales orders, and so forth.

Typically, there will be a network of interacting multipliers. Therefore the level of backlog may affect the rate of employing staff, which will affect cash utilization, which will affect the level of investment, which will affect the rate at which orders leave the order level, which will affect cash generation, and so on.

Taking a system dynamics perspective on the simulation of business processes will generally lead to very different questions being asked when compared with discrete event-based simulation, and these different questions are necessary for a good understanding of the processes at work.

As with many forms of analysis, OPR modeling is helpful to understand the technique, and create a framework to perform completeness and consistency checking.

System dynamics models may include charts. These are instances of a formal language, therefore it should be possible to express that linguistically by creating a language with objects, properties, relationships, and statements.

Table 13.4 shows the range of objects that may be included in system dynamics diagrams, based on such diagrams in Forrester (1969, 1971). He explains (1969) that, "The system dynamicist starts most effectively from intensive discussions with a group of people who know the system firsthand … some of the information describes cause—effect chains. Other information identifies system levels".

Object	Description
Source or Sink	A generalized source or destination for the material that flows in or out of a system level
Rate	The absolute amount of flow in or out of a level
Flow	The flow in or out of a level—if flowing in, it originates from a rate and is utilized by a level; if flowing out, it originates from a level and is utilized by a rate. A key system variable for something that can be considered to exist in some quantity
Constant	A constant value that can be applied to a rate or multiplier
Multiplier or Auxiliary	A variable that affects another variable or a rate
Feedback loop	A connection between constant, rate, or multiplier
Variable name	The symbolic name given to a level, rate, constant, or multiplier, as used in the formulation of equations
Equation	An equation that defines how the value of a level, rate, or multiplier can be computed

Table 13.4 System dynamics objects

There are slight variations from this list. For example, Roberts *et at* (1983) use the term "Cause-and-Effect Link". ModellData (1994) talk about delayed and initialization links. Roberts *et al.* and ModellData use the term Auxiliary rather than Multiplier.

The relationships in system dynamics diagrams are few, and consist of flows from sources to levels to sinks via rates, and cause—effect or feedback (positive or negative) loops to show interrelationships. Therefore primarily two relationships are seen as explained in Table 13.5: ORIGINATES/ ORIGINATED BY and UTILIZES/UTILIZED BY. These are generalized relations that can be applied to either flows or feedback.

The connections between rates, multipliers (or auxiliaries) and constants are defined by equations. These equations are implemented by system dynamics simulation packages such as DYNAMO (see Richardson and Pugh, 1981) or Powersim (see ModellData, 1994). Therefore as the analyst proceeds it is very helpful to define VARIABLE names for levels, rates, multipliers and constants along with a NAME IS relation. It is also helpful to define EQUATIONs as separate objects along with EQUATION IS/ USED IN relations. Therefore appropriate objects and relations are added to Tables 13.4 and 13.5.

Relation	Reverse relation	Description
Originates	Originated by	Used for flows: links source to rate, rate to level, level to rate, or rate to sink
Utilizes	Utilized by	Used for feed back loops: links constant to rate or multiplier, level to multiplier, multiplier to rate, or multiplier to multiplier
Equation is	Used in	Connects a level, rate, or multiplier to the equation describing its computation
Name is	Used to name	Links any object to the mnemonic or short form as used in equations

Table 13.5 System dynamics relationships

Concluding remarks

Experimentation and simulation are essential components of the business process analyst's repertoire of techniques and tools. Where possible, experimentation is more likely than simulation to yield good data about the likely consequence of new or modified processes. There are some important principles to be observed when defining and conducting "good" experiments. However, there are several reasons why it may not be possible to experiment with the real world. Therefore the analyst must experiment instead with models of the real world, that is simulations.

Simulations are important for the opportunity to check out all of the operational characteristics of the system models. In some cases, it may prove difficult to develop full simulation models. In any case, starting to develop models for the purpose of simulation can yield very good insight into process behavior even if the simulations are not completed.

Simulations are usually either (i) discrete, stochastic, event-driven, or (ii) deterministic, continuous, time-sliced. Each type yields different insights into process characteristics and requires different information to be collected and formulated into different models. Enterprises can be viewed either in terms of collections of business process chains or in terms of continuous flow.

OPR modeling can be used to collect information and represent static discrete or continuous models, but additional computational capabilities are needed to explore resource consumption and system dynamics. Many contemporary computer-based simulation tools provide animated displays of process behavior, and these are particularly useful for conveying to people how a process may operate in practice.

CSCW studies have shown how models developed for simulations represent plans and accounts of processes, but the actions of processes themselves are situated by context and the complexity of the real world of work. Therefore simulations should be considered as exploratory and perhaps indicative of abstract behavior, but generally will be unable to capture the whole richness of the processes.

Literature on BPW, competitive strategy, and so forth, can easily portray the world as a relentless struggle against massive, unpredictable, and chaotic forces, frequently outside the control of the best-laid plans and strategies.

Many world-scale corporations, after applying the best available thought to decision making, have taken disastrous decisions and been unable to control their destinies. The same has happened to financial and commodity markets where predicting the next boom or slump evades precise calculation. This should introduce caution into relying on simulations and forecasts.

It is not only the natural world that is difficult to control (and is frequently impossible), but also the human-made world of markets and economics.

Many people wanting new business processes hope that more order can be brought to the chaotic world. For this reason, it will be increasingly important for the business process analyst to keep up with emerging techniques such as the application of chaos theory. This is described by Chorofas (1994) as "applying fractals, fuzzy logic, genetic algorithms, swarm simulation and the Monte Carlo method to manage market chaos and volatility". Another capability that is emerging from the deployment of IT to support simulation and related techniques is the increasing complexity that can be handled by new tools.

Therefore experimentation and simulation are necessary for the analyst's toolkit, but they may not be sufficient, particularly when the goal is to handle complexity and understand chaos.

This chapter concludes the collection of specific techniques and tools to support the business process analyst or engineer. Describing business processes, and checking them for completeness and consistency, follow.

Chapter 14

Business process specifications

The principal deliverable from business process analysis work is likely to be some form of process specifications (and in many cases, ultimately, new processes). The analyst has been looking at existing or proposed processes, and relevant data have been collected. Appropriate analysis techniques have been applied to examine the situation, analyze the data, and reach some conclusions about future new or modified business processes.

There is a very strong thread in the BPW literature about business process innovation requiring very radically different processes, and often a complete transformation of the enterprise.

Business process analysis *per se* does not include design as well, although there is likely to be feedback between analysis, design, and construction. For example, the business process analyst may well have investigated the behavior of customers and staff in a banking hall. Useful information about processes (such as queue and service characteristics) may be available however, implementation of the banking hall, counters, queue barriers, and so forth, is activity that would follow the analytical work.

As such, the analyst is very much concerned with presenting to others how the business processes are expected to work. This usually needs to be done before the processes have been implemented completely.

The practitioner most certainly must support projects that have the primary goal of describing existing business processes. However, the longer term goal of most BPW projects is to improve something. Therefore the practitioner needs to be able to explain techniques that yield replicable results in the form of well-designed, improved business processes, and needs to be able to explain the reasons why any proposed processes are supposed to be "good".

This chapter brings together suggestions for documenting business processes, and for including in the documentation explanations of the basis for proposals to rationalize or improve processes.

Process specifications

The analyst generally needs to know what to put into a process specification or description. What is a good specification? The BPW literature is rather light about how to document business processes. Some ideas have been adapted from elsewhere.

The question of what is a good *software* specification has been addressed by several authors. For example, Blazer and Goldman, in their paper *Principles of Good Software Specification and their Implications for Specification Languages* (in Gehani and McGettrick, 1986), enumerate eight principles of a good specification:

1. separate functionality from implementation;
2. a process-oriented systems specification language is required;
3. a specification must encompass the system of which the component is a part;
4. a specification must encompass the environment in which the system operates, similarly, the environment in which the system operates and with which it interacts must be specified;
5. a system specification must be a cognitive model (that is, describe a system as perceived by its user community);
6. a specification must be operational;
7. the system specification must be tolerant of incompleteness and augmentable;
8. a specification must be localized and loosely coupled.

On reflection, these points contain many important principles for the specification of business processes. The principle that seems to be the odd one out is that concerning a specification being "localized and loosely coupled". The question of coupling is addressed earlier (in chapter 8). From an *analytical* perspective, the decoupling of processes is important. In other words, processes "should" be designed to be as self-contained as possible. In the design and construction of information systems, decoupling may be compromised for reasons of performance optimization, and by analogy, this may be the case for business processes.

Further discussions of requirements generally, are numerous and many are helpful for business processes (for example, Davis, 1993).

Cognitive models

The analyst must be able to represent the results of analysis in terms of what may be termed good cognitive models. This means that the resulting output should convey a good and accurate impression of the target system, and how it will appear to the "victims", or users, of the system.

Most output will be in the form of documentation; however, it is increasingly difficult for documents to convey good cognitive models. As described in chapter 13, tools are increasingly providing animations of processes. The fact that these convey good cognitive models is one reason for their popularity. Where documentation is the output, the analyst needs to make a careful match between purpose and audience to provide the best available cognitive model.

This chapter is heavily biased towards process *documentation*. However, computer-based models in particular, can often enhance the understanding of how processes work, or how it is proposed that they should work.

A preference is for the analyst to deliver documentation along with relevant underlying analysis databases and multimedia presentations of how business processes are likely to work. Therefore the analyst will produce output, and not just documentation.

Purposes of process descriptions

The analyst will need to produce output for many different purposes, a range of which is set out in Table 14.1.

Audiences

The output of BPA will go to different audiences. Earlier in the book was a discussion whether an enterprise can be characterized by 10-30, or 10,000-30,000 processes. How much detail should be included in process descriptions? The answer lies primarily in the level of the audience.

On the whole, the higher the level of management, the greater the degree of consolidation and abstraction. Therefore describing an enterprise in terms of 10-30 processes is likely to be very suitable for senior management audiences, typically board level. Much BPW literature is aimed at very senior management, therefore it is targeted at such a level of abstraction.

The next level of management will need more detail about processes and business functions, therefore the next level of de-composition is likely to contain more than 10-30 processes, probably nearer 100-200 processes, and this is multiplied by the number of departments or functions.

Purpose	Explanation
Contract	As part of the contract between the process sponsors and those who will develop and implement the processes. The Business Process Specification will be combined with a Statement of Requirements, Design Specification and Project Plan. The Business Process Specification document is a document for the sponsors and developers to agree on the nature of the target business processes to be implemented
Design	As the basis for design of the target business processes (TBPs). Ideally, the Process Functional Specification will be convertible into a Business Process Design Specification. A Process Functional Specification will be used by consultants and project leaders to propose one or more design approaches to building the TBPs—this means that the Functional Specification should avoid as far as possible any binding to specific implementations. The Functional Specification should contain design constraints but not design decisions
Communication	As a means for communication between those involved in the business processes. Developing the Functional Specification will aid everyone in understanding what the TBPs will do and ensure that the specification of the TBPs meets completeness, consistency, and behavioral standards
Testing	As a basis for identifying testing requirements, a separate test plan could be developed for the TBPs based on the information in this document
Resource management	Understanding the use of resources in relation to various business processes; providing information to make judgments about economies of scale; providing standards for resources
Documentation	As a prerequisite to producing support documentation for the TBPs. The functional specification document will be a part of the overall system documentation
Process support	This document should be maintained over the life-cycle of the process just as other components of the process are maintained. Thus any changes to the process must be reflected in this document where applicable
Justification	There should be sufficient information to identify the basis for the rationalization of any processes

Table 14.1 Business process description uses

At the most detailed level, a complete enterprise may need 10,000-30,000 processes (or even more). That level of detail is needed in order to implement a whole enterprise. Usually, business processes are being redesigned while retaining many components. Alternatively, the BPW project is targeted at part of the enterprise. This is another reason to maintain analysis information separately from design information. Even though in reality only certain aspects of business processes or certain parts of an enterprise are likely to be changed by a BPW project, it may be necessary to maintain descriptions of associated processes in order to perform tasks such as impact analysis. Even those cases that claim to be examples of radical business process innovation tend to retain much of the lower level detailed processes, which are generally more stable than the higher level organizational structures.

Typical audiences for business process specifications include:

- sponsors of BPW projects;
- consultants with the responsibility for specifying business processes;
- those who are involved in producing the specifications of business processes;
- analysts who are preparing functional specifications, and checking those for completreness and consistency;
- project managers;
- process portfolio consultants;
- resource managers and controllers;
- business process designers and constructors.

Correctness

The correctness of a business process specification relates to the property that, if implemented, the proposed process will meet its business goals. That is, the results of the process will be "correct" in business terms.

Checking a specification for correctness is a difficult exercise because there are no independent criteria that can be put into machine-processable form so that a specification can be verified. Where an OPR specification language is used, the specification can certainly be verified in terms of the structure of the language, and this is explained below in terms of completeness and consistency. There is little by way of independent criteria that can be used to measure correctness. The discussion in chapter 12 explains effectiveness measures. The operation of "incorrect" processes should be detectable by low scores on a range of effectiveness measures.

In software engineering, there are some situations where formal methods can be used to verify a specification, but in business process work, the number and nature of variables are such that computing correctness is almost impossible for the models, but more practicable when the processes are running.

Therefore, the analyst needs to understand that although demonstrating the correctness of specifications is important, the techniques to do so for business processes remain essentially qualitative at the analysis stage.

The analyst should obtain verification from experienced and knowledgeable people that there is a reasonable expectation that proposed business processes are correct. The analyst needs to alert the client to this problem, and not promise more than can be done. Operational metrics can be used for running processes.

Completeness

One of the most difficult tasks for the analyst is to determine appropriate completeness standards for each level of abstraction. For example, in the early stages of a BPW project, information is likely to be highly aggregated with very few objects and relationships. A simple process flowchart only needs process, comes_before/after, part_of, consists_of, and perhaps if condition_true/false—and yet this conveys sufficient information for a very high-level view.

Therefore, when constructing a process flowchart, one completeness criterion would be that every process is involved in at least one comes_before/after relation (the first process only comes_before, the last process only comes_after, and all the others must participate in both comes_before and comes_after relationships). Simple process flowcharts (such as shown chapter 7) do not generally show triggers, therefore a completeness criterion that every process must be triggered by at least one event is too rigorous for that level. However, at a more detailed level, it is essential to know how each process is started.

Meta models are described in earlier chapters of the book. A meta model presents the full range of completeness standards that can be applied for any modeling technique.

The criteria used in establishing completeness standards are listed in Table 14.2.

Criterion	Description
Existence	One or more of the object instances must exist in the database (for example, there must be at least occurrences of PROCESSes)
Coexistence	If one kind of object exists in the database, then at least one of another kind must also exist (for example, for PROCESSes, there should also be INPUTs and OUTPUTs)
Insertion	When an object is inserted into the database, it must be, or may be, part of a relationship; the classical database management system concepts of automatic and manual are useful for this (for example, PROCESSes should be TRIGGERED BY something)
Retention	Once an object has been connected in a relationship, can it be disconnected, reconnected, or must it be left in place? This corresponds to the database management system concepts of fixed, mandatory, and optional (for example, there may be a change in what TRIGGERS a PROCESS, but it should always be TRIGGERED BY something)
Uniqueness	Each object can only be included in the model once; in other words, the names of objects should be unique

Table 14.2 Completeness of meta models

The Level I and II process descriptions explained in chapter 4 are very explicit examples of completeness standards that evolve as a project unfolds. The meta model for a Level I process description is simpler than that for Level II. A set of completeness standards for Level I process descriptions could look like:

- every process must be triggered by at least one event;
- a process must transform identified inputs into identified outputs;
- the transformation process of every process must be described (at least briefly);
- every process must have a processor;
- every process must have some effect on its environment;
- a process may have conditions associated with its functioning.

When it comes to a Level II process description, there are additional completeness standards, such as:

- every process is part_of a higher level process and consists_of lower level processes, except the highest and lowest level processes;
- every process must have quantitative data about its frequency of operation;
- inputs, outputs, and events must have quantitative characteristics stated;
- there must be information to show how processes can be chained together in sequence or parallel.

Consistency

Consistency usually goes hand in hand with completeness. As with completeness standards, consistency standards can usually be derived from analysis or document meta models. The models identify the permitted objects and relationships. For example, it may be possible for processes to be related to each other in a comes_before relationship, which is a two-part relationship. In other words, each occurrence of the relationships has two processes linked together, so that one comes before the other, such as process P1 comes before process P2. It would then be inconsistent to make an additional statement that process P2 comes before process P1. However, the meta model could be amended to place the two process in a three-part relationship with something such as context. Then it would be possible to say that process P1 comes before process P2 in context C1, and process P2 comes before process P1 in context C2.

A concrete example of this rather abstract discussion could proceed as follows. In an order fulfillment system the process of creating an accepted, valid, customer order comes before the process of shipping the goods to the customer. That is the normal case, and seems to be a reasonable procedure—until a very well-known, reliable, trustworthy customer telephones and says that the goods are required very urgently, please ship them, and the paperwork will be delivered later!

In practice, computer-based OPR tools have been used for analysis work, therefore inconsistent statements can be detected automatically. Some tools will take a first statement (such as A comes before B) and then reject any subsequent inconsistent statement (such as B come before A), while other tools merely replace one statement with a subsequent inconsistent statement. It is trivial to state that the analyst should be alerted to inconsistent statements in order that proper consideration can be given to selecting the correct version, rather than allowing computer tools to operate some default.

Ultimately, completeness and consistency rules can only be derived from the business rules represented in the meta model.

When the analyst is dealing at a high level of abstraction, there is likely to be more real or potential inconsistency. It is important that techniques are tolerant of inconsistency by capturing the statements and alerting the analyst, rather than merely imposing some arbitrary rules.

Defining standards

The field of BPW is hampered by the absence of standards. To some extent, this is understandable because the field is young, and no general approaches have emerged as "de facto" standards. Therefore the corollary is present that if there were standards perhaps standards would be hampering BPW! It is certainly the case that many enterprises have hampered themselves with ISO 9000 certification by institutionalizing standards that do not really contribute to the quality of the final goods and services, but are now locked into defined processes that really need to be changed.

The nearest discipline that has grappled with standards for the specification documents of abstract objects is probably software engineering. Most of the standards for software specifications are what can be termed "table-of-contents standards", meaning that the standards typically set out one or more document structures, identifying such things as chapter and section headings.

Perhaps the most comprehensive set of such standards which is publicly available is the IEEE Software Engineering Standards. The documentation standards in this collection are table-of-contents standards.

One essential problem with standards is that they are generally a repository of experience. In a field that is evolving rapidly, and where problems of increasing novelty and complexity are being addressed, the evolution of standards will lag behind the evolution of approaches to solving the new or more complex problems. It is generally not a good idea to create and enforce standards before good knowledge and experience is gained of what really works and what does not.

However, in the area of BPW, the techniques and approaches used are so new that standards do not yet exist. On the contrary, a large amount of experience has accumulated for most of the techniques that the analyst is likely to use.

One frequent criticism of standards is that they impose an unreasonable overhead on projects. Unfortunately, many standards are arbitrary table-of-contents definitions of documents, and complying with these often involves a significant deviation from the critical path of the project. 'Good' standards assist rather than hinder projects. Standards should be designed in such a way that they flow naturally from one stage to another.

In taking a meta model approach to projects, a machine-processable encyclopedia of information about an enterprise or project is preferred (and may be essential if dealing with hundreds or thousands of processes). This encyclopedia (which may be a virtual encyclopedia in that the physical form is represented in many different but linked ways) contains everything needed by all abstract representations. Each document is then a subset of the information in the encyclopedia, where the subset is selected for its particular value to a combination of audience and purpose.

In defining standards the analyst needs to recognize where tool support is available for the analysis and where it is not. In creating business process specification documents, the most common software tool used is probably a word processor, followed by some kind of graphical editor (to produce flowcharts and such like).

The principal reasons to define standards are to reduce the number of degrees of freedom available when teams of analysts are used for a project and to set out minimum completeness and consistency standards.

Several equally valid ways exist to model many aspects of processes. Therefore when several analysts are working on a set of business processes, there is a substantial risk that they will each adopt a different mapping between the process information being analyzed and the features of the tools or techniques being used. Standards are a very important way to provide a consistent way to model business processes. In other words, standards are used to reduce the number of degrees of freedom.

This is a subtle but important point for analysts and the definers of standards. Defining standards is only part of the standards problem. Presumably, once a standard is in place stating the level of completeness and consistency needed for the description of processes, it is possible to use a variety of tools and techniques to produce specifications that comply with the standard. However, for each tool or technique there may be too many degrees of freedom available to ensure consistency of analysis Therefore it is also necessary to produce mapping standards between documentation standards, and the tools and techniques used to implement those standards.

Linked to the question of the use of IEEE standards is the whole question of information systems development (for a summary of such issues, see Maddison et al., 1993). For many BPW practitioners, information system develoment has provided inspiration and metaphors for methods.

Implementing standards: a case study

The process of implementing standards is much more complex than just defining the standards, promulgating their use, and training people.

In this section, one example of starting from software engineering for the implementation of a requirements definition standard and moving to a business process standard, is presented as a case study. Many aspects of this approach were used in developing standards for business process specifications.

The scenario is that it was necessary to provide automated support for the capture of business process requirements of the organization, and then automate the generation of a process specification document from a specification database.

The first problem to solve was defining the process specification standard. There are no published standards for business processes and few for software engineering, therefore the starting point was the IEEE Standard 830-1983, Software Requirements Specifications.

Several audiences for the specifications were identified, including senior management and user representatives who needed an overall view of the proposed processes for approval and understanding. The other main audience was process designers who needed to take the specification and be able to produce a design with a reasonable expectation that if implemented, the design would meet the requirements.

These are very different audiences. The target output document was divided into earlier overview chapters that are more appropriate to those who need a summary and overall architectural view. The later chapters are much more detailed and are intended to provide information to process designers to take design decisions about appropriate ways in which an adequate solution could be designed.

The expectation was that most process requirements would be met by the modification of existing processes or design of new processes. This meant that the specification had to provide enough information to make choices about implementation options (such as where machine or computer support can help). Computer programmers need to know about data structure, algorithms for the processing of information, and control information to handle the sequencing of operations. Organizational designers need to know about those parts of the processes that cannot be computer-based applications. Therefore a process specification needs to contain "enough" information for designers and programmers to know what the target systems is supposed to do, and how often it is supposed to do it. Other nonfunctional information (such as security and integrity requirements; how to maximize work satisfaction; how to create 'happy teams', and so forth), also need to be provided as these impose important constraints on design and coding.

The major differences between software and business processes are that implementation is likely to involve much more than just software, and the inputs to the system are likely to be a lot more than just information. Apart from that, the system designer needs "enough" information in a business process requirements specification to be able to identify different feasible ways in which the process can be performed (to meet process requirements) and constraints on the possible designs (to meet nonfunctional requirements).

A major requirement for the business process specification standard was that the resulting processes needed to be distributable, that is to support distributed and networked businesses, where processes need to be moved around, replicated, dispersed, and so forth, to meet changing business needs.

The business process specification standard has a minimal outline structure as shown in Table 14.3. This would be extended as necessary. This was modified from the IEEE software standard for use in the field by a large number of people.

The next implementation task was to try and automate the generation of process specifications that comply with the standard.

The standard as initially designed was a classical table-of-contents standard, and was insufficient to be able to automate production. What was needed was a database that contained sufficient information that the contents of the various business process specification sections could be "computed" from the available requirements information.

A meta model was created for the various requirements. This was then expressed to the analysts as a set of formal OPR statements that could be made to meet the requirements of each section of the standard. The meta model was a more complex version of those for the Level I and Level II process descriptions set out in appendices. This resulted in a mapping document that any analyst could use to determine how to model each part of a document.

Chapter	Title	Description
	Front Matter	Title page, copyright page, change history, signatures/approvals, table of contents, preface sections
1	Introduction	Purposes of document, intended audiences
2	System Summary	Terms and definitions, description of system, objectives, scope, key volume information, related systems, environment, critical factors, constraints, variants
3	System Architecture	Interfaces, functions, major business events, topology, inputs, outputs, performance requirements, acceptance criteria, security requirements, ad hoc processing, human work satisfaction requirements
4	Component Requirements	For each requirement: description, topology, inputs, transformations, outputs, interfaces, performance criteria, design constraints, acceptance criteria
5	Resource Requirements	OPR models or models of variables, dimensions, and metrics
6	System Dictionary	A dictionary of all objects
	Back Matter	Appendices, index

Table 14.3 Functional specification standard outline

An OPR approach is linguistic, meaning that normally an analyst needs to learn the language to originate source statements. A language-sensitive editor was used, constructed around the specification language, thus eliminating much of the need to learn a language. An easy alternative to a language sensitive editor is a set of online forms implemented in a browser. By doing this, the analyst only needed to identify what construction was required, or which part of a specification. The language-sensitive editor (and equivalent browser forms) then displayed a template and the analyst only needed to fill in the parts where object names needed to be placed. The relationships were already a formal part of the language, and displayed by the language-sensitive editor (and when a browser is used, only the available parts of the language valid for what is being defined are made available).

A very important side-effect of this approach is that when all the OPR statements from each section of the specification standard were combined, the analyst could also work by defining all the various aspects of the processing requirements.

The automation of the generation of process specifications was approached in this way, because different analysts (and not only the analysts) work in very different ways.

There is a very real danger in documentation standards. The existence of detailed documentation standards often changes the behavior of people working on a project, so that the goal becomes meeting the documentation requirements. A process specification is the result of a great deal of analysis work, which needs to be done independently of the final form in which it will be represented. Unfortunately, many projects start an analysis phase by filling in the sections of the required documentation. Writing a process specification should not commence until much required analysis has been done. When analysis is being done, it is usually not with reference to the structure of the resulting documentation, therefore analysis tools need to support analysis work independently of any resulting documentation.

While people are discussing a new system, the level of the discussion can change very rapidly in the course of one conversation. For example, while talking about the overall business needs to be met by the system, someone may talk about the kind of interface needed by system users of a computer-based application. The analyst needs to capture all of these discussions as they take place.

In practice, an encyclopedia is built up during a project, by placing in it representations of the many topics discussed and decisions taken. Therefore definitions of completeness and consistency standards needed to be created so that periodic checks can be made on the contents of the encyclopedia and reports generated to let the analysts know what information still needed to be collected.

Different completeness and consistency checks are needed for different levels of detail. Hence the checks for management information are not the same as those for the system designers.

The completeness and consistency standards are made from a match between purpose and audience, and then expressed in software as a set of interrogations of a requirements database. The software generates output that is a combination of information about the state of completeness and consistency, along with document formatting tags. This output can then be processed by markup language processing software to produce a completeness and consistency report. Such a report indicates to the analysts what information is still required in order for the encyclopedia to contain "enough" information, which also needs to be structured correctly.

This approach to completeness and consistency reporting supports collaborative work towards defining and refining requirements. A problem commonly occurs when the relationship between requirements and development is treated contractually. It is very difficult for people who want a new system to be able to say exactly, and in complete detail, what is needed. Similarly, very few business process engineers are able to articulate how requirements should be stated. What is acceptable usually requires careful management of uncertainty and expectations.

When the completeness and consistency reports showed sufficient detail, or the analysts could accept existing deficiencies, another piece of software was used to interrogate the encyclopedia and construct the document source code[1] for the process specifications. A source code was delivered to enable

---

1 Here, document source code means something like simple text, or of more use for subsequent processing, could be HTML, SGML, XML, or something like those.

the analyst to insert any additional document components, such as diagrams or appendices.

This approach to process specifications requires the following documentation:

- business process specification standard;
- completeness and consistency standards;
- mapping document: to map source material to the components of analytical tools;
- user guides for supporting methods, techniques, or software;
- support documentation for methods, techniques, and software.

It also requires the following software components:

- requirements database management system;
- language schema generator;
- language-sensitive editor for linguistic input, or web pages for browser input;
- graphical tools for graphical input;
- completeness and consistency check procedures;
- encyclopedia reporting;
- business process specification standard schema;
- business process specification document source generator;
- document processing.

Suggestions for business process documentation

If the target system is a set of business processes then what documentation should be produced?

The original specification environment was modified for describing business processes, and this has provided a very useful part of my analytical toolkit.

The specification outlined in Table 14.3 needed some modification, therefore chapter 5 refers to a resource model and not just a, data model. Many sections were found to be appropriate when extended to all aspects of business process, even though they were originated from software development.

A specification for business processes is only one document; other documents may be generated depending on the needs of the project. The following documents have been produced in addition to the documents listed above in the case study:

- existing process audit;
- management requirements;
- user requirements;
- functional requirements;
- nonfunctional requirements;

- logical specification;
- design constraints;
- physical specification (organization, manual, automated);
- risk assessment and management;
- implementation plans.

All of these documents are in addition to normal project documentation that covers terms of reference, scope, and project plans. As well as the more formal documents, the analyst will need workbooks to hold notes, and records of the analysis of data.

It is important for the analyst to document the reasons why proposed business processes are considered to be efficient and effective. This justification should be incorporated into the documentation. Figure 14.1 presents a chart of possible key documents.

Reports

Business Process Specifications
Consistency and Completeness Reports
Business Process Design Specifications
Business Process Metrics
Tool X Mapping Document

Standards

Business Process Requirements Specification Standards
Completeness and Consistency Standard
Analysis Tools Mapping Standard
Business Process Design Specification Standard
Business Process Language Reference Manual

Figure 14.1 BPA key documentation.

Of course, this may all seem very intimidating on initial reading! However, keep in mind that business process engineering may be addressed to a complete organization. That is a non-trivial task. Returns on investment in BPW can be spectacular, or merely modest. The acid test is that the returns on investment from a project exceed the returns otherwise available using the money for some other organizational purpose. In many examples of BPW in recent years, substantial returns on investment have been achieved improving a limited number of processes; it is not necessary to take on the whole organization to obtain beneficial results.

The next chapter explores business process architecture, engineering, and management.

Business process architecture, engineering, epistemology, management, maturity, ontology, etc.

Throughout this book, the term BPW has been used. BPW means Business Process Work. This is in no sense a derogatory term. It was chosen simply because the term business process is followed by many different other words BPW is used as a generic expression to mean any or all of those terms beginning with BP. That term was established in the first edition of the book. Since then, more words have been added after 'business process' making it even more useful to have onw expression to include all such terms.

Some words that followed BP have more extensive use than others. For example, business process analysis, business process architecture, business process engineering, business process management, business process redesign, business process re-engineering, business process improvement, and so forth.

So far, most of the book has been concerned with business process analysis skills, which has been taken to cover a very wide range of activities.

This chapter looks in more detail at several other terms commencing with BP.

There is much overlap in the subject matter covered by the way the various terms are used. Therefore choice of term is more in the hands of the user, and the reader should look at a variety of materials whatever term they are delivered under.

Business process engineering

In the early days of BPR, many writers interpreted the R as meaning re-engineering (the other interpretation for the 'R' is redesign). As pointed out earlier, if BPR is business process re-engineering, in what sense were processes engineered in the first place?

There is very wide scope for the interpretation of the word engineering. A relatively strict interpretation is found in the Oxford English Dictionary which suggests that engineering is regarded as a field of study especially that part which can be treated according to the laws of mathematics and physical sciences.

Generally, BPW activity is not concerned with the laws of mathematics and physical sciences! That observation gives rise to comments to the effect that the word engineering implied by one interpretation of the expression BPR is inappropriate because of the unlikelihood that there was ever any engineering in the first place, and that engineering is not an appropriate term covering the replacement of existing business processes, or the creation of new business processes.

Are there any interpretations of the word engineering which would permit a much more liberal application of the word?

Nadler (1992) suggests for engineering that "its meaning is synonymous with technology and the economic application of the materials and forces of nature". The editor of the book in which Nadler's book section appears takes an even wider interpretation. His view (Salvendy, 1992) suggests engineering is about "...the application of knowledge to solving real-world problems". There is no doubt that all activity falling under the BPW banner can be classified as the application of knowledge to solving real-world problems. In this sense, BPR can accommodate the concept of engineering.

At different points in this book, the term business process engineer has been used where the term business process analyst would be equally applicable. Therefore, to all intents and purposes this book takes the view that there is no added value from using the term engineering, but writers should feel free to do so if they feel that helps the points they are trying to make. Interpretation of the term BPR as business process reengineering is stretching use of the word engineering to the limits of a liberal interpretation.

It seems that use of the word engineering dates from around late 18th century. However, the word engineer has much earlier origins. The Oxford English Dictionary attributed it to Middle English or old French. An engineer is a person "who contrives, designs, or invents". It is reasonable to assert that the person who does BPW work is contriving, designing, or inventing!

Thus, although for many people, use of the word engineering in a context of BPR is deprecated, there is no good reason why it should not be tolerated or accepted.

Business process architecture

There are hints in the literature about the concept of a business process architecture.

It is somewhat surprising that such a concept has not received more attention. It may be that many BPW practitioners see little difference between concepts such as business process architecture, enterprise architecture, or information architecture.

As with other sections of the book, let's take a journey back in time to see if there are any prior ideas we can start to build on.

What is 'architecture'? As with other terms, the Oxford English Dictionary is a helpful starting point. Architecture is "The art or science of building or constructing edifices of any kind for human use" (OED, 2009). The dictionary goes on to point out that the word is frequently qualified by an adjective to indicate what kind of architecture is the subject of concern. Thus they go on to explain that some branches of architecture are "civil, ecclesiastical, naval, military", and thus by implication, there are different types of architecture.

Moving into the modern world, the OED indicates the use of architecture with reference to computing: "The conceptual structure and overall logical organization of a computer or computer-based system from the point of view of its use or design; a particular realization of this".

Webster's Dictionary does not go beyond buildings (but it does have a very interesting full-page table of different forms of building architecture).

Building on the OED entry for computing architecture suggests something along the following lines: "Business process architecture is the conceptual structure and overall logical organization of business processes or business process based systems from the point of view of its use or design; a particular realization of this [the business process architecture]".

This definition, building on the OED ideas, is interesting because it hints immediately at the use of business process architecture at different constructor levels corresponding to Figure 4.1 (see Table 15.1).

There is a discussion about business process architecture in Barros (2007). That paper identifies a number of ways in which processes have been grouped by different commentators in the field. They go on to identify a set of macro processes that they claim is based on an empirical base of projects "...covering all the processes and enterprise needs to perform in a coordinated way". Process architecture may be equated to an enterprise-wide process view of the business (Hegedus, 2008).

The macro processes in various papers are very similar to the business processes shown horizontally in Figure 2.3 (originally from Darnton & Giacoletto, 1992).

Everything in the Barros paper can be modelled by the OPR approach described in this book, but the paper sets out what is primarily a graphical language. The contents of the Barros general BP architecture and subsequent sections discussing that architecture, can be related directly to the layers in the meta-meta language pyramid (figure 4.3).

However, to make extensive use of the Barros approach for any significant project, and be able to have confidence that models could be checked for completeness and consistency, would require translation from those graphical language elements to an appropriate OPR (metaPSL generated) linguistic (i.e. not diagrammatic) language.

Hegedus (2008) has a classification of three process categories: core; management; enabling (p59).

Two architecture frameworks that have evolved from the IS/IT worlds are: Zachman (Zachman, 2008 evolved from Zachman 1987 and his work in IBM) and Darnton and Giacoletto (1992 evolved from their work in DEC—Digital Equipment Corporation).

The evolution of the Zachman Framework is described in Zachman (2009), incorporating some of his personal overheads used in addition to publications, going back to 1984. The original published version was 1987. A major extension to the 1987 version was published in 1992 (Sowa and Zachman, 1992). At that point it was still called an Information Systems

Architecture. However, in terms of both structure and content, Fig 6 of that 1992 paper (p600-1) would be instantly recognizable because of its substantial similarities to today's Enterprise Architecture Framework. Around 2004, the top row of Data, Function, Network, People, Time, and Motivation was changed to today's What, How, Where, Who, When, and Why, although that mapping appeared in Table 7 of the 1992 paper. Presumably, work started before 1984.

Constructor Level	Business Process Architecture Instantiation	Discussion
metameta-language	OPR	This is the high-level starting point to be expanded and instantiated at different layers. This will ensure that consistency is enforced at all layers, and enable the definition and execution of related completeness and consistency checks however large the model.
metalanguage	Business Process Architecture Language	A meta language for business process architectures. Some components may be stated as mandatory, and some may be optional.
model or language	Business Process Architecture of a particular organization	The business process architecture language is used to describe the business process architecture of a particular organization.
subject	The business processes of a particular enterprise	Different enterprises will want their own specific business process architecture

Table 15.1 - Business Process Architecture Metamodelling Levels

Zachman's architecture, although its chart has 7 rows, is really a 5-level architecture, the 5 levels being Business (that was called Enterprise in 1992), Systems, Technology, Implementation, and Operations. For copyright reasons, the Zachman framework is not reproduced here, but it is easy to see online.

During the 1980s IBM was working on its Information Systems Architecture, and DEC was working on its Information Architecture.

At the beginning of the 1980s, work on DEC Europe's Information Architecture started with an Enterprise Planning Framework (EPF - see Figure 15.1) inspired by the work of Pascale and Athos (1981) and Waterman et al. (1980). This early architecture model was created to support:

- vertical integration from business needs to operational systems;
- horizontal integration at the business and systems levels to ensure the definition of cooperating cross-functional processes;
- horizontal integration at he technology and product levels to define and implement common infrastructure.

This was used to align the business, systems (manual or automated), organization, competencies (called skills for simplicity, but in reality more than skills), processes, monitoring, etc.

Figure 15.1 Enterprise Planning Framework (EPF)

Work was done to explore what critical success factors were implied by that EPF. The result is shown in Figure 15.2.

The EPF was examined to extract the elements of *information relevance* in order to construct an information architecture. As with all such constructs, there is some arbitrariness in the final choices made, but the overall scheme for the information architecture is shown in Figure 15.3:

- the Business Architecture sets out the overall information needs of the enterprise (or, as is often the case, a specific strategic business unit where the architectural work is being done);

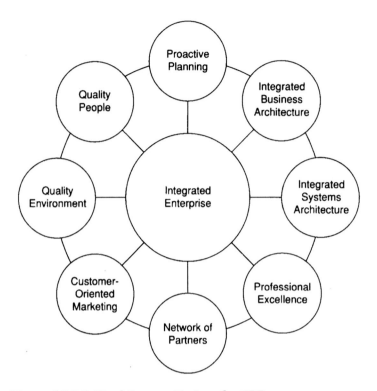

Figure 15.2 Critical Success Factors for EPF

■ a Systems Architecture identifies the interrelated set of information processing systems, along with associated priorities and organizational success criteria—note that this does not imply only computer-based information processing systems; some will have computer support, and some will not;

■ a Technical Architecture that is a product-independent identification of information processing environments and the design principles that apply to them; again, this is not restricted to computer-based technology—in many situations, paper is an appropriate technology, or any other information machines set out in Machlup's classification scheme (Machlup, 1962: 295-322); the Technical Architecture is perhaps the most difficult to conceptualize—it is NOT a technology architecture—it is concerned with technological principles that will guide the selection among technical choices;

■ a Product Architecture that sets out the technological choices made to realize the technological principles in the Technical Architecture.

There is always a substantial risk that something like an Information Architecture is seen primarily in technological terms. That is a fundamental error when of all information work (or play) done in an enterprise, only about

10% is computer-based, and much information work has no computer or technology support at all.

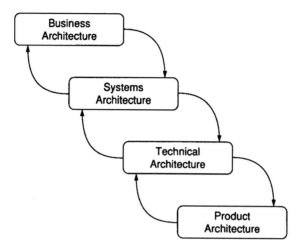

Figure 15.3 Information Architecture

For this reason, a variant was produced (shown in Figure 15.4) indicting that in an enterprise there are computer-supported information systems, and aspects of enterprise organization. Even non-computer-based activities, may be computer-supported, by IT infrastructure and some automated business procedures.

Thus, 'architecture' incorporates issues such as business, systems, technology, technical principles, products, organization, operations, people, resources, and competence. Business process architecture is concerned with processes that affect all of these issues. A business process architecture covers processes that apply to some or all of these.

Business Process *Architecture* is about describing and designing processes; it is not the processes themselves. An architect is not a builder. Architectural drawings are not finished buildings. A business process *architecture* sets out what business processes to implement.

Business process epistemology

Business process epistemology is the 'black sheep' of the BPW family because there is no BPW field in which that term is 'mainstream'. In itself, that may not be a problem, but what is ironic is that there is an emerging field of business process ontology but not business process epistemology. Why not? In many senses, because BPW is very much concerned with the real world and real world processes, it is far more logical that a business process epistemology should have evolved rather than a business process ontology, which must start from a profoundly abstract concept (business process ontology is discussed below).

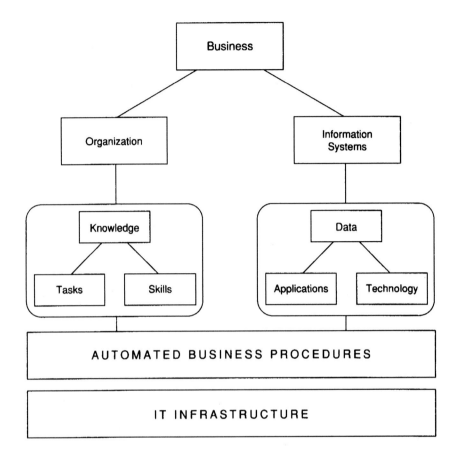

Figure 15.4 Enterprise Information Management Model with IT

Epistemology can be considered to be "The theory or science of the method or grounds of knowledge" (OED, 2009). Webster is in substantial agreement with that. However, a definition like that does need some unpacking to help the reader!

Putting on one side, the complex philosophical debates about how we can ever know that anything is real or true, in very down-to-earth practical terms, epistemology is concerned with knowing things and having proof, or experience, to underpin our knowledge, so that knowledge goes beyond mere belief or faith; i.e. validated knowledge.

So many management decisions are acts of faith, not knowledge, because they don't know whether their decisions will be successful or not until they have tried. A harsher statement in the context of this book, is that some writers who advocate various things related to business processes, but in reality, until they have been tried, they don't *know*. Perhaps this is why there is a preference for ontology and its implicit abstraction rather than epistemology with its implication of evidence!

When process descriptions are generated for processes we know happen, we are not really talking about process *ontology*, we are talking about process *epistemology*. When I look at the hierarchical scheme of wine in Noy and McGuiness (2001), it looks to me much more like epistemology than ontology - but it's called ontology. In several analytical worlds, not only business process, there is a distinct subculture of ontology emerging which is using the term 'ontology' in a very idiosyncratic way—if you are in love with the word ontology, be careful!

Business process epistemology should be at the very heart of BPW, because we really need to *know* whether our ideas are good ideas or not. So many companies have failed following their strategy into oblivion. Why?—because the strategy was based more on *belief* and *faith* than on *knowledge*.

Core competence probably requires a systemic view of the organization, not a process view. An organization that is particularly successful in what it does is a complex system that behaves in particular ways with benefit from the emergent properties of the system. This is epistemological reality. The managers may or may not know what is the 'magic' that makes the organization particularly more successful than its competitors. A neo-ontological[1] approach involving decomposition of higher level processes into lower levels, with formal definitions of those processes, is at extremely high risk of throwing away all the emergent properties of core competence. It's the age old question—if company X is highly successful in its industry and ahead of its competition in some important respects, why can't other companies simply replicate company X's processes and be at least equal? The answer lies in the emergent properties of the Company *viewed as a system*. That is an epistemological issue, not ontological.

Having said that, ontology can come to the rescue by building metametamodels, metamodels, and models in such a way that captures and reflects the emergent properties of the system as well as the process views.

Thus, epistemological and ontological views can be brought together by adding those views to Figure 4.1, resulting in Figure 15.5.

Business process management

The emerging field of business process management (BPM) has several interesting dimensions to it. For this reason, it is a field of study that is not yet well-defined in that different people and organizations, take different views about what it means (Hegedus, 2008; Wolf & Harmon, 2012)

The current lack of a clear definition of BPM has not prevented (and indeed maybe it inspired) the emergence in recent years of some interesting and useful empirical studies that give good background to what issues various organizations consider as falling within the remit of BPM (Hegedus, 2008;

---

1 The term 'neo-ontological' is being used for modern 'ontologies' and approaches to ontology, which are not based soundly on highly abstract objects with constructor principles applied when generating lower levels.

Patig & Casanova-Brito 2012; Wolf & Harmon 2012).

Keep in mind that we are talking about *Business Process* Management; we are NOT talking more generally about *Business* Management.

Taking a classical life-cycle view, this means that the matters of concern are the creation, use, maintenance, and cessation of *business processes*. We will return to this shortly to propose a definition of BPM.

For the purpose of considering this, let me set out a discussion I have had with many students when talking about business processes. The situation is replete with some very modern technology to enhance the discussion.

What is the life-cycle involved in a carton of milk? We are talking about milk obtained from cows. The life-cycle of an alternative such as soya milk is different. Business processes can be derived from knowing the product life cycle.

Assume that the carton of milk has a barcode on it, at a minimum to support retailing activities, although it may have wider functions such as product tracing. A consumer has a very smart barcode reading capable refrigerator and garbage can. The consumer has hooked up the barcode reading capabilities of the refrigerator and garbage can, to a supermarket online ordering system.

The consumer throws away the used carton of milk in the garbage can. The 'intelligent' garbage can reads the barcode. The refrigerator stock is checked, and the domestic stock control system adds more milk to the online order for the supermarket. The supermarket delivers the new carton of milk, and has its own stock control system to manage re-ordering from the milk distributor co-op. The milk distributor co-op orders from the farmer who has the cows who produce the milk. The farmer is connected back to the veterinary surgeon who needs to call from time to time to the farm to impregnate the cows. The vet needs to go from time to time to obtain more sperm from bulls for the cow impregnation service.

Firstly, a side comment. Having run this exercise with students a few times, it was astonishing how many students (and some colleagues!) did not realize that cows do not simply walk around fields eating grass and making milk; they need to be pregnant to make milk! They had no understanding of why many vegans take moral objection to the milk industry because of the slaughter of calves to retain as much milk produced by the cows as possible. In India, where cows can be sacred, there is widespread belief that cow milk can be shared between calves and humans, removing any need to slaughter calves. There can be many unexpected dimensions to some business processes.

The fundamental issue about this milk supply chain from bull to consumer garbage can is what is the business process? Is it one process, or many processes?

This problem is not only milk. How about a car from a car dealer? The car has a manufacturer badge on it, but it is almost certain that various products and services were outsourced. The final car manufacturer may not even know the whole chain of other companies involved in the supply chain to produce the finished vehicles they sell. It is probably only the aircraft manufacturing industry that is supposed to have complete traceability of all components in an aircraft.

This problem is fundamental to BPW at this point in time. The vast majority of BPW literature is concerned with business processes *within* an enterprise. This begs the question, is BPW only concerned with *intra*-company processes, or does it include *inter*-company processes also?

Of course, when it comes to the manufacture of a car with extensive outsourcing of components and services, the final manufacturer as supplier of the finished product, is only demarcated by being a distinct legal entity. That also has important consequences as far as business process management is concerned, because there may well be no management of the complete set of business process to produce the final product. Therefore, demarcation of legal entities in a process, is mirrored by demarcation of process management responsibilities. However, that does not remove the analytical problems arising from trying to understand the high-level business process of 'supply milk to the consumer', or 'supply a car to the end-user'.

This problem of business process scope is being recognized slowly in the literature, including some empirical investigation (Patig & Casanova-Brito, 2012; for example, their Table 4-1, and conceptually, Figure 4-1).

The BPTrends report (Wolf & Harmon, 2012, and their earlier reports) is extremely helpful in understanding the current state of practice. Their discussion in terms of CMMI is less convincing in the absence of any data showing a statistically significant correlation between business process maturity (see below) and successful business process management. Until there is such empirical evidence, BPMM remains an ideological artefact, and much less reliance can be placed on the report's "What is much more exciting is the increase in process maturity" (p6). If there is a negative correlation between maturity level and quality, as can be inferred by an interpretation of the original CMM published data, this 'increase in process maturity' would be bad news, not good. As discussed elsewhere, the trick at the moment in making good use of BPMM is considering their characteristics as a flat menu, ignoring the classification into maturity levels. However, putting that on one side, there is much interesting information in that report and it should be read by every BPW practitioner and academic.

The BPTrends report also classifies the BPM activity resulting from their survey in a way reminiscent of the 'Anthony Pyramid, or triangle (Anthony, 1965) with Strategy, Process, and Implementation as the levels, rather that Strategic, tactical, and Operational as levels of management.

An interrerting feature of the BPTrends report is the absence of data from Asia. Is this because Asia was not surveyed, or because the attitude to process in Asia is radically different from the West?

Given the current lack of consensus about the scope of BPM, and indeed the very scope of business processes, a definition of BPM based on a business process life-cycle may be the most appropriate:

'BPM is the *management* of the creation, use, maintenance, and cessation of business processes.'

Thus, current debates about methods, methodology, classification schemes, maturity, and so forth can be side-stepped with a definition that provides a 'broad church' for all the approaches currently being explored.

The various foci of BPM can be derived from the discussion above, about business process architecture.

Business process maturity

In terms of one of the cartoons in Chapter 14, the Object Management Group's Business Process Maturity Model (BPMM, 2008) certainly passes the poundage test at 496 pages!

BPMM follows a long line of maturity models that have been developed following the initial work and outputs from the work at Carnegie Mellon University in the late 1980s. This origin is acknowledged explicitly in the BPMM document. Therefore, it may be worthwhile just taking a quick look at those origins to see if there are any important lessons for maturity models generally, and to reflect on whether such lessons have been taken on board.

The Software Engineering Institute's (SEI) original proposal for a Capability Maturity Model (CMM) was published in 1987 followed by consolidating publications (Humphrey and Kitson, 1987; Humphrey, 1988; Humphrey, 1989). The 'problem' to be solved was that the US Department of Defense had experienced high variability in the quality of delivered software, and wondered if there was some way to pre-screen potential contractors at the bidding stage. SEI's CMM has 5 levels of maturity.

The SEI started on the back of a remarkable comment that "The quality of a software product is governed largely by the quality of the process used to develop and maintain it" (SEI Bridge Fall/Winter 1987). No data was offered about the software products studied, qualitative measures used, or variance calculations to show how the assertion that the quality of the process was actually the most important factor (what about the skill levels of those doing the work?). This begins to have an aroma of ideology and faith about process, rather than looking at outputs. Even more remarkably, two years later in 1989 the SEI published data claiming that a study of 113 projects had yielded 85% at level 1, 14% at level 2, 1% at level 3, and none at levels 4 or 5. At the time, there was a lot of 'tut-tutting' about how terrible it is that no organizations are yet at levels 4 or 5. Of course, the more hard-nosed statistician, living more in an epistemological world than ontological would ask, "if there are no projects at levels 4 or 5, where is the empirical evidence that those levels exist and are more than a mere figment of someone's imagination and more a creation of ideology and prescription?".

As if that was not enough to raise alarm bells about the lack of a satisfactory empirical underpinning of the CMM, another two years later in 1991, a paper comparing US and Japanese software projects was published (Humphrey et al., 1991). After commenting about how good the Japanese projects were, and application of CMM to those projects resulted in many being in the bottom quartile of CMM Level 1. This all raises very serious doubts about the reliability and validity of CMM. Indeed, it even makes it reasonable to put on the table an hypothesis that software quality is inversely correlated with assessed maturity level!

Since that early history of CMM there has been a proliferation in maturity models. In the absence of sound empirical data, the principal conclusion that can be drawn is that at a minimum, achieving certification of some maturity level is a business issue, and not necessarily a technical issue—get certification if you can't bid for work without it—whether the quality of work is good or not, may well be a different issue. In pure business terms, the next best thing to having high-quality outputs is conveying the illusion of high-quality outputs.

Now, what about BPMM (Business Process Maturity Model)? The basic document contains no references to empirical data to show any statistically significant correlation between maturity level and other dimensions of managing business processes, or more particularly, improving them. If there is no such empirical data, then BPMM is essentially only a conceptual construct and it is not easy to know if achieving higher levels of maturity would lead to improved processes, which are performing better than if those processes had been improved without the maturity level.

There may be commercial reasons why certain maturity levels are needed. If this is the case, then pursue them.

Looking at all the things that could be done according to the BPMM, there is a lot of advice to be considered. Therefore, my personal view is that as a flat menu of things to think about, the BPMM contributes much value. It will be interesting to see results when empirical studies can be carried out.

Business process ontology

As hinted in the discussion above about business process epistemology, another term that has emerged and which can be included in the BPW family of terms, is 'business process ontology'.

In recent years, the term ontology has been used increasingly in a variety of analysis worlds, often by way of some hierarchical system of classification.

In a way similar to the way the word 'technology' is now a homonym for both the study or science of using things to help achieve objectives, and the things themselves, the word 'ontology' is also now a homonym. An '-ology' is the study or science of something. So, ontology, in the sense of a study or science of something, is "The science or study of being; that department of metaphysics which relates to the being or essence of things, or to being in the abstract" (OED, 2009).

Recent years have seen the emergence of many 'ontologies'. That is a use of the word not yet recognized by the Oxford English Dictionary, but is recognized by Websters (Gove, 2002): "a particular system according to which problems of the nature of being are investigated", and, "a theory concerning the kinds of entities and specif. [sic] the kinds of abstract entities that are to be admitted to a language system".

Further assistance can be obtained from philosophy literature, for example, Feibleman (1951):

> "Ontology proper is a field of enquiry and not the name of a particular philosophy. In Bentham's definition, ontology, "the field of supremely abstract entities, is a yet untrodden labyrinth." Bentham's "supremely abstract entities" the categories of traditional metaphysics, or, as we should say in reference to a modern mathematical system,

the undefined terms employed in the unproven propositions which constitutes the postulates of the system. Ontology, then, is a speculative field, for there is more than one set of abstract entities claiming to be the set of "supremely abstract entities"; in other words, there are rival ontologies and non is generally accepted by common agreement." [p4]

Following the discussion earlier in the book, it is clear that Carnap has the "supremely abstract entities" in place prior to the modern computing world to be able to support an assertion that Carnap's ontology is the most likely source for the computing world's approaches to statements, requirements modelling, relational database concepts, and object oriented concepts. The highest abstract entity in Carnap's scheme is 'object' or 'thing' corresponding with the top layer in Figure 4.1, metametametalanguage, or meta^3 language. Hence, on first examination, OPR fits into an ontological view of the world.

A modern use of the term 'ontology' can be found in the overview of the tool Protégé (Protégé, 2012) (an open source tool for creating 'ontologies').

"An ontology describes the concepts and relationships that are important in a particular domain, providing a vocabulary for that domain as well as a computerized specification of the meaning of terms used in the vocabulary. Ontologies range from taxonomies and classifications, database schemas, to fully axiomatized theories. In recent years, ontologies have been adopted in many business and scientific communities as a way to share, reuse and process domain knowledge. Ontologies are now central to many applications such as scientific knowledge portals, information management and integration systems, electronic commerce, and semantic web services."

Of course, that definition refers explicitly to process domain *knowledge*. Thus, we come full circle to the point made earlier when discussing business process epistemology, that many modern uses of the word 'ontology' are muddled. This will not help in the long term, and it is unlikely that modern concepts blurring the distinction between epistemology and ontology will unseat the well-established philosophical foundations and distinctions between those terms. Of course, 'ontology' may emerge as a helpful symbol for the analyst, even if detached from its original meaning.

Modern uses of 'ontology' such as these, are examples of another 'psychological epidemic' sweeping the world of analysis with a word people like the sound of, and perhaps feel it conveys an illusion of being more precise.

From the same source as Protégé, is a tutorial for creating ontologies (Noy and McGuiness, 2001). It is evident that their ontology is completely consistent with OPR modelling, and indeed the vocabulary is substantially the same as discussed earlier in this book identifying Carnap as the likely source for much of the vocabulary and analysis techniques used in the computer application development world. Also consistent with that discussion is the point that the wine ontology used by Noy and McGuiness (2001) does not restrict the ontological approach to computer-based applications.

Indeed, the application of ontology in such a way, does beg the question why, instead of ontology, was the term epistemology not used - particularly when we see an ontology tutorial based on different categories of wine! Perhaps that's the next BPW term - *business process epistemology*!

An example of the application of a Protégé approach to business process ontology can be found explicit in Jenz (2003). However, Jenz asserts " There is no single tool on the market, which is built on a comprehensive meta model to express process-related functional requirements, let alone non-functional requirements, such as "performance" and "reliability""; the only sense in which that is correct, is that PSL/PSA is not currently (i.e. 2003) on the market, but there is no doubt that as early as the 1970s and 1980s, PSL had exactly those properties. More to the point, creating such a 'comprehensive meta model' is a relatively trivial task with metaPSL which is on the market, albeit only in conjunction with a meta modelling project.

Reconciling business process epistemology and ontology

The previous sections discussing business process epistemology and ontology raised the point that some of the current modern uses of ontology are not strictly correct. Many people will say, "so what?", but the long term impact, and it can be seen already, is a slow steady drift away from the well-established philosophical field of ontology and the previously well-established meaning of ontology. There is no need for that.

Ontology starts from "supremely abstract entities"; epistemology starts from "validated knowledge". In terms of Carnap and constructor principles, this can be represented by annotating Figure 4.1, as is shown in Figure 15.5.

Carnap's supremely abstract entity is object or thing, which is almost all that is needed as a metametametalanguage (meta^3 language) shown at the pinnacle of the pyramid. That is instantiated by an object-property-relationship (OPR) language as a metametalanguage. OPR is used to define languages at the metalanguage level. That means the OPR language enables the definition of objects, properties, relationships, and the syntax needed to represent those. In the case of a language developed using metaPSL, the syntax is entirely linguistic using a highly structured subset of English. In the case of a language such as UML, the syntax is mainly graphical using diagrams annotated with linguistic expressions. The way UML's M3 metametalanguage is defined means that really it is a hybrid metametalanguage and metalanguage, thus it would benefit from more work to create a clean separation of those layers.

The metalanguage, whether it is PSL-lite, PSL, or UML is used to describe or model a real life situation. When it starts to do that, it is moving into the realm of validated knowledge, or epistemology. Obviously, the subject matter (the bottom layer in Figures 4.1 and 15.5) is the real world, therefore it is very firmly validated knowledge, and hence a matter of epistemology. Thus, we are moving down the arrow in Figure 15.5 from ontology to epistemology. In object-oriented terminology, the nearest we can get to that is 'instantiation' from the top supremely abstract object, down to the validated knowledge of the real world.

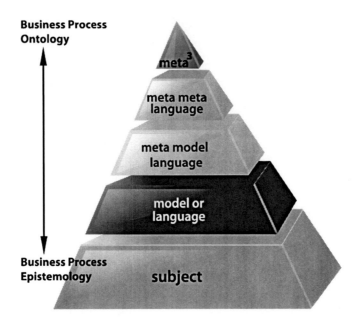

Figure 15.5 Reconciling Business Process Ontology and Epistemology

When we start from the subject layer, or real world, we are starting with validated knowledge, that is a matter of epistemology. Then the processes of generalization and abstraction start as we move up the layers. We select what we want from the real world to create our systems of classification, description, and analytical summaries. We move first into the next layer up— our model, or language. That is still firmly linked to validated knowledge. Then we can generalize our model to an abstract way of describing the real world, our metalanguage, and that can be used to describe other real-world situations. We have now abstracted sufficiently from validated knowledge into abstract objects. We are moving from epistemology to ontology. We are moving up the arrow in Figure 15.5. Again, in object-oriented terminology, the most appropriate term is 'generalization'.

There are no absolutely correct ways to move from ontology to epistemology, or from epistemology to ontology. There are many valid ways an analyst could achieve this.

The person who uses a metametalanguage to create a metalanguage is performing the role of *Language Definer* (that is the term I use for someone using metaPSL). A Language Definer requires a specific skill set, and very few people have that (or need it). A language definer should also be able to provide consulting services to an organization to explore if the modelling language used by that organization is capable of creating 'good' representations of the organization.

Business Process Modeling Notation (BPMN)

The Object Management Group (OMG) have a standard for modeling business processes.

Given the relationship between OMG and UML, it should not be surprising that the Business Process Modelling Notation (BPMN) is a graphical language.

A history of BPMN is set out in Allweyer (2010) along with a comprehensive presentation of the language. An additional source of material is Silver (2011).

BPMN is undoubtedly useful for limited and localized discussion of some business processes and their context. However, as with all graphical notations, it is inevitable that as the size of the set of business process specifications increases, it is unsuitable for the management of process information about many processes. The notation provides a useful checklist of things to think about when analyzing business processes.

Business Process Outsourcing (BPO)—and Insourcing

There are at least two dimensions to the question of business process outsourcing (BPO):

1. Many enterprises decide to outsource some or all of their processes;
2. For the enterprises who provide the outsourced service, service fulfilment is itself probably the most important business process.

It is impossible to separate a discussion about BPO from the earlier discussion about levels and components of business process in Chapter 2 (figs 2.1-2.3).

When outsourcing takes place, it is certain something was outsourced, but without further examination, it may not be clear whether what was outsourced was a business process, a process, an activity, a task, etc. It depends to some extent on whether your preference is for a recursive concept of process as suggested in this book, or something consistent with BPMN suggestions.

For example, if what is outsourced is a call centre, is it the outsourcing of all call handling, in which case it is something like a common process call handling which is outsourced, or is it only some aspects of call handling, such as calls related to customer account queries?

HR is another function which is often outsourced, such as recruitment or payroll. However, although these may be termed business process outsourcing, if a business process is a truly cross-functional process, recruitment and payroll are processes, not business processes. Does this matter? This book does not offer a strong view, but merely alerts the reader to problems of process classification when dealing with discussions about BPO.

Logistics is a process outsourced by many enterprises, but normally, logistics is only part of a business process such as order fulfilment.

It is highly likely that the term BPO is used for all kinds of process outsourcing, whether or not the process is a business process as determined by independent classification criteria. Figure 2.3 shows several business processes that cut across multiple, if not all, enterprise functions (or departments). It is highly unusual to see any of these outsourced (except, perhaps, servicing?).

Of course, there is nothing wrong with this outsourcing. There are some extremely good reasons to outsource various processes or activities (whatever they are called). The point is that for the purposes of a business process analyst or engineer, it is necessary to have sufficient precision in the terminology used.

Common reasons for choosing what to outsource include economies of scale and core competence. As mentioned earlier, there is a paradox of core competency; if an enterprise is particularly good at doing something, why is it so difficult to replicate if all business processes can be described? In the UK, many supermarkets outsource their logistics. It's not that they couldn't run a fleet of trucks; it's that they can't run a fleet of trucks as efficiently, or cheaply, as an outsourcee.

Outsourcing also has the effect of converting a master-servant relationship as between employer and employee, into a contractual relationship between supplier and customer.

When done on an international basis, outsourcing is one way to avoid local regulation over things such as rates of pay, working conditions, or employee rights. Some high-tech products are made by people working in appalling conditions and for below poverty rates of pay, such as would be totally unacceptable in a developed economy. WTO (World Trade Organization) rules are in place to ensure that this is likely to remain as an option for outsourcing for the foreseeable future; remedy lies in the hands of the voluntary social responsibility of enterprises.

Providing outsourcing solutions is very big business. A range of processes that are outsourced is set out by Kulkarni (2005) including contact (or call) centres, healthcare information, transaction processing, human resources, media and entertainment, and publishing.

It is interesting to look at BPO from the perspective of the places where outsourcing services are provided. Kulkarni helps to do that. Other examples of looking at India as a supplier are the books by Anandkumar and Biswas (2008), and, Thite and Russell (2009). Anandkumar and Biswas have an interesting classification of outsourced processes into voice and non-voice, setting out reasons why they think the characteristics of those two classes are very different. Thite and Russell present a collection of evidence-based papers by themselves and other authors, looking at HR issues in Indian call centres. They papers also look at comparisons between Indian call centres, and those in US, Canada and Australia

There are several books available which the business process analyst can use for ideas about business process outsourcing. For example, Duening and Click (2005) offer one set of reasons for adopting BPO as cost savings, bringing in expertise, increasing market flexibility, improving scalability, and reducing time to market. They also discuss the point that core competence is more likely to be tetained in-house with other processes or activities being candidates for BPO. They suggest setting up a BPO analysis team (BAT) in some situations, to identify and decide about BPO.

Further reasons for outsourcing are suggested by Clements et al. (2004) who say *"Many companies have progressed well beyond using outsourcing simply to reduce costs; today they are using it as a tool to promote enterprise-wide change"*, and, *"Many companies are concerned that outsourcing will lead to less control over their business and therefore expose them to greater risk"*. Clements et al., go further, showing that the economies of scale developed by companies providing outsourcing services, can be available to small companies outsourcing. Thus, outsourcing can provide small companies with economy of scale benefits if large-scale outsourcing providers are used. However, great caution is necessary. Where the principal reason for outsourcing is cost, the outsource service provider may not really have the skills necessary to do the job properly. For example, much software development is outsourced to low cost countries. However, if the outsourcing supplier does not have people trained properly, particularly in technical issues such as normalization for database design, the delivered solutions may be sub-optimal, and what is worse, costs of modification can be higher, and there may be time bombs in the delivered solution which are triggered when some, possibly very minor, upgrades are performed.

An approach to looking at outsourcing different from articulating a range of benefits, is presented by Blokdijk (2008) who offers a number of discussion points about BPO; the style is a little like a FAQ for outsourcing.

When going down the outsourcing route, it is important to establish a Service Level Agreement (SLA) and decide how the relationship is monitored and managed. Important elements of any SLA include data protection and confidentiality.

It is easy to imagine that outsourcing refers primarily to information work of some kind, but of course it may be any aspect of enterprise such as manufacturing. China has built its economy in recent years, with substantial contribution coming from work outsourced there.

A surprising country that lags in the outsourcing provision is the Philippines, particularly given its substantial strengths in English.

Continuing a theme earlier in the book of looking at historical origins, it can be seen that outsourcing is not a new phenomenon. To some extent, the emergence of the idea of an economy having different economic sectors is likely to have started because of specialization and outsourcing.

For example, in the early days of the industrial revolution, many manufacturing facilities will have done all their accounting and legal work in-house. That work would be included when assessing the size of the manufacturing sector of the economy. As soon as the manufacturing facility outsources activities such as accounting and law, total economic activity remains the same, but the emergence of a service sector can be seen. Similarly for the emergence of a knowledge or information sector, when computers are deployed, the work done by them becomes part of an 'information age', beyond the services sector. Attempting to quantify this was an important element in Machlup's (1962) work.

BPO is a business in its own right, also with order and service fulfilment as core business processes. There are discussions of these as businesses, for example Kulkarni (2005).

For the business process analyst, studying outsourcing operations at home and abroad gives many things to think about, even if some processes are to be 'insourced' by setting up a distinct business unit to perform some business process.

The concept of insourcing is related to the discussion earlier about coupling and cohesion from the software development world applied to business process analysis. Whether to insource or outsource may be more of a business decision than analytical; the business process analyst needs to set out the characteristics of the processes involved, wherever they are to be performed. However, if some processes are to be outsourced, the analyst should check if there are any contextual matters (for example, see: Anandkumar and Biswas, 2008; Kulkarni, 2005; Thite and Russell, 2009) in the external environment which may affect the operation of the processes when outsourced.

Chapter 16

Journey's pause—epilogue

It is time to pause this BPW journey again, until the next book edition. As stated in the Preface, it is not possible to address in a book of normal size all the detail to help everyone. However, a wide range of analytical approaches has been investigated and used. Other techniques undoubtedly exist which will also help the analyst. Consulting, training and seminars are available from me for those who wish to study the subject matter more deeply.

This Epilogue presents summaries of the key dimensions of business process analysis: the roles of the professional analyst, core skills and techniques, and desirable functionality in a business process analyst's workbench. It has a section hinting at possible futures.

Much of the book has assumed that business process analysis will be done by some in-house or external team with a view to defining required processes that will then be implemented. A very different alternative would be to use someone else's process model rather than developing one's own.

Following the observation that most of the BPW work encountered has been run as a project, the chapter sets out a view for BPA to be a core strategic, ongoing process, rather than "merely" a project.

General commentary

In looking for the analytical skills needed to support BPW, a fundamental conclusion is that there is nothing particularly new today. Indeed, the fundamental concept of BPW is not new either, and what is presented today under the BPW banner is a continuation of a very long historical trend in the radical transformation of ways in which people do their work.

In terms of an analysis of the *technical* characteristics of business processes, the core skills are derived from fields developed earlier than the current BPW focus, such as statistics, work study, organization and methods, and operational research. In addition, it is necessary to understand the *microeconomic* characteristics, derived from financial and management accounting and economics. The emphasis on information technology means that it is also necessary to analyze the *technological* characteristics. The creation of new or modified business processes often involves a substantial transformation of the world of work, involving changes to organization, teams, collaboration, and the 'human use of human beings'[1]. Therefore there is a need to understand the *human, social and organizational* characteristics. More extensive, complex, and distributed enterprises combined with the emergence of virtual enterprises lead to the need to understand the *communications and control* characteristics obtainable from fields such as managerial cybernetics and applied information theory.

What seems to be new today is the extensive and intensive proactive search for ways in which present work can be transformed into something more efficient or more profitable. This is the case whether the goal is radical transformation of the enterprise or continuous improvement.

BPW activity is as old as enterprise. Significant BPW work frequently follows the invention and deployment of new technology. As mentioned earlier in the book, the key technology that most writers implicate in today's BPW activity is the technology generally labeled information technology. In reality the implicated technology is not just information technology, but a massive convergence of interacting technology of many kinds.

For the business process analyst faced with new and complex business processes enabled by a wide range of technologies, perhaps the greatest challenge is the need for a broad, multidisciplinary set of core skills. In many instances, the set of skills must be provided by a team because the

1   To use the title of Wiener's book (1954).

totality is beyond the capabilities of individual analysts. There is scope for the evolution of business process analysts into generalists and specialists.

Since the first edition of this book, there has been a whole host of other dimensions to BPW, as shown in the previous chapter.

The professional business process analyst

This book illustrates the very wide range of skills and techniques needed to support BPA work. Not all techniques are needed for every engagement, but they will probably be needed for every *significant* engagement. Individuals cannot be expected to possess all the skills to a substantial depth. However, the most capable analysts generally possess demonstrably good skills in more than one of the disciplines identified.

In most professional practices, such as engineering, medicine, law, accounting, architecture, dentistry, statistics, and so forth, the practitioners have received extensive and intensive training and obtained appropriate academic qualifications. Practice qualifications or certification usually require a period of competent practical work, under the supervision of experienced and qualified practitioners dealing with real problems. In the BPW and information systems world, many practitioners have little more than attendance at some short courses followed by practice. This is generally inadequate preparation for a professional approach to BPW work.

Advice to those embarking on BPW projects includes checking the academic and professional qualifications of anyone employed to do the work. However, be very careful about new certification and accreditation schemes. There is a whole new industry around certification and accreditation. Unfortunately, many such schemes require the acquisition and use of many untested, unresearched, ideological and prescriptive approaches. Mere experience is insufficient, and given the serious classification problems associated with BPW, it is easy to assert that any experience in changing the way work is done is relevant BPW experience!

The professional business process analyst will possess a range of skills and competencies. Literacy is expected in a wide range, and in-depth abilities in at least one area, for each person undertaking the work.

For a complex project, either there should be a team of people with an appropriate mix of in-depth skills, or those skills that are missing should be available from some other source when required.

The main professional attributes of a business process analyst are:

- possessing at least some of a range of analytical abilities that are needed for business process analysis work;
- being able to advise on and perform a range of fact-finding techniques to support the collection of information relating to existing or proposed business processes;
- being able to apply a range of techniques to summarize and present facts about existing or proposed processes;

- being able to apply a range of analytical techniques to a collection of business process data to deduce conclusions and make comparisons about existing or proposed processes;
- being able to design a set of business operations performance metrics that can be used in conjunction with business process analysis;
- being able to produce appropriate descriptions of business processes and how they relate to each other;
- being able to define and implement an appropriate range of completeness, consistency, and correctness standards for the documentation or description of business processes;
- being able to take operational data about business processes, and apply appropriate techniques to generate and support proposals for new or modified business processes;
- knowing enough about a range of analytical techniques to be able to decide which are appropriate to use for the problem in hand;
- knowing when to call in supporting specialists;
- being able to support the production of useful reports and recommendations resulting from a business process analysis engagement.

The analyst also needs to display professional behavior such as an emotional detachment from analysis results and recommendations that are given. There needs to be a separation between giving the advice and the business decision of whether to act on the advice or not. Generally, the analyst will not be taking the business decision. After all, the lawyer may advise that a particular case is hopeless, but the client decides to continue in any event. Similarly, those with responsibility for business decisions are well advised to seek the results of good business process analysis work in order to understand the possible consequences of various possible decisions about how to implement particular processes.

Those who become the best business process analysts start their analytical lives having developed good analytical skills in a relevant discipline. It does not matter too much what that discipline is—finance, operations research, organization and methods, information systems, or some branch of engineering—what is important is that the analyst has a sense of what the techniques can and cannot do. Of the categories listed the greatest learning difficulties were encountered among those with an information systems structured analysis background. This is perhaps because as an area of analysis it is neither rigorous nor well defined. However, it almost all analysts from any background benefit from a much broader base of analysis.

For a broader view of a business process practitioner, Harmon (2012) sets out an interesting perspective of practitioner work from the 1960s onwards. This pre-dates the 1990 commencement of the BPR world. His observations about industrial engineering are also interesting in that the ISDOS project and its operationalization of metametamodelling took place within a university industrial engineering department.

Have multidisciplinary teams to support BPW. Junior analysts tend to have some good specialization with a realization of a wider analytical world. Senior analysts are usually literate in a broader range of analytical techniques and possess competency in multiple specialist techniques.

Core skills and competencies

The subject areas discussed elsewhere in the book are significant contributors to the core skills needed by business process analysts. The list should be supplemented where necessary by additional skills from areas such as engineering. A non-exhaustive list of core skills is shown in Table 16.1.

Skills are applied to do something, and the application of skills to achieve a desired result is what is termed a competency. This is similar to the idea of the core competency of a business, which is the ability of the business to apply its skills and resources to achieve desired results.

Table 16.2 presents a sample list of core competencies that are important for the business process analyst. A core competency is similar to a statement of what someone is able to do, or to do well; some people refer to descriptions of core competencies as "can do" statements.

Methods and techniques

Skills and competencies are frequently employed within the context of more general methods for problem solving. BPW is relatively young, and there is not yet a corresponding public literature about proven BPW methods. For example, one method available publicly is in the book by Harrington (1991) who offers five phases (organizing for improvement; understanding the process; streamlining; measurements and control; and continuous improvement). That method combines actions by management with particular techniques that may be useful for process improvement. Another example is that of Petrozzo and Stepper (1994) who divide the contents of their book into four phases (discover; hunt and gather; innovate and build; and reorganize, retrain, retool). A more general method for addressing issues from strategic planning to implemented information systems is set out in Darnton and Giacoletto (1992).

Many consultancies have substantial practices based on BPW. However, because these are often substantial fee-earning activities, such methods tend to be proprietary, and hence not available more widely to the interested practitioner.

The method to be employed in any particular enterprise is contingent on both the problem to be solved and the context for the BPW project. Therefore, methods are likely to be at a very high abstract level with a small number of phases, and not too much detail for those phases. The field is not yet mature enough to assert any overall BPW method that the analyst can follow for all projects.

Skill	Description
Process visualization	Creating a mental model of how a process (or set or interrelated processes) operates in practice, including an understanding of the role of technology.
Listening	Taking in the significance of other people's accounts of processes.
Facilitation	Helping other people to articulate processes.
Cross-examination	A more formal ability that recognizes where people have not stated what needs to be said or where they do not actually mean what they have said—often based on the results of formal completeness and consistency checks.
Creativity	Envisioning new ways in which processes could be performed or organized.
Semantic representation	Producing a well-structured, more formal description of processes, from a variety of sources expressed in very different ways.
Analysis	Approaching process descriptions with an inquiring mind that is looking for models of processes.
Inference	Taking descriptions of processes and being able to infer other system components or processes that have not yet been articulated.
Presentation	Explaining processes to other people in terms that they can use to create their own effective mental models.
Domain specificity	In-depth skills in one or more of the analysis subjects which have been identified (or others as appropriate).
Process thinking	Visualizing processes in terms of events, processes, and conditions, linked together to provide process or workflow.
System thinking	Visualizing processes as continuous within a system where there are multiple processes running continuously, and interacting together.
Professional detachment	Treating analysis as a profession, presenting considered and justifiable opinions, and not being upset when others ignore advice or recommendations.

Table 16.1 Core business process analyst skills: suggestions

In some cases, methods must be linked into existing processes (for example where there is an existing quality program, or ISO certification that restricts changes to certified processes).

Following a theme developed earlier in the book, the need for BPW was articulated by Canning (1956) although he did not use any *term* such as process engineering—he referred to a *systems engineer*. He advocated that a systems study "should be approached from the scientific method viewpoint ... make a thorough study of the company's methods and procedures ... it might be possible to revise the methods and procedures ... ". He then discussed minor and major changes to processes before introducing data processing-aided automation this comparison is remarkably similar to the current debate about the difference between business process improvement and business process innovation.

Competency	Explanation
Obtain process requirements	Exercise several of the skills shown previously to acquire a comprehensive understanding of what a process is supposed to do, and the possible ways in which it could do them.
Do analysis	Take a range of process source information and perform appropriate analysis on it.
Prepare analysis reports	Create relevant analysis reports that are well matched to purpose and audience.
Create process specifications or descriptions	Create comprehensive specifications or descriptions of processes that are well structured and comprehensive enough to suit a range of purposes and audiences.
Define completeness and consistency standards	Apply different levels of completeness, consistency, and correctness criteria for different stages of an analysis project to generate reports or specifications.
Predict process behavior	Use source materials and analysis skills to predict how a process is likely to perform.
Assist process design	Help designers to produce appropriate and feasible ways to implement process specifications.

Table 16.2 Business process analysis core competencies: examples

Canning's work was one of the earliest references in the field known as data processing (and its successors) that articulated a waterfall life cycle for changes to the *business* (and not just the software).

As with other cases of creating new systems, new or modified business processes are created on the basis of various requirements, articulated or not. The business process analyst is advised to keep an eye on the developing field of *requirements engineering* because it deals with many difficult aspects of identifying requirements in the face of uncertainty or a large number of degrees of freedom. The emergence of this field is evidenced by various new series of conferences, for which there are publications such as Theyer (1990), and the ICRE and ISRE conference proceedings.

Experimentation is discussed in chapter 13 in a context where it is possible to try alternative ways of performing a process. At the requirements stage, perhaps the most sophisticated method to help with clarifying requirements, as well as identifying and managing risks, is the spiral method of Boehm, reprinted in Boehm (1995) and modified slightly in Boehm (1989). Essentially this involves iterative prototyping until enough is known about requirements, operation, and feasibility, to be able to commit the development of a new system, and to have a good idea of what it will look like.

This book has focussed on underlying analytical techniques that the analyst will find useful independently of the method employed. Making analysis techniques and BPW methods orthogonal, can help the analyst to obtain a set of skills and competencies that can be applied in the context of most methods likely to be encountered.

The skills outlined above are based on reasonably well-defined subject areas. Within these areas (and in some cases by combination) are techniques set out in Table 16.3 (a non-exhaustive list).

Technique	Descripton
Accounting	Particularly cost accounting, and activity-based costing
Data envelopment analysis	To compute the most efficient way of executing a process that is performed in different places or replicated in some way
Data modeling	In particular, applying basic skills to the development of object property relationship models or meta models (or equivalent of OPR)
Diagram analysis	Constructing formal linguistic representations of diagrams; explaining what a diagram type can be used for
Document analysis	Understanding the structure of a document and mapping it to sources of the document contents
Ethnography	Exploring and understanding the real world of work; how actions are performed in reality
Experimentation	Design, conduct, and analyze processes where it is possible to experiment with the real thing
Information analysis	Applications of information theory (such as attenuation, amplification, and decision making) to business processes
Interviewing and questionnaire design	Construction, testing and analysis using these techniques; understanding how to check validity and reliability
Managerial cybernetics	Examining process control and communications

Object property relationship modeling	Creating meta models from a variety of sources
Operational research	Traditional techniques including operational analysis and linear programming
Organizational design	Relationships between process performance and organizational structure
Organization and methods (O&M)	Traditional techniques from this field
Performance measurement	Design and use of relevant measures of process performance linked to any measurement need ranging from strategy to operations
Process and system de-composition	Expressing systems and processes as a collection of interacting components (that may themselves be decomposed further)
Process mapping	Showing sequences of processes and flows of information, materials, and control
Simulation	Both discrete and continuous simulations
Software engineering principles	In particular, the application of cohesion, coupling, decision splitting, and information hiding to business processes
Statistics	Traditional techniques from this field
Strategy definition	Mission, vision, objectives, SWOT analysis, critical factor, and the implementation of these in business processes; links between processes and enterprise goals
Systems analysis	Traditional techniques from this field
Text analysis	Production of OPR models from text sources
Variance analysis	Sources of deviations from plans and actual results
Wallcharting	Capturing the results of facilitated techniques
Work and process flowcharting	Traditional techniques from this field
Work study	Traditional techniques from this field
Workshop facilitation	Scoping a workshop and defining procedures to capture ideas and experience efficiently

Table 16.3 BPA techniques

The analyst's workbench

As explained in chapter 11, the role of computers in BPW is two-fold. Firstly, computers are part of the enabling technology that is driving so much contemporary business process reorganization. Secondly, many of the essential techniques that underpin BPW projects could only be applied with the aid of computers because of complexity, or the volume of information which needs to be handled.

Data capture remains a somewhat messy process, because data are received from many kinds of source and in very different formats. Various tools have different types of front-end, but these are specific to the tool meta model. Therefore data need to be adapted, and where it helps, feeders need to be built between the various tools. Ideally there would be a seamless set of tools, but at the moment there is not. The problem faced in building a workbench is reminiscent of the CASE workbench problem of fitting together a comprehensive set of tools to support software engineering.

Analysis requires a collection of tools. The main areas of functionality suggested, are:

- statistical analysis (and presentation);
- linear programming and data envelopment analysis;
- object-property-relationship language modeling along with completeness and consistency checking;
- context-sensitive editors, or web-based forms;
- document processing;
- simulation;
- accounting (particularly cost accounting);
- database.

Workbench functionality can be divided into front-end, analysis and back-end components.

The front-end components are responsible for client[2] functionality. The principal elements of this functionality are depicted in Figure 16.1. The view integration functionality is used to support the creation of corporate data models because several of our projects included the need to consolidate a range of information about data. (This can be applied to the consolidation of information about resources more generally, not just data.)

The analysis work is performed by servers[3] as shown in Figure 16.2.

The back-end of the workbench is essentially server work. Its main responsibility is to package the results of analysis in the most appropriate form for the next stage of work. The principal functionality is shown in Figure 16.3.

---

2 A client is responsible for (i) presenting the capability of the processing available, (ii) enabling the capture of necessary data, (iii) assisting with the formulation of semantically and syntactically correct requests for processing, (iv) propagating these requests to the appropriate server mechanisms to do the work, and (v) receiving responses and presenting them to the requester. (From Darnton and Giacoletto, 1992.)

3 A server receives requests from clients, and either carries out the request, or propagates other requests to other servers, and manages the request and responses

Much workbench output is in the form of documentation. Therefore the ability to define documentation standards and implement those standards by completeness and consistency checks along with document schemas is paramount. Most of the PC-based (or other) WYSIWYG (what you see is what you get) word processors that have embedded control and formatting information are not helpful. The most appropriate approach to documentation is the markup language route, combined with document processing capability where the nature of the output can be defined with a very high degree of independence from the source. Also, it is relatively trivial to compute the markup tags needed, whereas the idiosyncratic internal structures of most word-processing packages mean that integrating them into a BPA workbench involves too much investment.

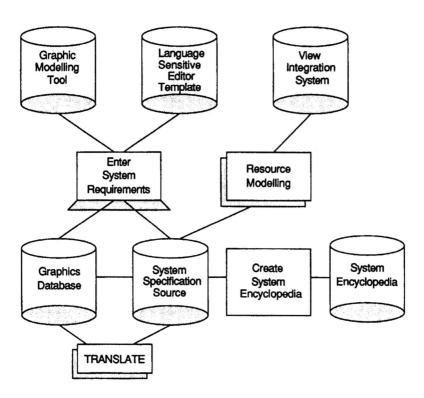

Figure 16.1 Workbench front-end.

Additional output is in the form of images (static or dynamic) that can be viewed by humans. Therefore attention needs to be paid to producing good cognitive models (that is, representations that make it easy for people to understand the analysis results). For example, in modeling a bank, one approach would be to present block diagrams of system components (such as counters, customers, tellers, mortgage processors, and so forth) along with communications links, whereas another approach might be to provide animations of, say, a bank branch showing icons of customers arriving, going to the counter, being served, waiting.... UML diagrams are, generally, very poor cognitive models and are not understood easily by many stakeholders in BPW projects.

Where part of the system is to be computerized, the workbench should also be able to provide output in machine-processable form for any subsequent stage of analysis or design (and eventually to support code generation).

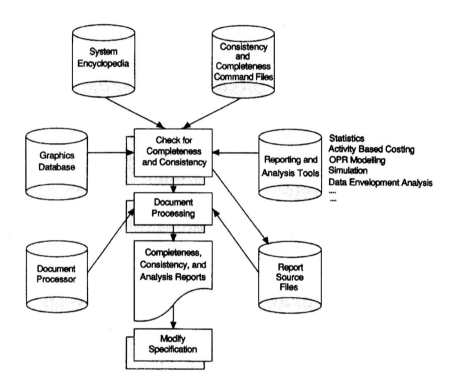

Figure 16.2 Workbench analysis.

An early tool workbench produced an environment that is able to provide skeleton source code for database management systems and transaction processing monitors from a specification database containing process requirements, this is known to be feasible (Darnton, 1987). Achieving the same result from a BPA database involves more steps because the implementation of a business process usually involves a lot more than software, extending approaches inspired by writers such as Teichroew and Sayani (1971).

New processes: build or buy?

A significant amount of the BPW literature assumes that the best thing to do is examine current processes, identify better ways of doing them, and then implement the required changes. As with many system components, there may be a realistic build or buy decision to be made.

Some factories make their own machine tools for the production of the goods that they sell. However, many (perhaps most?) buy general-purpose machine tools from a specialist manufacturer and then jig the tools for the specific required production. Many enterprises have internal software development organizations to create most computer applications; however, many buy in software packages and only do development where a package cannot be found.

There are many models, particularly by way of complex software packages, that can be bought by enterprises. In such a case, rather than adapting the package to the business, the business is adapted to the package. Typical examples of this are the massive manufacturing, logistics, and planning packages being purchased and installed by many large manufacturing enterprises. Similarly, most application domains have vendors of packages who have specialized in their area and can provide comprehensive support capability at a fraction of the cost that would be needed for in-house or bespoke development.

BPA as a core strategic process

Most BPW projects encountered have been in the nature of a project. In other words, an existing situation or proposed new business is brainstormed, analyzed, investigated, simulated, or whatever. The resulting output of the project is a set of process descriptions along with information about how to implement the new or revised processes. The next stage of work is implementation. This is a more classical waterfall project approach to BPW.

The most frequent problem facing the business process analyst is the absence of long series of operational data for the processes. This absence of historical data means that much analysis must be technically naive.

The same problem exists for organizations that want to use techniques such as activity-based costing or data envelopment analysis. The problem for activity based costing is not the absence of accounting records, or even severe problems in identifying different ways to allocate fixed costs. The real problem is usually the absence of good data from which statistically valid cost drivers can be derived, and the implementation of operational procedures to continue collecting high-quality operational data to refine the activity-based costing processes.

The motivation for a BPW project is usually urgency or opportunity. For those situations, it is necessary to run BPW projects. However, business process analysis can be set up as an ongoing strategic service to the enterprise. In this way, it is possible to build up high-quality data for longer periods, and this is certainly of value to subsequent analysis work. To help understand the mystery of enterprise core competence the collective knowledge of an enterprise can be understood better by a more refined collection of financial and operational data over a long period of time.

Top-down design or redesign of business processes by senior management teams, facilitated by consultants, is the most common approach.

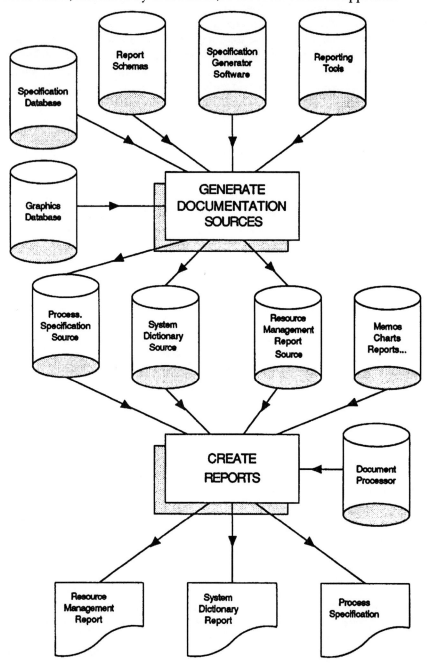

Figure 15.3 Workbench back-end.

The value in such an approach is that it draws on the experience and knowledge of broadly based teams. The scope of the resulting decompositions is usually substantial, and normally most areas are covered[4]. The most serious disadvantage of top-down approaches is that a lot of operational detail and experience is missed out or indeed lost. This detail and experience are in the real world of work, and are needed for the organization to function properly.

Therefore I advocate bottom-up at the same time as top-down approaches to analysis. In several projects, I have used both approaches, but independently of each other to begin with, as the two sets of results provide very good initial benchmarks for each other.

Speculation about the future of BPW

As demonstrated in the previous chapter, since the first edition of this book, quite a few new terms have joined the BPW stable.

It is difficult to identify any specific new approach or idea that has contributed to building up a new business process field. Much more empirical research is needed to test all the ideas that are not based on any concept that has self-contained logic (such as many modelling techniques).

Analysis in terms of diagram techniques has not moved on, except for various attempts to introduce UML diagrams to the BPW world. That is likely to be more a retrograde step than helpful. There are now many ideological UML advocates in the world! The fundamental technical problems with UML remain: the meta metalanguage is ill-formed mixing levels, and the UML, as a language does not implement the constructor principles that are necessary to be able to take a system described using UML and check it thoroughly for completeness and consistency. There is no easy way to combine all the semantics of the different diagram types into any unified whole. This is very surprising given that one early motivation for object oriented techniques in the first place was the dysfunction separation of data and process modelling. In UML that has now been replaced by an even more dysfunctional proliferation of diagram types. In terms of appeal to as many stakeholders as possible involved in a BPW project, UML diagrams just don't have it.

Flowcharts are still used, and at high levels of abstraction, can be accessed by a broad range of BPW project stakeholder.

Thus, the harsh reality of 20-40 years ago is still in place today, that the only way to solve these fundamental presentation and analysis problems, is an underlying linguistic solution, such as OPR, so that business process models can be as complex as they need to be, and can be checked for completeness and consistency - using an approach that is completely scalable.

---

4 However, sometimes a disaster can result—in one case in a very large international corporation, while redesigning the order fulfillment process, invoicing was forgotten! The result was a substantial drop in revenue and cash flow. It took a check of confirmed sales reports, and product shipments, to identify that in fact there had been an increase in business and the delivery of goods, but the problem was that they were not being billed!

Since the first edition of the book, there have been dramatic improvements in available 3D modelling and animation. These could make a dramatic improvement in terms of providing a capability to provide dynamic modelling that gives substantially improved cognitive models of processes, and animation of working processes. This may be one key to developing dynamic models, rather than static.

The BPW field is still not yet developed well enough to establish credible certification and accreditation schemes.

There are some very helpful contributions to consolidating information about BPW, such as BPTrends and a Business Process Management Journal (started in 1995). Hopefully, the Journal is resistant to the scourge of academic papers produced more to contributed to a published paper count, than move the subject matter forward!

Final comments

The BPW journey has gone a long way in the past few years. It is not yet complete, but a useful "refuelling" point has been reached, at which more can be shared with others.

Hopefully, the book strengthens an operational concept of business process, and the foundations on which the business process analyst can build.

A key message is for the analyst to become more professional by the adoption of both a collection of more rigorous techniques and at least an implicit professional code for the conduct of work. The analyst should also be aware of the debate about the value of BPW approaches (for example, Mumford and Hendricks, 1996)

The book introduces a range of techniques that is orthogonal to BPW methods. In other words, the techniques should be useful whatever the method and context within which the BPW work is being done. Fundamental engineering skills are applicable to a wide range of contexts and standards within which the work must be done. Accounting and statistical skills are applicable in many situations.

In this turbulent world of work, where there seems to be a massive change from contracts of employment towards individuals providing services on a temporary basis, it is even more necessary for the practitioner to have a basis of skills that can be applied in many situations. In the nineteenth century, many people were classified as a "journeyman" (that is, someone who was paid by the day's work), and sought work where it might be available. Today, many more people are working in the same way.

It would be good to see the emergence of formal curricula in universities to provide the basis of professional analysis across the spectrum outlined in this book, as well as more formal research to provide a wider empirical basis for advocacy in BPW projects.

Hopefully, you have enjoyed this book, and that it has at least been useful in some respects. Suggestions and feedback are welcome. The goal of the book is to evolve the subject matter to provide more detail, depth, and illustration.

Acronyms

Acronyms

ABC	Activity-Based Costing
AD	Anno Domini
ADS	Accurately Defined Systems
ANSI	American National Standards Institute
ASIC	Application Specific Integrated Circuit
BAL	Business Architecture Language
BAT	BPO Analysis Team
BC	Before Christ
BFS	Business Flight Simulator
BISAD	Business Information System Analysis and Design
BPA	Business Process Analysis
	Business Process Analyst
BPE	Business Process Engineer
BPI	Business Process Improvement
	Business Process Innovation
	Business Process Insourcing
BPL	Business Process Language
BPM	Business Process Management
	Business Process Mapping
	Business Process Maturity
BPMM	Business Process Maturity Model
BPMN	Business Process Model and Notation
BPO	Business Process Outsourcing
BPR	Business Process Redesign
	Business Process Reengineering
BPW	Business Process Work
CAD	Computer Aided Design

CAM	Computer Aided Manufacturing
CASE	Computer-Aided Software Engineering
	Computer-Aided Systems Engineering
CD-ROM	Compact Disk-Read Only Memory
CEF	Critical existence factor
CEO	Chief Executive Officer
CFF	Critical Failure Factor
CFO	Chief Finance Officer
	Commission on Filipinos Overseas
CIV	Calculated Intangible Value
CKO	Chief Knowledge Officer
CML	Competence Management Language
CMM	Capability Maturity Model
CMMI	Capability Maturity Model Integration
CODASYL	Conference on Data Systems Languages
CSCW	Computer-Supported Collaborative Work
	Computer-Supported Cooperative Work
CSF	Critical Success Factor
DEA	Data Envelopment Analysis
DEC	Digital Equipment Corporation
EDI	Electronic Data Interchange
EPDP	Executive Planning for Data Processing
ERA	Entity Relationship Attribute
FIFO	First-In First-Out
FMS	Flexible Manufacturing System
GDP	Gross Domestic Product
GNP	Gross National Product
GUI	Graphical User Interface
HRM	Human Resources Manager
HTML	Hypertext Markup Language
IBM	International Business Machines
ICAM	Integrated Computer Aided Manufacturing

IDEF	ICAM Definition Method
IEEE	Institute of Electrical and Electronics Engineers
IS	Information System
ISDL	Information System Description Language
ISDM	Information System Description Model
ISDOS	Information System Design and Optimization System
ISO	International Organization for Standardization
ISP	Information Systems Planning
	Internet Service Provider
IT	Information Technology
JIT	Just In Time
LDM	Language Definition Manager
LIFO	Last-In First-Out
MIA	Multivendor Integration Architecture
MIS	Management Information System
MIT	Massachusetts Institute of Technology
MU	Monetary Unit
NTT	Nippon Telephone and Telegraph
O&M	Organization and Methods
OECD	Organization for Economic Co-operation and Development
OED	Oxford English Dictionary
OMG	Object Management Group
OPR	Object Property Relationship
PC	Personal Computer
PSA	Problem Statement Analyzer
PSL	Problem Statement Language
QPL	Quality Process Language
SADT	Structured Analysis and Design Technique
SEI	Software Engineering Institute
SEM	System Encyclopedia Manager
SGML	Standard Generalized Markup Language

SLA	Service Level Agreement
STDL	Structured Transaction Definition Language
SWOT	Strengths Weaknesses Opportunities Threats
TAG	Time-Automated Grid
TBP	Target Business Process
TOWS	Threats Opportunities Weaknesses Strengths
TQM	Total Quality Management
UML	Unified Modeling Language
VHDL	VHSIC Hardware Description Language
VHSIC	Very High Speed Integrated Circuit
WTO	World Trade Organization
WWW	World Wide Web
WYSIWYG	What You See Is What You Get

BPA Services

A range of services is available from the author, varying from a full-scale project for the creation of an organization's own modelling language, to a short seminar/workshop going over either a summary of techniques, or a particular theme.

This Appendix gives example opportunities, but readers are invited to contact the author and discuss requirements and possibilities. This Appendix starts from the most complex and ends with the simplest.

Consulting and Projects

Bespoke metalanguage—the most effective way to understand your organization, what it deals with, and how to have an integrated view of all processes, is to create a metalanguage for your organization. The nearest alternative to a bespoke metalanguage would be to use an existing language (or subset), such as BPL (business process language), CML (competence management language), IAL (information architecture language), PSL (problem statement language), or PSL-lite where that is a good match to what your organization does. The approach to this is OPR as discussed in this book.

Modelling Audit—using an OPR approach, check if your current process modelling approaches are sufficiently comprehensive, or if there are any important gaps.

Completeness and Consistency Standards definition—define a set of completeness and consistency standards that can be used for two main purposes: (1) support your analysts by having a set of period checks to support the development of your own process models.

Workshops, Seminars, and Training

These can be tailored to suit your needs. Topics that can be included are:

- What is BPR?
- Creating the business vision
- IT Opportunities
- Organizing and re-organizing
- Business process improvement
- Making BPR happen

- Modelling business processes
- Process context and quantification
- Analyzing text
- Analyzing diagrams
- Analyzing costs
- Performance measurement
- OPR modelling
- Creating metalanguages
- Business process epistemology and ontology
- Creating the corporate data model
- Normalization
- Business process architecture
- Business process management
- Contemporary issues in business process analysis
- Information Architecture
- Competence Management

Process Description Forms

This Appendix sets out two key forms that are recommended in various places in the book, as starting points for collecting what are termed Level I and Level II Process Descriptions.

These process description forms are only suggestions. There is more detail to be collected about processes than suggested by these two initial forms. Also, an analyst may prefer to start analysis from perspectives other than processes. They are only suggested as possible starting points.

The Level I form captures a minimal set of information about one process in isolation from others.

The Level II form is typically printed on the back of Level I, and it is used to collect information *additional* to that on the Level I form.

For a more complete description linking together a number of rocess descriptions, it is far more satisfactory to use a tool such as PSL-lite or PSL/PSA to store all system description information.

Level I Process Form

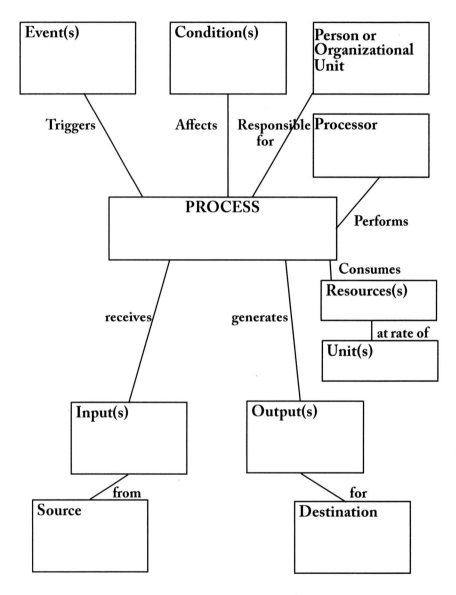

This is a diagrammatic representation of the contents of the sugested Level I process description. A linguistic equivalent follows.

Level I process Form - Linguistic Equivalent

As with all diagrammatic representations of process, they can be very helpful in understanding a single, or small number, of processes. It is when a full-scale system, or large number of processes, is required that the only satisfactory way to store the information is in a database so that all necessary completeness and consistency tests can be performed.

One possible linguistic equivalent[1] is:

DEFINE PROCESS process-name ;
   TRIGGERED BY event-name(s);
   AFFECTED BY condition-name(s);
   RESPONSIBILITY OF responsible-person-or-unit;
   PERFORMED BY processor-name;
   RECEIVES input-name **FROM** interface-name;
   GENERATES output-name **FOR** interface-name;
   CONSUMES resource-name(s) **AT RATE OF** unit-name(s);

In creating a metalanguage for an organization to use for its modelling, the organization can select thewords used to model it processes.

---

1 For a full set of examples, see the PSL-lite User Guide (forthcoming).

Level II Process Form

The additional information for Level II process descriptions is to put a process into a context of other processes, and add further quantification information.

Structure

PART-OF	CONSISTS-OF	COMES BEFORE	COMES AFTER

Quantification

Object	HAPPENS n TIMES	PER	UNIT(S)
EVENTS			
INPUTS			
OUTPUTS			
PROCESSES			

DEFINE PROCESS process-name;
  PART OF process-name;
  CONSISTS OF process-name(s);
  COMES AFTER process-name(s);
  COMES BEFORE process-name(s);
  HAPPENS number **TIMES PER** unit-name;

References and sources

References and Sources

This appendix is not a bibliography in the classical sense; it is not a systematic survey of the literature as it affects the matters discussed in the body of the book. Only those books and articles that have been referenced explicitly in the text are included here.

Ackroyd, S., Harper, R., Hughes, J.A., Shapiro, D. and Soothill, K. (1992) *New Technology and Practical Police Work,* Open University Press.

Adams, R., Carruthers, J. and Hamil, S. (1991) *Changing Corporate Values,* New Consumer and Kogan Page.

Allweyer, Thomas (2010) *BPMN 2.0 - Introduction to the Standard for Bus9iness Process Modeling,* Norderstedt: Herstellung und Verlag: Books on Demand GmbH.

Alschuler, L. (1995) *ABCD...SGML,* International Thomson Computer Press.

American National Standard ANSI Y15.3M-1979 (1980) (reaffirmed 1986), *Process Charts,* American Society of Mechanical Engineers.

Anandkumar, V. and Biswas, S. (2008) *Business Process Outsourcing: Oh! BPO—Structure and Chaos, Fun and Agony,* New Delhi: Response Books.

Anderla, G. and Dunning, A. (1987) *Computer Strategies 1990-9,* John Wiley & Sons.

ANSI (1980) *Standard flowchart symbols and their use in mformation processing (X3.5)* New York: AmemcanNational Standards Institute.

Anthony, R.N. (1965) *Planning and Control Systems: A Framework for Analysis,* Harvard University Press, Cambridge, MA.

Argyris, C. (1966) "Excerpts from Organization of a Bank", in *Some Theories of Organization,* (eds. Rubenstein, A.H. and Haberstroh, C.J.), Irwin-Dorsey.

Arnold, J. and Hope, T. (1990) *Accounting for Management Decisions,* 2nd edn, Prentice-Hall, Englewood Cliffs, NJ.

Barrow, M. and Wagstaff, A. (1989) Efficiency Measurement in the Public Sector: An appraisal. *Fiscal Studies.*

Bachman, C.W. (1969) " Data structure diagrams" in ACM SIGMIS Database, Vol 1 No. 2 Summer 1969 pp4-11.

Bachman, Charles W., Batchelor, Richard E., Beriss, I. Marvin, Blose, Charles R., Burakreis, Turgut I., Valle, Vincent Delia, Dodd, George G., Helgeson, William, Lyon, John, Metaxides, A., McKinzie, Gerald E.,

Siegel, Paul, Simmons, Warren G., Sturgess, Larry L., Tellier, Harrison, Weinberg, Sharon B., Werner, George T. (1969) *Data base task group report to the CODASYL programming language committee,* New York: ACM

Barros, Oscar (2007) "Business Processes Architecture and Design", BPTrends, Newton, MA: BPTrends May 2007.

Basham, A.L. (1967) *The Wonder That was India,* Sidgwick and Jackson.

Beardshaw, J. and Palfreman, D. (1986) *The Organization in its Environment,* Pitman.

Beer, S. (1979) *The Heart of Enterprise,* John Wiley & Sons, New York.

Beer, S. (1981) *The Brain of the Firm,* 2nd edn, John Wiley & Sons, New York.

Beer, S. (1985) *Diagnosing the System for Organizations,* John Wiley & Sons, New York.

Bennion, Francis (2008) *Bennion on Statutory Interpretation,* London: LexisNexis.

Bentley, R., Rodden, T., Sawyer, P., Sommerville, I., Hughes, J.A., Randall, D. and Shapiro, D. (1992) Ethnographically-informed systems design for air traffic control. *Proceedings of CSCW92,* ACM Press, Toronto.

Bertalanffy, L. von (1968) *General System Theory,* George Braziller, New York.

Blokdijk, G. (2008) *Outsourcing 100 Success Secrets - 100 Most Asked Questions: The Missing IT, Business Process, Call Center, HR -Outsourcing to India, China and more Guide,* Newstead QLD: Emereo Publishing.

Boehm, B.W. (1989) *Software Risk Management,* IEEE Computer Society Press.

Boehm, B.W. (1995) A spiral model of software development and enhancement. *IEEE* Engineering Management Review, *Winter.*

Booch, G. (1991) *Object Oriented Design with Applications,* Benjamin/ Cummings.

Born, G. (1994) *Process Management to Quality Improvement,* John Wiley & Sons, New York.

Bosak, R., Clippinger, R.F., Dobbs, C., Goldfinger, R., Jasper, R.B., Keating, W., Kendrick, G., Sammet, J.E. (1962) "An information algebra: phase 1 report - language structure group of the CODASYL development committee", Communications of the ACM, Vol 5 (4) April 1962

Bowers, J.M. and Benford, S.D. (eds) *Studies in Computer Supported Cooperative Work,* North-Holland, Amsterdam.

BPMM (2008) *Business Process Maturity Model v1.0,* Needham, MA: Object Management Group Inc. (OMG).

Brinkley, P.A., Meyer, K.P. and Lu, J.C. Combined generalized linear modelling-nonlinear programming approach to robust process design—a case-study in circuit board quality improvement. *Applied Statistics, Journal of the Royal Statistical Society (Series C)*, 45(1), 99-110.

Buchanan, D.A. and Huczynski, A.A. (1985) *Organizational Behaviour*, Prentice-Hall, Englewood Cliffs, NJ.

Burgess, C. (1980) *The Age of Stonehenge*, Dent, London.

Canning, R.G. (1956) *Electronic Data Processing for Business and Industry*, New York: John Wiley & Sons,

Carlson, S. (1991) *Introduction to HDL-based Design using VHDL*, Synopsis.

Carnap, R. (1928) Der Logische Aufbau der Welt, Berlin-Schlachtensee: Weltkreis Verlag.

Carnap, R. (1937) The Logical Syntax of Language, London: Kegan Paul, Trench, Trubner & Co. Ltd.

Carnap, R. (1958) Introduction to Symbolic Logic and its Applications, (1st English ed.) New York: Dover Publications, Inc.

Carnap, R. (1967) The Logical Structure of the World and Pseudoproblems in Philosophy, (2nd (1st in German 1928)) London: Routledge & Kegan Paul.

Cash, J.I., McFarlan, F.W. and McKenney, J.L. (1983) *Corporate Information Systems Management: Text and Cases*, Richard D. Irwin.

Cash J.I. Jr., McFarlan, F.W. and McKenney, J.L. (1988) *Corporate Information Systems Management*, Dow Jones-Irwin.

Champy, J. (1995) *Reengineering Management*, HarperBusiness.

Chapman, J. (ed.) (1996) *IT Support in the Productive Workplace*, Stanley Thornes in association with Unicorn.

Chapple, E.D. and Sayles, L.R. (1961) *The Measure of Management*, Macmillan, New York.

Charnes, A., Cooper, F.F. and Rhodes, E. (1978) Measuring the efficiency of decision making units. *European Journal of Operational Research*, 2(6).

Charnes, A., Cooper, W., Lewin, A.Y. and Seiford, L.M. (1994) (eds), *Data Envelopment Analysis: Theory, Methodology, and Applications*, Kluwer.

Checkland, P. (1981) *Systems Thinking, Systems Practice*, John Wiley & Sons, New York.

Checkland, P. and Scholes, J. (1990) *Soft Systems Methodology in Action*, John Wiley & Sons.

Chen, P. P.-S. (1976) The entity-relationship model—toward a unified view of data. *ACM Transactions on Database Systems*, 1(1) March.

Child, J. (1984) *Organization: A Guide to Problems and Practice*, Paul Chapman.

Chorafas, D.M. (1994) *Chaos Theory in the Financial Markets*, Irwin.

Clements, S., Donnellan, M., and Read, C. (2004) *CFO Insights: achieving high performance through finance business process outsourcing,* Chichester: John Wiley & Sons Ltd.

Cobb, I., Innes, J. and Mitchell, F. (1992) *Activity Based Costing Problems in Practice,* London: Chartered Institute of Management Accounting

Cochran, W.G. and Cox, G.M. (1957) *Experimental Designs,* 2nd edn, John Wiley & Sons.

Couger, J.D. (1973) Evolution of business systems analysis techniques. *Computing Surveys,* Sept, 167-98.

Couger, J.D. and Knapp, R.W. (1974) *System Analysis Techniques,* John Wiley & Sons, New York.

Cover, T.M. and Thomas, J.A. (1991) *Elements of Information Theory,* John Wiley & Sons, New York.

Cox, D.R. (1958) *Planning of Experiments,* John Wiley & Sons, New York.

Crump, D.W. (1976) *Dix on Contracts of Employment,* 5th edn, Butterworths, London.

CSCW 86, 88, 90, 92, 94, *Proceedings of the Conference on Computer Supported Cooperative Work,* ACM Press.

Cutaia, A. (1990) *Technology Projection Modeling of Future Computer Systems,* Prentice-Hall, Englewood Cliffs, NJ.

Darnton, G. (1987) *Automating the Generation of Functional Specifications,* Proceedings of the PRISE Conference, Meta Systems, Ann Arbor, MI.

Darnton, G. (1995) Working together: a management summary of CSCW. *Computing & Control Engineering Journal* February.

Darnton, G. and Giacoletto, S. (1992) *Information in the Enterprise,* Burlington, MA: Digital Press.

Date, C.J. (1981) *An Introduction to Database Systems,* 3rd edn, Addison-Wesley.

Date, C.J. (2007) *Logic and Databases: The Roots of Relational Theory,* Oxford: Trafford Publishing (UK) Ltd.

Davenport, T.H. and, Short, J.E. (1990) The new Industrial engineering: information technology and business process redesign, *Sloan Management Review,* Summer.

Davenport, T.H. (1993) *Process Innovation: Re-engineering Work through Information Technology,* Harvard Business School Press, Boston, MA.

David, D. (1989) U.S. giants run a $50 billion IS tab. *Datamation,* 15 November.

Davis, A.M. (1993) *Software Requirements: Objects, Functions, and States,* Prentice Hall, Englewood Cliffs, NJ.

Davis, G.B. and Olson, M.H. (1984) *Management Information Systems,* 2nd edn, McGraw-Hill, New York.

Davis, S.M. (1987) *Future Perfect,* Addison-Wesley, Reading, MA.

De Marco, T. (1978) *Structured Analysis and System Specification*, Yourdon.

Donovan, J.J. (1993) *Business Re-engineering with Technology: An Implementation Guide*, Cambridge Technology.

Drury, C. (1992) *Management and Cost Accounting*, 3rd edn, Chapman & Hall, London.

Duening, T.N., and Click, R.L. (2005) *Essentials of Business Process Outsourcing*, Hoboken, NJ: John Wiley & Sons, Inc.

Dumaine, B. (1991) The Bureaucracy Busters. *Fortune International*, 123(13).

Dworkin, G. (1967) *Odgers' Construction of Deeds and Statutes*, 5th edn, Sweet & Maxwell.

Dyson, R.G., Thanassoulis, E. and Boussofiane, A. (1990) Data envelopment analysis. *Operational Research Tutorial Papers*, Operational Research Society.

Earl, M.J. (1989) *Marketing Strategies for Information Technology*, Prentice-Hall, Englewood Cliffs, NJ.

Eason, K. (1988) *Information Technology and Organizational Change*, Burgess Science Press.

Eccles, R.G. (1991) The performance measurement manifesto. *Harvard Business Review*, Jan—Feb.

Espejo, R. and Harnden, R. (eds) (1989) *The Viable Systems Model: Interpretation and Application of Stafford Beer's VSM*, John Wiley & Sons, New York.

Farrell, M.J. (1957) The measurement of productive efficiency. *Journal of the Royal Statistical Society Series A*.

Fayol, H. (1949) *General and Industrial Management* (English translation by Constance Storrs), Pitman (Original French edition published 1916).

Feibleman, James K. (1951) *Ontology* Baltimore: The Johns Hopkins Press.

Fitzgerald, L., Johnston, R., Brignall, S., Silvestro, R. and Voss, C. (1991) *Performance Measurement in Service Businesses*, Chartered Institute of Management Accountants.

Forrester, J.W. (1961) *Industrial Dynamics*, MIT Press, Cambridge, MA.

Forrester, J.W. (1969) *Urban Dynamics*, MIT Press, Cambridge, MA.

Forrester, J.W. (1971) *World Dynamics*, Wright Allen Press.

Galbraith, J. (1973) *Designing Complex Organizations*, Addison-Wesley, Reading, MA.

Galbraith, J. (1977) *Organization Design*, Addison-Wesley, Reading, MA.

Galbraith, J. (1987) Organization design, in Lorsch, J.W., *Handbook of Organizational Behaviour (ed.* J.W. Lorsch), Prentice-Hall, Englewood Cliffs, NJ.

Galbraith, J.K. (1967) *The New Industrial State*, Hamish Hamilton.

Galliers, R.D. and Sutherland, A.R. (1991) Information systems management and strategy formulation: the 'stages of growth' model revisited. *Journal of Information Systems.*

Gane, C. and Sarson, T. (1979) *Structured Systems Analysis: Tools and Techniques*, Prentice-Hall, Englewood Cliffs, NJ.

Gehani, N. and McGettrick, A. (1986) *Software Specification Techniques*, Addison- Wesley, Reading, MA.

Gilbreth, F.B. and L.M. (1924), [see pointers in Ferguson, D "Therbligs:The Keys to Simplifying Work" in an undated web publication available at: http://web.mit.edu/allanmc/www/Therblgs.pdf]

Gove, P.B. (ed.) (2002) *Webster's Third New International Dictionary of the English Language Unabridged*, Springfield MA: Merriam-Webster Inc.

Gray, J. and Reuter, A. (1993) *Transaction Processing: Concepts and Techniques*, Morgan Kaufmann.

Gross, D. and Harris, C.M. (1985) *Fundamentals of Queueing Theory*, 2nd edn, John Wiley & Sons, New York.

Hall, A.D. III (1989) *Metasystems Methodology*, Pergamon Press, Oxford.

Hammer, M. (1990) Reengineering work: don't automate, obliterate. *Harvard Business Review*, July/August.

Hammer, M. and Champy, J. (1993) *Re-engineering the Corporation: A Manifesto for Business Revolution*, Nicholas Brealey.

Hammer, M. (1994) In Depth (interview). *Computerworld*, 24 Jan.

Hammer, M. and Stanton, S.A. (1995) *The Reengineering Revolution*, HarperCollins.

Handy, C.B. (1985) *Understanding Organizations*, Penguin Books.

Harmon, Paul (2012) "What is a BPM Practitioner?" in *BPTrends* Vol 10 (11). Available at: http://www.bptrends.com/publicationfiles/advisor20120612.pdf.

Harrington, H.J. (1991) *Business Process Improvement*, McGraw-Hill, New York.

Hatley, D.J. and Pirbhai, I.A. (1987) *Strategies for Real-time System Specification*, Dorset House.

Hegedus, Imre (2008) *Business Process Management—Insights and Practices for Sustained Transformation*, London: Ark Group.

Herzberg, F. (1968) One more time: how do you motivate employees? *Harvard Business Review*, 46(1).

Hirshleifer, J. and Riley, J.G. (1992) *The Analytics of Uncertainty and*

Information, Cambridge University Press, Cambridge.

Holstein, W.K. and Berry, W.L. (1970) *Work Flow Structure: An Analysis for Planning and Control* quoted in *The Structuring of Organizations* (1979) (ed. H. Mintzberg), Prentice-Hall, Englewood Cliffs, NJ.

Holt, Jon (2009) *A Pragmatic Guide to Business Process Modelling,* Swindon: British Informatics Society.

Holtham, C. (1996) A groupware-based framework for learning organizations: the BFS project, in *IT Support in the Productive Workplace* (ed. J. Chapman), Stanley Thornes in Association with Unicorn.

Honeywell (1968) *Business Information Systems Analysis and Design,*

Hope, T. and, Hope, J. (1995) *Transforming the Bottom Line,* Nicholas Brealey.

Horngren, C.T. and Sundem, G.L. (1987) *Introduction to Management Accounting,* 7th edn, Prentice-Hall, Englewood Cliffs, NJ.

Hoverstadt, Patrick (2008) *The Fractal Organization: creating sustainable organizations with the Viable System Model,* Chichester: John Woley & Sons Ltd.

Hughes, J.A., Shapiro, D. and Randall, D. (1991) *CSCW Discipline or Paradigm? A Sociological Perspective,* Proceedings of ECSCW'91, Kluwer.

Humphrey, Watts S. (1988) "Characterizing the Software Process", IEEE Software 5 (2) pp73-79, March 1988.

Humphrey, Watts S. (1989) *Managing the Software Process,* Reading, MA: Addison-Wesley Publishing Company.

Humphrey, Watts S., and Kitson, D.H. (1987) "Preliminary Report on Conducting SEI Assisted Assessments of Software Engineering Capability", SEI Technical Report SEI-87-TR-16.

Humphrey, Watts S., Kitson, D.H., and Gale, Julia (1991) "A comparison of U.S. and Japanese software process maturity", SEI Technical Report CMU/SEI-91-TR-27.

IEEE (1993), *Software Engineering Standards Collection,* IEEE

Innes, J. and Mitchell, F. (1990) *Activity Based Costing,* Chartered Institute of Management Accountants.

Innes, J. and Mitchell, F. (1991) *Activity Based Cost Management—A Case Study of Development and Implementation,* Chartered Institute of Management Accountants.

James, P. and, Thorpe, N. (1994) *Ancient Inventions,* Michael O'Mara Books.

Jenz, Dieter E. (2003), *Business Process Ontologies: Speeding up Business Process Implementation,* Erlensee: Jenz & Partner. [available online at: http://www.bptrends.com/publicationfiles/07-03%20WP%20BP%20 Ontologies%20Jenz.pdf]

Johansson, H.T., McHugh, P., Pendlebury, A.J. and Wheeler, W.A. 111

292

(1993) *Business Process Re-engineering,* John Wiley & Sons, New York.

Juran, J.M. (1988) *Juran on Planning for Quality,* Free Press, New York.

Kaplan, R.S. and Norton, D.P. (1992) The balanced scorecard—measures that drive performance. *Harvard Business Review* Jan—Feb.

Kaplan, R.S. and Norton, D.P. (1993) Putting the balanced scorecard to work. *Harvard Business Review,* Sept—Oct.

Kaplan, R.S. and Norton, D.P. (1996) Using the balanced scorecard as a strategic management system. *Harvard Business Review,* Jan—Feb.

Katzenbach, J.J. and Smith, D.K. (1993) *The Wisdom of Teams,* Harvard Business School Press, Boston, MA.

Keen, P.G.W. (1998) *Competing in Time,* Ballinger, Cambridge, MA.

Kilgannon, P. (1972) *The Student's Systems Analysis,* Edward Arnold, London.

Klir, G.J. (1991) *Facets of System Science,* Plenum.

Kohn, A. (1993) *Punished by Rewards—The Trouble With Gold Stars, Incentive Plans, A's, Praise, and Other Bribes,* Houghton Mifflin Co., Boston, MA.

Kulkarni, S. (2005) *Business Process Outsourcing,* Mumbai: Jaico Publishing House.

Landauer, T.K. (1995) *The Trouble with Computers,* MIT Press, Cambridge, MA.

Langley, A. (1995) Between "paralysis by analysis" and "extinction by instinct". *Sloan Management Review,* Spring.

Lee, A., Cheng, C.H. and Chadha, G.S. (1995) Synergism between information technology and organizational structure: a managerial perspective. *Journal of Information Technology,* March.

Lorsch, J.W. (ed.) (1987) *Handbook of Organizational Behaviour,* Prentice-Hall, Englewood Cliffs, NJ.

Lynch, H.J. (1969) ADS: a technique in systems documentation. *Database* 1(1).

Machlup, Fritz, (1962) *The Production and Distribution of Knowledge in the United States,* Princeton, NJ: Princeton University Press.

Maddison, R.N., Baldock, R., Bhabuta, L., Darnton, G., Feldman, P., Fitzgerald, G., Hindle, K., Kovacs, A., Lane, A., Mansell, G., Stokes, N. and Wood, R. (1993) *Information Systems Development for Managers,* 2nd edn, Open University.

Maddison, R.N. and Darnton, G. (1996) *Information Systems in Organizations,* Chapman & Hall, London.

Maisel, H.T. and Gnugnoli, G. (1972) *Simulation of Discrete Stochastic Systems,* Science Research Associates.

Marca, D.A. and McGowan, C.L. *SADT Structured Analysis and Design Technique,* McGraw-Hill, New York.

Martin, D., and Estrin, G. "Models of Computations and Systems-Evaluation of Vertex Probabilities in Graph Models of Computations". Journal of the ACM Vol. 14. No. 2. April 1967.

Martin, J. with Leben, J. *Strategic Information Planning Methodologies*, Prentice-Hall, Englewood Cliffs, NJ.

Maslow, A.H. (1954) *Motivation and Personality*, Harper & Row, New York.

Maslow, A.H. (1968) *Toward a Psychology of Being*, Van Nostrand Reinhold, New York.

Maslow, A.H. (1971) *The Farther Reaches of Human Nature*, Viking Press.

McGee, W. C. (1963). "The Formulation of Data Processing Problems for Computers", in F. L. Alt and M. Rubinoff, (eds.), Advances in Computers vol IV. Academic Press, pp. 1-52.

Melan, E.H. (1993) *Process Management*, McGraw-Hill and ASQC Quality Press.

Meyer, B. (1988) *Object-Oriented Software Construction*, Prentice-Hall, Englewood Cliffs, NJ.

Meyer, N.D. and, Boone, M.E. (1987) *The Information Edge*, McGraw-Hill, New York.

Mintzberg, H. (1979) *The Structuring of Organizations*, Prentice-Hall, Englewood Cliffs, NJ.

Mintzberg, H. (1994) *The Rise and Fall of Strategic Planning*, Free Press, New York.

Mintzberg, H. and Quinn, J.B. (1991) *The Strategy Process: Concepts, Contents, Cases*, Prentice-Hall, Englewood Cliffs, NJ.

ModellData, (1994) *Powersim User's Guide and Reference*, ModellData, 1994.

Morgan, G. (1986) *Images of Organization*, Sage Publications, Beverly Hills, CA. Morgan, G. (1989) *Creative Organization Theory*, Sage Publications, Beverly Hills, CA.

Morgan, G. (1993) *Imaginization: The Art of Creative Management*, Sage Publications, Beverly Hills, CA.

Mumford, E. and Hendricks, R. (1996) Business process re-engineering RIP. *People Management*, May.

Nadler, Gerald (1992) "The role and scope of industrial engineering", in Salvendy, G. (1992) *Handbook of industrial engineering (2nd Ed.)* New York: John Wiley & Sons Inc

Neuschel, Richard F. (1950) *Streamlining Business Procedures*, New York: McGraw-Hill

Neuschel, Richard F. (1960) *Management by System*, New York: McGraw-

Hill

Nolan, R.L. (1973) Managing the Computer Resource: A Stage Hypothesis. *Communications of the ACM*, 16.

Nolan, R.L. (1979) Managing the crisis in data processing. *Harvard Business Review*. Oakland, J.S. (1989) *Total Quality Management*, Butterworth Heinemann, Oxford.

Noy, Natalya F. and McGuinness, Deborah L. (2001) ``Ontology Development 101: A Guide to Creating Your First Ontology". Stanford Knowledge Systems Laboratory Technical Report KSL-01-05 and Stanford Medical Informatics Technical Report SMI-2001-0880, March 2001.

Oakland, J.S. (1991) *Total Quality Management*, Butterworth Heinemann.

OED (2009) *Oxford English Dictionary Second edition on CD-ROM Version 4.0*, Oxford: Oxford University Press.

Ould, M.A. (1995) *Business Processes*, John Wiley & Sons, New York.

Pall, G.A. (1987) *Quality Process Management*, Prentice-Hall, Englewood Cliffs, NJ.

Parnas, D.L. (1972) On the criteria to be used in decomposing systems into modules. *Communications of the ACM*, 15(12).

Pascale, R.T. and Athos, A.G. (1981) *The Art of Japanese Management*, Penguin Books.

Patig, Susanne and Casanova-Brito, Juliana Vanessa (2012) *BPM Software and Process Modelling Languages in Practice: results from an empirical investigation*, Berlin: Frank & Timme

Perry, D.L. (1991) *VHDL*, McGraw-Hill, New York.

Peters, T.J. and Waterman, R.H. (1982) *In Search of Excellence*, Harper & Row, New York.

Petrozzo, D.P. and Stepper, J.C. *Successful Reengineering*, Van Nostrand Reinhold, New York.

Phlips, L. (1988) *The Economics of Imperfect Information*, Cambridge University Press, Cambridge.

Pidd, M. (1992) *Computer Simulation in Management Science*, 3rd edn, John Wiley & Sons, New York.

Porter, M.E. (1980) *Competitive Strategy*, Free Press, New York.

Porter, M.E. (1985) *Competitive Advantage*, Free Press, New York.

Porter, M.E. and Millar, V.E. (1985) How information gives you competitive advantage. *Harvard Business Review*, July—Aug.

Protégé (2012), *Protégé Overview* available at: http://protege.stanford.edu/overview/ [accessed 2012-04-19]

Rath, Tom (2007) *Strengths Finder 2.0*, New York: Gallup Press.

Rath, Tom, and, Conchie, Barry (2008) *Strengths Based Leadership*, New

York: Gallup Press.

Reinhardt, A. (1994) Managing the new document. *Byte,* August.

Richardson, G.P. and Pugh, A.L. (1981) *Introduction to System Dynamics Modeling with DYNAMO,* MIT Press, Cambridge, MA.

Rivett, P. (1994) *The Craft of Decision Modelling,* John Wiley & Sons, New York.

Roberts, N., Andersen, D.F., Deal R.M., Garet, M.S. and Shaffer, W.A. (1983) *Introduction to Computer Simulation,* Addison-Wesley, Reading, MA.

Rockart, J.F. (1979) Chief executives define their own data needs. *Harvard Business Review,* March—April.

Rockman, S. (1995) Ready, steady, flow. *Personal Computer World,* Aug.

Roszak, T. (1986) *The Cult of Information,* Lutterworth Press, Glasgow.

Rubin, M.R. and Huber, M.Y. with Taylor, E.L. (1986) *The Knowledge Industry in the United States, 1960-1980,* Princeton University Press, NJ.

Rumbaugh, J., Blaha, M., Premerlani, W., Eddy, F. and Lorensen, W. (1991) *Object- Oriented Modeling and Design,* Prentice-Hall, Englewood Cliffs, NJ.

Salvendy, Gavriel (ed.) (1992), *Handbook of Industrial Engineering (2nd ed.),* New York: John Wiley & Sons, Inc.

Sammet, Jean E. (1969), *Programming Languages: History and Fundamentals,* Englewood Cliffs: Prentice-Hall, Inc.

Savage, C.M. (1990) *Fifth Generation Management,* Digital Press.

Sayani, H.H. (1990) PSL/PSA at the age of fifteen, in *System and Software Requirements Engineering,* (eds R.H. Theyer, and M. Dorfman) IEEE Computer Society Press.

Scarbrough, H. and Corbett, J.M. (1992) *Technology and Organization,* Routledge, London.

Schein, E.H. (1988) *Process Consultation: Its Role in Organization Development* (2nd edn), Addison-Wesley, Reading, MA.

Schreiber, R. (1995) Workflow imposes order on transaction processing. *Datamation,* July 15.

Scott Morton, M.S. (ed.) (1991) *The Corporation of the 1990s: Information Technology and Organizational Transformation,* Oxford University Press, Oxford.

Shannon, C.E. and, Weaver, W. (1949) *The Mathematical Theory of Communication,* University of Illinois Press.

Silver, Bruce (2011) *BPMN Method & Style (2nd ed.) with BPMN Implementer's Guide,* Aptos, CA: Cody-Cassidy Press.

Simon, H.A. (1957) *Administrative Behavior,* 2nd ed., Macmillan, New

York.

Slemaker, C.M. (1985) *The Principles and Practice of Cost/Schedule Control Systems*, Petrocelli Books.

Solomon, S.L. (1983) *Simulation of Waiting-Line Systems*, Prentice-Hall Englewood Cliffs, NJ.

Sowa, J.F., and Zachman, J.A. (1992) "Extending and formalizing the framework for information systems architecture" in IBM Systems Journal Vol 31 No 3 pp590-616.

Stebbins, M.W., Sena, J.A. and Shani, A.B.R. (1995) Information technology and organization design. *Journal of Information Technology*, June.

Stewart, T.A. (1991) Brainpower. *Fortune, 123(11)*.

Stewart, T.A. (1995) Trying to grasp the intangible. *Fortune*, 2 Oct.

Stewart, T.A. (1996) The coins in the knowledge bank. *Fortune*, 19 Feb.

Stieger, W., and Teichroew, D. (1968). *A Problem Statement Language Preliminary User's Manual*, Case Western Reserve University, Cleveland, Ohio.

Strassman, P.A. (1990) *The Business Value of Computers*, Information Economics Press.

Strassman, P.A., Berger, P., Swanson, E., Kriebel, C.H. and Kauffman, R.J. (1988) *Measuring Business Value of Information Technology*, International Center for Information Technologies.

Suchman, L.A. (1987) *Plans and Situated Actions*, Cambridge University Press.

Synnott, W.R. and Gruber, W.H. (1981) *Information Resource Management*, John Wiley & Sons, New York.

Taylor, Frederick Winslow (1911). *The Principles of Scientific Management*. New York, NY, US and London, UK: Harper & Brothers

Teichroew, D. (1972) *A survey of languages for stating requirements for computer-based information systems*, in Fall Joint Computer Conference, 1972.

Teichroew, D. (1974) Problem statement analysis: requirements for the problem statement analyzer (PSA), in *Systems Analysis Techniques* (eds J.D. Couger and R.W. Knapp), John Wiley & Sons, New York.

Teichroew, D. and Hershey, E.A. (1977) PSL/PSA: A computer-aided technique for structured documentation and analysis of information processing systems. *IEEE Transactions on Software Engineering.*

Teichroew, D. and Lubin, J.F. (1966) Computer simulation—discussion of the technique and comparison of languages. *Communications of the ACM*, Oct.

Teichroew, D. and Sayani, H.H. (1971) Automation of system building. *Datamation* 15 Aug.

Teichroew, D. , and Steiger, W. (1967). ISDOS - A Research Project to Develop Methodology for the Automatic Design and Construction of Information Processing Systems. Case Western Reserve University, Cleveland, Ohio.

Teichroew, D., Macasovic, P., Hershey, E.A. and Yamamoto, Y. (1980) Application of the entity-relationship approach to information processing systems modelling, in *Entity-relationship Approach to System Analysis and Design,* North-Holland, Amsterdam.

Thé, L. (1995) Now you can automate BPR. *Datamation,* March.

Theyer, R.H. and Dorfman, M. (eds) (1990) *System and Software Requirements Engineering,* IEEE Computer Society Press.

Thite, M. and Russell, B. (eds.) (2009) *The Next Available Operator: Managing Human Resources in Indian Business Process Outsourcing Industry,* New Delhi: Response Books.

Thom, A. (1967) *Megalithic Sites in Britain,* Oxford University Press, Oxford.

Toffler, A. (1990) *Powershift: Knowledge, Wealth and Violence at the Edge of the 21st Century,* Bantam Books.

Turney, P.B.B. (1996) *Activity Based Costing: the performance breakthrough,* Kogan Page.

Vacca, J. and Andrews, D. (1994) BPR tools help you work smarter. *Byte,* Oct.

Venkatraman, N. (1994) IT-enabled business transformation: from automation to business scope redefinition. *Sloan Management Review,* Winter.

Vincent, D.R. (1990) *The Information Based Corporation,* Dow Jones Irwin.

Ward, P.T. and Mellor, S.J. (1987) *Structured Development for Real-time Systems,* Yourdon Press.

Waterman, Robert H. Jr., Peters, Thomas J., and Phillips, Julien R. (1980) "Structure is not Organization" in Business Horizons, June 1980 pp14-26.

Weihrich, H. (1982) The TOWS matrix: a tool for situational analysis. *Long Range Planning,* 15(2).

Wiener, N. (1954) *The Human Use of Human Beings—Cynernetics and Society,* Houghton Mifflin Co.

Wilson, B. (1984) *Systems: Concepts, Methodologies, and Applications,* John Wiley & Sons, New York.

Wilson, D.C. and Rosenfeld, R.H. (1990) *Managing Organizations,* McGraw-Hill, New York.

Wilson, D.C. (1992) *A Strategy of Change: Concepts and Controversies in the Management of Change,* Routledge, London.

Wolf, Celia, and Harmon, Paul (2012) *The State of Business Process*

Management 2012, Newton, MA: BPTrends. Available online at: http://www.bptrends.com/members_surveys/deliver.cfm?report_id=1006&target=2012-_BPT%20SURVEY-3-12-12-CW-PH.pdf&return=surveys_landing.cfm.

Yates, J. (1989) *Control through Communication: The Rise of System in American Management*, Johns Hopkins University Press, Baltimore, MD.

Young, J. W., and Kent, H. K. (1958). "Abstract Formulation of Data Processing Problems." Journal of Industrial Engineering, IX(6), pp 471-479.

Yourdon, E. and Constantine, L.L. (1979) *Structured Design*, Prentice-Hall, Englewood Cliffs, NJ.

Yourdon, E. (1989) *Modern Structured Analysis*, Prentice-Hall, Englewood Cliffs, NJ.

Zachman, John A. (1987) "A framework for information systems architecture" in IBM Systems Journal Vol 26 No.3 pp276-292.

Zachman, John A. (2008) *The Zachman Enterprise Framework²*, available from: http://test.zachmaninternational.com/

Zachman, John P. (2009) *The Zachman Framework Evolution*, available from: http://test.zachmaninternational.com/index.php/ea-articles/100-the-zachman-framework-evolution.

Zuboff, S. (1988) *In The Age of The Smart Machine*, Heinmann Professional Publishing.

Index

300

Lightning Source UK Ltd.
Milton Keynes UK
UKOW05f1918181114

241821UK00001B/42/P